ParanoidParenting

FRANK FUREDI

ParanoidParenting

Abandon Your Anxieties
and be a Good Parent

ALLEN LANE
THE PENGUIN PRESS

ALLEN LANE
THE PENGUIN PRESS

Published by the Penguin Group
Penguin Books Ltd, 27 Wrights Lane, London w8 5tz, England
Penguin Putnam Inc., 375 Hudson Street, New York, New York 10014, USA
Penguin Books Australia Ltd, Ringwood, Victoria, Australia
Penguin Books Canada Ltd, 10 Alcorn Avenue, Toronto, Ontario, Canada m4v 3b2
Penguin Books India (P) Ltd, 11 Community Centre, Panchsheel Park, New Delhi – 110 017, India
Penguin Books (NZ) Ltd, Private Bag 102902, NSMC, Auckland, New Zealand
Penguin Books (South Africa) (Pty) Ltd, 5 Watkins Street, Denver Ext 4, Johannesburg 2094, South Africa

Penguin Books Ltd, Registered Offices: Harmondsworth, Middlesex, England

First published 2001
1

Copyright © Frank Furedi, 2001

The moral right of the author has been asserted

Set in 10.5/14 pt Linotype Sabon
Typeset by Rowland Phototypesetting Ltd, Bury St Edmunds, Suffolk
Printed and bound in Great Britain by Clays Ltd, St Ives plc

A CIP catalogue record for this book is available from the British Library

ISBN 0–713–99488–6

Contents

Contents

Acknowledgements

After a radio debate on parental anxieties, a listener e-mailed me, stating, 'You got to write a book on this subject'. I instinctively realized that she was absolutely right but hesitated before embarking on this project. It was my partner, Ann, who convinced me that I ought to put my academic training towards something as practical and worthwhile as a book on *Paranoid Parenting*. I received great encouragement from mothers and fathers that I interviewed and talked to. The unwavering support of my agent Maggie Pearlstine somehow made this project more real. Margaret Bluman is every author's dream editor and helped me keep focused throughout the writing of *Paranoid Parenting*. Bruno Waterfield and Ellen Raphael assisted with the research and managed to discover more material than I needed. My five-year-old son, Jacob, has convinced me that childhood does not need to be colonized by adults. This one is for him.

Introduction

I am not sure if this is a book written by a sociologist who happens to be a father of a 5-year-old or by a father who possesses an intense sociological curiosity about the relationship between generations. My academic training did not prepare me for the strange world of parental anxiety that seems to afflict so many fathers and mothers. Since my son Jacob was born, just over five years ago, I have been reminded time and again that life is perilous and that the peril starts at birth.

The alarm began almost at once. At the hospital nurses carefully explained the in-house measures to thwart baby snatchers. Concerned friends then made sure that we were fully aware of the latest cot death advice. Relatives weighed up the risks of different childcare arrangements, debating the dangers of nannies (potential baby batterers) versus the dangers of nurseries (potential neglect). But it was when my mother announced that she could no longer bring herself to watch any television programmes about babies because they made her nervous about Jacob that the intensity of parental paranoia was fully brought home. It was as if my child's survival was constantly under threat.

It does not take long for parents to realize that everyone today seems to hold strong opinions about the problems of raising a child. While the politicians regularly hold forth about what they believe makes a 'good' or 'responsible' parent, there is an industry of experts who bombard us with 'helpful' insights drawn from the science of child-rearing. This science produces an endless stream of manuals, pamphlets and leaflets that claim to provide crucial knowledge for the now terrified mother and father.

Paradoxically, it seems as if the only people who feel unconfident in their opinions about what is good for children are the parents themselves. The role of bumbling amateurs has been assigned them by the self-appointed experts. Consequently, a lack of self-belief tinged with an intense level of anxiety informs the parenting style of our times. Most parents I know are not just worried about how they are performing as fathers and mothers: they are paranoid about it. Having a child appears to change people's worldview. Once a man becomes a 'father' and woman becomes a 'mother' other adults are suddenly transformed into potentially threatening strangers. As one mother explains:

I took James to Tesco's this morning and a man about 50 years old was talking to him. The first thought that came into my head was, 'Get away from my child!' and of course he was probably only being nice. I hate it but I can't let anyone touch him or talk to him without getting suspicious.

Parents not only seek to protect their children from strangers – they distrust even those they charge with the care of their offspring. Neighbours, nannies, nursery workers and children: no one is above suspicion.

Although the mistreatment of children by their carers is thankfully an extremely rare occurrence, and certainly no more frequent than it was in past decades, it only takes one high-profile case of nanny abuse to unleash a wave of parental anxiety. Sadly, in recent years security has become one of the primary concerns of parents choosing pre-school care for their children. A 1997 study on this subject indicated that they rated security second only to 'caring staff' in a list of ten things they would look for if choosing between two similar places.[1] Not surprisingly, many nurseries now vie with minimum-security prisons in their security arrangements. Take one London nursery, Happy Times. This 119-place nursery boasts the latest security technology, including a palm-recognition system. Adults who wish to enter the nursery must type in their personalized four-digit PIN number and place their hand on a scanner that will either let them enter or keep them out depending on whether it recognizes the palm print. Happy Times also boasts closed-circuit television cameras directed at the nursery entrance.

This sort of hi-tech security has become a marketing device used by private nurseries looking for customers. Crawford Kindergarten in London was the first nursery in Britain to allow parents to monitor their children from home or the office through closed-circuit television cameras installed in the classroom. In September 1999, Bolton School Nursery in Manchester announced that it had installed a webcam to allow parents to keep an eye on their children via the Internet. A camera fitted into a room at the nursery relays pictures that can only be accessed by parents with individual passwords. In the United States, an Orwellian sounding Parentwatch, Inc. has set up a web site that allows parents to view live video images of their children.

Incredibly, the practice of spying on nannies, care workers and children has become associated with good parenting. It shows that you care. In America, parents are bugging their children's telephones, installing secret cameras in their bedrooms and sending strands of hair retrieved from pillows for analysis at drug laboratories. Parental paranoia leads to mistrust and renewed demands for even more drastic security measures. Predictably, the commercial sector is more than happy to feed parents' appetite for more security.

In August 1999, the British supermarket chain Tesco announced that it would launch an experimental programme to electronically tag young children in order to allay their customers' fears that their children could stray out of sight or be snatched by paedophiles. They were merely catching up with their North American counterparts, where electronic tagging is already used widely in shopping malls and nurseries, and anxious parents welcome it as a means of always knowing where their children are.

All this new technology is wonderful and no doubt many working mothers and fathers would take pleasure from sneaking off for a few minutes to watch their children play in their nursery. But do parents really need to know just exactly what their youngsters are up to? Do they need to constantly monitor their activities? Is there not something a little sordid in parents spying on their children and those who look after them? There was a time when all mothers and fathers assumed that nurseries were safe places where caring teachers looked after their toddlers. Thankfully, most still trust their nannies and nursery teachers. But the very fact that many of them are inclined to rely on a camera rather than a teacher's word does not bode well for the future.

Unfortunately, there are no technological solutions to parental anxieties. Even if it were desirable, it is humanly impossible for parents to monitor the lives of their children 24 hours a day. The new gadgets of surveillance are far more likely to intensify rather than allay parental fears. A parent who has no means to check on the carer has to trust or suspend their suspicion. Someone who cannot do that is likely to grow increasingly neurotic. A mother with access to a webcam is likely to feel guilty when she does not check it. The very fact that it has been installed suggests to her that there is a need for it.

This obsessive fear about the safety of children has led to a fundamental redefinition of parenting. Traditionally, good parenting has been associated with nurturing, stimulating and the socialization of children. Today, it is associated with monitoring their activities. Parents are continually advised to supervise their children. An inflated sense of risk prevails, which demands that children should never be left on their own and that they should preferably be within the sight of one of their parents. An army of professionals advises that children are never safe. Today, allowing a child to play outside on its own is seen as an act of neglect.

The media plays a significant role in provoking these irrational attitudes. Every incident involving a child serves as a pretext for demanding greater vigilance and new forms of supervision. Even stories that would seem to illustrate 'good news' are interpreted as problems. In August 1999, a report published by the European Review of Injury Surveillance and Control provided evidence that British children are among the safest in Europe. It showed that childhood mortality due to accidents has halved in Britain over the past decade. But instead of greeting this news with joy, so-called safety experts used it as an opportunity to warn against complacency and demand even more parental supervision of children. 'It is important for parents to supervise their children as much as possible,' was the comment of the spokesman for the Royal Society for the Prevention of Accidents on this report.

Fatal injuries to children are fortunately very rare and the numbers are falling, but when they occur they provoke an outcry for new regulation. After 15-month-old Dillon drowned in a pond and another toddler was left fighting for his life, the *Mirror* launched a campaign –

backed by a number of MPs and public figures – urging parents to fill in their garden pools. 'This is a vitally important message,' Esther Rantzen stressed; 'toddlers can die in the shallowest of water.'[2] It is true that young children can drown in shallow water – and a relatively small number will tragically die this way. But does one accident require that we all reorganize our lives and abolish water from our children's experience? Is there not a danger that if we so desperately try to protect children from every possible risk we may end up causing more harm than good?

The demand for constant parental supervision creates an impossible strain on fathers and mothers, serving as yet another reminder of the perils facing their children and helping to reinforce their already intense sense of insecurity. Since supervision can never be constant, the pressure to monitor every aspect of children's lives contributes towards reinforcing paranoia. Mothers and fathers have responded to this pressure by fundamentally altering their relation to their children.

In order to oversee the activities of their children, parents have reorganized children's leisure time around the home. A growing proportion of them refuse to allow their children to play outdoors on their own. Activities that were normal even in the seventies – children walking to school on their own or playing outdoors with friends – have become increasingly rare. Instead, parents drive their children to school, cart them to after-school care or take them to other forms of organized activities supervised by adults.

The cruel irony is that many of those concerned with the problems facing the institution of the family complain that parents do not spend enough time with their children. It is widely believed that a new generation of selfish career-oriented adults are refusing to take responsibility for the upbringing of their children. But such complaints fail to engage with reality. One of the big myths of our times is that mothers and fathers spend less time with their children than previously. The new cultural norms demanding the constant supervision of children represent a major claim on the time of parents. And yet mothers and fathers spend so much time supervising their youngsters that children have little time available for free play. Research conducted by Stuart Waiton, a Scottish social scientist, showed that parents' worries led to a loss of an average of one hour's play time every day.[3]

Allowing children to play unsupervised or leaving them at home on their own is increasingly interpreted as a symptom of irresponsible parenting. No doubt, some parents are neglectful and take decisions that put their children at risk. However, chaining children to their parents benefits no one. Allowing children to play on their own is essential for their personal development. Children thrive when they have the freedom to explore the world with their friends. For their part, parents also need their own space.

Unfortunately, those who question the merits of the constant supervision of children are sometimes accused of reckless parenting. Parents who allow their children to walk to school unsupervised may find themselves the subjects of local gossip. 'Good Parenting' now seems to mean protecting children from the experience of life – supervising them and chaperoning them to keep them safe.

This book explores this phenomenon of 'paranoid parenting' and tries to explain why parenting has become such a troublesome enterprise. It is hoped that through making sense of this worrying development, more parents will be encouraged to believe in their innate capacity to act as capable fathers and mothers. There is little basis to the fears that fuel parental paranoia. Children are far healthier and safer than at any other time in history and, if we can resist the pressure of subjecting them to our anxieties, they are likely to thrive and turn into well-balanced adults.

Anxious parents – battery children

The damaging consequences of paranoid parenting are finally being recognized in Britain. Since 1997, numerous studies have drawn attention to the impact of parental anxieties on children. There is now a consensus that parents' concern with their children's safety has acquired obsessive proportions. According to most of the available evidence the main focus of this obsession is 'stranger-danger' – a fear that has haunted British parents since the 1980s. In 1993, the campaign group Kidscape produced a report, 'How Safe are our Children?', that showed that 95 per cent of 1000 adults interviewed put fears about the possible abduction of their child by a stranger at the top of a list of concerns. Two years later, the charity Barnardo's published a survey which claimed that nearly 70 per cent of parents felt that their neighbourhood was unsafe, and half said they never let their children play outside without adult supervision. In 1998, a Mori poll of more than 500 parents found that almost 80 per cent would not let their children play unsupervised in the park during their summer holiday. A Year later, in August 1999, an NOP poll indicated that 78 per cent of the respondents believed that the reason for so many children not being allowed to play outside was parents' fear of harm. Later that month, a study by the National Society for the Prevention of Cruelty to Children (NSPCC) claimed that eight out of ten parents were too frightened to allow their children to play unsupervised in the park.

Parental anxieties regarding stranger-danger have been widely commented on in recent years. Numerous studies decry this trend and experts have condemned parents who keep their children indoors for treating their offspring like battery hens. For some time now, educators and psychologists have been pointing to the danger of young children turning into couch potatoes, because 'timid parents' are stifling the sense of adventure of British children. A recent study published by the Mental Health Foundation concluded that children are failing to develop their self-confidence because of parents' fears about them going out to play.

It is evident that parental paranoia has a deteriorating effect on the quality of childhood. Supervised play is only virtual play at best. Children need to play on their own: unsupervised activity – where children can test their limits independently of an adult framework – is crucial for their development. They should be allowed to make mistakes, and to learn from them. Children must learn to make decisions for themselves, something they can never do under a parent's watchful eye – supervising children, cocooning them, can seriously damage their health. In fact, probably the greatest casualty of the totalitarian regime of safety is the development of children's potential. Playing, imagining and even getting into trouble has contributed to the sense of adventure that has helped society forge ahead. A community which loses the sense of adventure and ambition does so at its peril, and yet that is precisely what may happen when socializing children consists, above all, of inculcating fears in them.

There is little doubt that most parents are anxious about the safety of their children outdoors. But where does this anxiety come from? Surely one of the causes of this anxiety is the incessant demand for the constant supervision of children? Paradoxically, often the very same people who complain about the damaging effects of parental anxiety are active in promoting it.

Take the NSPCC. Its protests against overprotective parents sits strangely alongside its own 'panic mongering'. During the spring of 1999 the charity ran an alarmist television campaign on child abuse using 'shock tactics' specifically designed to disturb and scare parents about the scale of this problem. The NSPCC guidelines regarding child safety during the summer holidays issued later in the year were also unlikely to encourage parents to loosen restrictions on children's independent activity. These advised that young children should never be left unsupervised in public places. This advice is hard to reconcile with allowing children to walk to school or play outside – unless it is assumed that an adult should 'shadow' the children.

Other critics of parental anxiety are also complicit in contributing to the problem they complain about. One reason why a survey published in Community Care was critical of parents' preoccupation with strangers was because it diverted attention away from what it considered to be a far greater danger to children – 'abusers within their own families'. The Mental Health Foundation also pursued the approach of decrying one panic in order to propagate another. A recent study published by the Mental Health Foundation claimed that children have become intensely susceptible to mental illness. So now neurotically anxious parents have a new fear: not only are their children prey to threatening strangers, they are also at risk of losing their minds. One threat to children has been replaced by another.

Manifestations of parental anxiety are discreetly associated with the activities of the child protection industry. The army of professionals concerned with child protection take every opportunity to promote the message that children are constantly at risk. Safety campaigns around a bewildering variety of issues – from child abuse and cot death to stranger-danger and sunbathing – all reinforce the message that childhood is a particularly dangerous experience. Just about every aspect of the childhood experience has been recast as a safety issue.

And of course, once experts start to look for new dangers, they will find plenty to worry about.

So now that children spend so much time cooped up at home, it is the safety of their indoor environment that has come under intense scrutiny. Parents are continually warned about the danger that many toys represent to the well-being of their children. Consumer activists have labelled children's playhouses unsafe. 'Wendy Houses', trusted by generations of parents as a safe summer diversion for their children, have recently been depicted as potential death traps. Greenpeace has warned that tens of thousands of baby toys, including baby teethers, inflatable books, bath-time ducks and hand-held rattles put children at risk because they contain hazardous chemicals. Researchers have also called for a ban on baby-walkers on the ground that they cause serious injuries to toddlers. The Child Accident Prevention Trust even advises that parents keep a careful check on their babies' dummies so that they don't choke on a broken piece.

Scaring parents appears to be the mission of indoor safety advisors. Take the campaign oriented towards turning Wendy Houses into a major safety issue. The words children and danger tend to be linked together in the public imagination. Anyone casting a glance over an article in one Sunday paper entitled 'Built-in danger to children of death-trap Wendy houses' would have imagined that children had actually died or been severely injured.[4] In fact, on a careful read, it becomes clear that there have been no such incidents. The article did not refer to any actual deaths or cases of injury; it simply raised the *possibility* that the door and window hinges of playhouses could catch children's small fingers. It is not clear what this report was attempting to accomplish. Parents already know that little children are very good at insinuating their fingers in the wrong places. While it is not evident what the article aimed to do it is clear that its only possible effect was to scare parents about one more trivial aspect of their children's lives. Of course, one single newspaper article about playhouses makes little difference to the way we think. But today, almost everything that children do is discussed in terms of dangers and risks and, in this context, each absurd report adds to the sense of peril.

The message is that if you thought you could protect your children by keeping them indoors, then you had better think again. Even the home is a risky place for children. Outdoors or indoors there is no escape, and always plenty of groups ready to excite parental paranoia.

Relentless advice

Well-intentioned advice has become the bane of parents' lives. Virtually every week a new report is published that warns parents about yet another hazard threatening the well-being of their child. As I am writing, the radio has just announced the news that a new study has concluded that since children absorb up to 50 per cent more radiation from mobile phones than adults do, these gadgets represent a serious risk to their health. Dr Gerald Hyland, a physicist at Warwick University, warns that parents who 'dish' out phones as presents to their children are making a dangerous mistake. 'It's totally irresponsible for parents to allow their children to have these,' argues Hyland. Yet before this report, many parents had issued phones as a safety measure in case a child is stranded and needs a lift home.

Information on health scares affecting children are a particularly invidious source of anxiety to parents. It only takes one speculative study on a potential new risk to bring about another mini parental panic. In March 1998, many parents were terrified by a study which alleged that there was a connection linking the Measles Mumps Rubella (MMR) vaccine with Crohn's disease and autistic spectrum disorders among young children. Although the Chief Medical Officer tried to reassure the public that there was no link between MMR and autism, it was too late to prevent a panic. Thousands of parents reacted to this scare story by refusing to allow their children to be injected. When a year later another study again suggested that this vaccination might cause serious bowel diseases among children, a further substantial decline in immunization levels followed. Liam Donaldson, the Chief Medical Officer, was forced to issue a warning that unless parents had their children vaccinated there would be an epidemic of measles, mumps and rubella.

This MMR panic exemplifies the dilemma that health scare stories pose for parents. Who should they listen to: the 'experts' or the 'experts'? It is the proliferation of experts at a remove from the physical activity of parenting that is a prime cause of parental difficulties.

The most active source of destabilizing advice for parents is the media. Every parent is plagued by the media-fuelled anxiety that cot death or Sudden Infant Death Syndrome (SIDS) might suddenly snatch their child away in the night. These apprehensions are regularly reinforced by new studies that claim to have discovered yet another new cause of cot death. Small, obscure studies, which contradict previous findings, are reported as serious news. In 1998, there was widespread public discussion around a study claiming that cot death was caused by pollution from traffic and industry. This report was followed by a study insisting that quilts put babies at risk of cot death, then by another which indirectly suggested that babies flying on aeroplanes faced a significant risk of cot death. Despite eventual reassurances that flying does not kill babies, the continuous communication of cot death reports makes it impossible for parents to be equanimous.

The result of the relentless publicity surrounding cot death is a spate of anxieties that are disproportionate to the scale of the problem. Cot death is a very rare occurrence. There are fewer than 300 cot deaths out of an average 588,000 live births every year. Yet the campaigns around this issue help to generate a sense of insecurity among parents who fear a tragedy that is extremely unlikely to happen. This can only undermine their enjoyment of a baby's early life and potentially make parents over-attentive and over-protective. It almost seems that campaigns around cot death seek to guilt-trip parents. One doctor has even gone so far as to suggest that pathologists carrying out autopsies on babies who have died suddenly should 'think dirty' and assume that the tragedy was the outcome of deliberate harm by parents and carers. Writing in the *British Medical Journal*, Dr Michael Green claimed that up to 40 per cent of these tragedies may be caused by murder. The presumption that fathers and mothers are likely to be responsible for cot death can only serve to strengthen their insecurities on this matter.

It is a sign of the pervasiveness of parental fear that many scare stories about children's health often touch upon practices that were in the past advocated as beneficial to a child's development – now they have been recast as a major threat to their well-being. Parental advice is not rocket science. Reports on children's safety often contradict one another and experts seem unable to agree which end of the baby is up. Take the case of parents sleeping with their infants. In recent years, many professionals have advocated the practice of co-sleeping on the grounds that it is beneficial, promoting breast-feeding and strengthening bonds between parents and child. The practice has gained popularity with young couples who, absent during the day, are reluctant to be separated from their children at night. However, in September 1999, the US Federal Consumer Product Safety Commission issued an alarmist statement that warned parents not to sleep in the same bed with infants under the age of two. It claimed that sleeping together poses a significant risk of accidental smothering or strangling. 'Don't sleep with your baby or put the baby down to sleep in an adult bed,' counselled Ann Brown, the Commission's chairwoman. One would think that this pronouncement, which directly affects the daily practice of millions of parents, was based on research which conclusively showed that babies died solely because they were sleeping in their parents' bed. But the study did nothing of the sort. The authors of the study acknowledged that they did not take account of any other risk factors. They merely noted that 557 children under the age of two died while sleeping with their parents in their beds. Although the report could not substantiate a direct causal relationship between co-sleeping and infant death, it could clearly offer one more problem for parents to worry about.

Empathy is the only emotion appropriate for those parents confronted with this 'expert advice', who until now have been content with the words of child development expert Miriam Stoppard: 'I have never believed that taking the baby into our bed could do him or us any harm.' But this new report, taken together with some of the other advice on offer, forces parents to think again. In *What to Expect the First Year*, a successful manual written by three American mothers backed by an army of doctors and caring professionals, the argument is that those who opt for the 'family bed' need to be made 'aware of the possible risks' of letting their child sleep with them: sleep problems, developmental problems, peer problems, marital problems, safety problems, 'drawing the line' problems – even dental problems.

Yet there is support for Miriam Stoppard in *The Year after Child-*

birth, in which Sheila Kitzinger assures the reader that leaving a child to sleep alone 'may not be the safest arrangement . . . there is some evidence that a mother's movements during sleep, and the noises that she makes, stimulate a baby's breathing.' But just as mother rushes to bring baby into her bed, the *Which? Guide to Children's Health* raises the stakes still higher in the risk game, announcing that research shows 'bed-sharing with a parent or parents' to be one of the factors 'associated with a higher incidence of cot death'. So we are damned if we do and damned if we don't. The people who definitely will not get any sleep after reading all this are petrified parents.

Of course, getting babies to sleep has always been a fundamental problem. In his classic child-care manual *Baby and Child Care*, the late Dr Spock said that if you are having trouble getting your baby to sleep, the cure is simple: put the baby to bed at a reasonable hour, say goodnight affectionately but firmly, walk out of the room, and don't go back. What could be clearer than that?

Unfortunately, in her book *Baby and Child*, Penelope Leach is equally clear that 'tearing yourself away, leaving him to howl, cannot be the right answer.' If 'your baby cries when you leave, go back,' she counsels. But as you quietly make your way back to the baby's bedroom, Spock's warning rings in your ears: 'It's important not to tiptoe in to be sure the baby is safe or to reassure her that you are nearby. This only enrages her and keeps her crying much longer.' So you turn away again, only to be confronted by a recently published study which claims that leaving your baby to cry will not only spoil her night's sleep, but could ruin her entire life.

Toilet training has also become a battlefield for rival child experts. In the United States, John Rosemond, a bestselling author of parenting books, has published articles in more than 100 newspapers attacking wishy-washy parenting. Rosemond demands a return to traditional child-rearing practices and advocates that children should be toilet trained by the age of two. The process, he says should be as simple and straightforward as housebreaking a four-week-old puppy. Dr. T. Berry Brazelton, a well-known American parenting guru, is horrified by Rosemond's approach. He argues that parents who force toilet training can cause long-term problems for their children. In the meantime parents are left wondering whether they should let their children decide when they are ready to use the toilet or take matters into their own hands and train their offspring into the mysteries of this science. And whatever they decide, they will get a slap on the wrist from some expert for doing things wrong.

This slap may be a metaphorical one, but when it comes to the highly charged issue of parents smacking their children, the debate is venomous. Many child-protection experts believe that smacking children constitutes a form of abuse. Their sentiment was upheld in 1997 by the European Court of Human Rights in Strasbourg, when it awarded £10,000 damages to a British boy who sued his stepfather for the beating he received. For its part, the British government indicated that while it would make sure that children were protected from severe beatings, it would defend the right of parents to smack their children. This correlates with the belief of most parents, who think that it is acceptable for them to smack a naughty child. An ICM poll conducted during the summer of 1999 found that seven out of ten parents were in favour of smacking children. The poll was greeted with disappointment by organizations like Epoch (End Physical Punishment of Children) that believe that smacking children legitimizes violence in society. Parental insecurity about this subject has been exploited by a New Zealand company called Safe Smack Limited. In October 1997, they marketed a Safe Smack Parenting Programme, which included a patented leather strap known as 'Uncle Sam Smacker'. The company claimed that the use of this strap was 'the only safe way to smack children' and assured potential customers that the use of its product was good for children. Predictably, the NSPCC and other child-protection advocacy groups denounced the Uncle Sam Smacker as dangerous.

The controversy that surrounds the question of how adults should discipline their children exposes the highly politicized character of parenting. Advice on smacking has little to do with the specific needs of an individual child. Instead such advice is driven by competing ideologies about what constitutes an appropriate form of family life. Many opponents of smacking are suspicious of parents' motives towards the disciplining of their children. Those who support the right of parents to smack their children are often motivated by the objective of restoring traditional family values. Such highly polarized advice about smacking actually undermines the ability of mothers and fathers to negotiate the difficult choices they have to make when forced to discipline their children. There will always be some expert who will criticize parents for being too robust or too soft in their approach to child rearing.

The discussion on smacking is part and parcel of the current tendency to question every aspect of parental behaviour. Parents who place pressure on their children to perform well in sports or in school are sometimes denounced as 'emotional abusers', while those who leave their children's education to their teachers are stigmatized for neglecting their youngster's future. With the escalating frequency of advice, it is often assumed that parents who ignore it are highly irresponsible individuals. Those who advise also serve as a parenting police. Thus it is that the advice-givers – sometimes inadvertently – transform routine aspects of parenting into a major scientific or ideological issue. If their advice achieves anything, it is the intensification of parental paranoia.

The assumption of parental incompetence

At its most insidious, this barrage of advice causes parents to be labelled 'incompetent'. A study of 1,025 parenting articles and advice columns in the US, carried out by Mary McCaslin and Helen Infanti, indicated that parents were represented as the problem in 97 per cent of the entries. At the same time, although parents were deemed to be responsible for the problems, they were not perceived to have the competence to deal with them: 68 per cent of the entries advised parents to follow the advice of an expert, whilst parents were counselled to act on their own knowledge in just 29 per cent of the entries.[5] Most research carried out on parenting has as its premise the view that parents have less expertise on the subject than the professional mounting the research. Surveys of professional attitudes towards parents suggest they hold them in low regard and mistrust parental competence and commitment to the education and upbringing of their children.

Parenting experts often complain – only partly in jest – that child-raising is the only profession that does not require rigorous training or qualification. In May 1999, Barnardo's published a report at the launch of a campaign to highlight the need for 'parenting education'. The campaign aimed to increase awareness and acceptance of education for parents. It rhetorically asked, 'You get instructions for everything else in your life, why not children?' The impulse to transform parenting into a hugely complicated skill that requires special training can take on highly intrusive and totalitarian forms. In the US, some experts have proposed that parents be required to obtain a licence from the government to raise their children. Jack C. Westman's book *Licensing Parents: Can We Prevent Child Abuse Neglect?* offers an extreme variant of the conviction that many mothers and fathers are not fit to parent children. Such authoritarian experts seldom confront the problem of what they would do with women who became pregnant without a licence.

Thankfully, most experts are far more restrained in their advocacy of parenting education and stop well short of demanding parental licensure. They tend to confine themselves to simply drawing attention to parental shortcomings. For example, Professor John Gottman, author of *The Heart of Parenting*, pontificates that 'there is a big difference between wanting to do right by your children and actually having the wherewithal to carry it off.' Gottman's message is clear: 'read my book or you will fail as a parent.'[6]

Scolding parents for their incompetence usually serves as a prelude to scaring them with the terrible consequence that their failure represents to the future well-being of their children. Such advice serves to undermine parental confidence whilst inflating the responsibility of mothers and fathers for every aspect of their children's life. The paradox that drives parents paranoid is to be told that although they are hopelessly incompetent, they also bear greater responsibility for the well-being of their children than parents of previous generations. They need to be permanent supervisors, experts in literacy skills and possess a degree in counselling. The professionalization of parenting has served to undermine the confidence of fathers and mothers in their ability to parent. It has reinforced the notion that we all need outside professional help in order to cope with the basics of bringing up children. This professionalizing of child-rearing infantilizes parents, who in turn end up treating their offspring as an endangered species. The growth of the child protection industry has helped transform parenting from a routine experience into something that is seen as a highly complex skill. Even before a child is born parents are encouraged to study parent-craft skills. Every aspect of conceiving, bearing and raising children is subject to professional advice since, the experts agree, child-rearing is too important a task to leave to parents.

Since parenting has been transformed from an intimate relationship, involving emotion and warmth, into a skill, involving technical expertise, the role of the expert assumes a special significance. From this perspective, the solution seems clear: to take parenting out of the family so that enlightened professionals can put things right. And this, as we have seen, is exactly what is happening. Those who advocate parental training justify their proposal on the grounds that it helps to empower otherwise confused adults. In fact, despite the claims of empowerment, this approach can only have the effect of further undermining parents' confidence in their abilities. It is difficult to get on and parent when child-rearing has been mystified and recast as a skill. No doubt it has been assumed that all this professional advice and intervention would lead to a more confident and informed generation of proud new parents. Instead it seems that today's parents are more insecure and unconfident than their own parents ever were.

The reason why the professionalization of family life weakens the effectiveness of parents is that the relationship it tries to regulate cannot be reduced to a series of skills. A relationship between parent and child is a qualitative one that cannot be improved by the application of a technical formula. Such intervention can, however, undermine the integrity of the parent–child relationship. When professionals encroach on this relationship it necessarily weakens the authority of parents. And parents with weak authority are unlikely to become confident at handling their children.

Professional intervention rests on the bureaucratic conviction that, because parenting has to be learned, it must also be taught. This misguided approach fails to grasp the elementary relationship between human experience and learning. There are many things in life we learn in our own way through experience. Confident parents learn from their experience of life. Such lessons cannot be created through a course drawn up by experts. These courses only foster a climate where the parent develops a relation of dependence on the professional.

To make matters worse, child professionals do not merely give advice. They intrude into parents' lives and undermine their confidence. Recently, when my wife took Jacob into the nursery and explained that he had bruised himself falling over, one of the staff joked that social services would have to be informed. Everybody laughed – if a bit too nervously. Afterwards one of the mothers whispered to my wife, 'Amy had two bruises last week – you have no idea how nervous I was in case people jumped to the wrong conclusion.' This exchange of confidences is symptomatic of the temper of our times. Parental anxiety is not confined to the actual well-being of children. It extends to a preoccupation with how parents are seen by faceless professionals. Something has clearly gone wrong when parents live in fear that the most innocent incident can be interpreted as malign and lead to intrusive enquiries from nosy officials. In such circumstances, parents are quite entitled to feel paranoid.

During the course of researching this subject, I learnt a lot from the parents that I interviewed. Probably the main insight that I gained is that although not all of us are paranoid parents, none of us are immune from the climate of insecurity that afflicts child-rearing today. We can do very little about our fears and reactions. But hopefully if we can understand why we behave the way we do, we can do something about its dreadful effects on our youngsters.

One

Making Sense of Parental Paranoia

Tony is giving up teaching. Although he would not use the words, it was 'parental paranoia' that drove him out of the West Sussex primary school where he had taught for three years. During his teacher training, Tony had anticipated that he might be stretched by the challenge of dealing with rowdy children. But he was not prepared for the task of coping with 'difficult' anxious parents. The most taxing moments of his working life were to be spent dealing with 'worried mums'. He sighs as he tells of the mother who insisted on driving behind her son's coach to France to ensure that he arrived safely. He wearily recalls how a school trip to the seaside, planned for a class of 5-year-olds, was cancelled because two parents were concerned that the trip would involve their children in a 45-minute journey in a private car. Would the cars be roadworthy? Who would accompany a child to the lavatory? Who would ensure correctly fitting seat belts? Were these normally non-smoking cars, or would the children be made victims of passive smoking? The planned pirates' day on the beach ended up being confined to the school field – sea, sand and adventure confined to their imagination and many of the educational aims undermined. Exasperated by 'problems – all in the minds of parents', Tony sought, and found, a career outside teaching.

Of course, it is normal for parents to be concerned about the well-being of their children. Parental anxiety is nothing new. A brief inspection of the pages of *The Nursery World* from the 1920s and 1930s shows that our grandparents were haunted by many of the doubts, worries and preoccupations that torment fathers and mothers today. A frequently revisited topic was: 'Is my child's development normal?' Child tantrums, shyness, aggression, jealousy, thumb-sucking, nail-biting, refusing to sleep, were regularly raised in letters from concerned parents. Many begged an answer to what the publication's agony aunt called 'a problem as old as parenthood itself – that of how to get children to obey us'.

It might seem that not much has changed. But the superficial similarities betray some big differences. In the past, parental anxiety focused on problems within the family. Infant health – physical, psychological and moral – was an important preoccupation, as was preparing children for the outside world – school, career, marriage. And of course, the older generation was often anxious about their children falling in with bad company and generally 'getting up to no good'. But the concerns raised by our grandparents were voiced in a different tone from today.

Reading the worries of parents published in the 1920s, the overall impression is something like this: 'Family life is fine, but there is just this *one* little thing that we need to sort out.' Today the discussion in parenting magazines suggests that family life is far from fine, that most parents feel out of control and that everything is up for question. Instead of a specific concern, parents seem to be suffering a more general loss of confidence.

The parents who write to magazines today do not give the impression that they are troubled by one aspect of child-rearing. Many seem overwhelmed by the sheer scale of troublesome issues confronting them. These days it seems that every little issue – how to toilet-train a child, when you can leave them home alone, whether to force them to eat their greens – is made into a bigger problem by an overall crisis of parental nerve. This suggests that there must have been some major changes in the way that adults negotiate the task of looking after youngsters. The clearest symptom of this trend is the public panic about child safety.

In recent years, no issue has come under closer scrutiny than the question of children's safety. It has become so highly charged that a single incident can spark a major public debate and demands for new regulations. For example, the tragic murder of an English teenage girl while visiting France on an organized school exchange led to a major review of the safety of school trips – despite the fact that the incident was clearly a one-off event. There is no evidence of any increase in attacks on foreign (or French) students in France, and it is unlikely that such an attack will take place again regardless of whether the authorities take new precautionary measures or not. Such measures may make parents feel better, but a murderer intent on getting into a dormitory will probably do so as easily in France as he would in England. Thankfully, such outrages happen rarely – not because of security measures recommended by educational establishments, but because only a tiny number of people are motivated to commit such atrocities. In truth, a 15-year-old girl is probably far safer in a dormitory in St Gervais than in her 18-year-old boyfriend's Ford Fiesta on the M25.

Public concern with safety has reached obsessive proportions. The remote possibility that children might choke on small toys in packets of cereals, chocolates and crisps has provoked demands to ban them. Infants have a habit of swallowing just about anything that is lying about. Are we also going to ban coins, tissue paper, marbles . . . ? Baby walkers, which have been used for years to allow infants to whiz about before they can walk alone, have been condemned because of the possibility that children may topple over or fall down the stairs. Admittedly this danger is more 'real' than that of death by Pokémon-card ingestion, but it is still triggered by the potential risk that something might happen, and not by specific evidence that it has.

Once in place, parental paranoia easily attaches itself to any new experience concerning children. Take *in vitro* fertilization (IVF) – for many the only route to parenthood. Rather than celebrating the potential of IVF to create wanted children, researchers have recently warned about hypothetical dangers to the children being given life. There have been warnings that IVF could induce changes in children's genetic make-up and impair their mental development. There has been speculation about whether sperm that have to be assisted to fertilize an egg will produce babies as healthy as sperm that can swim on their own. Psychologists muse about whether people who become parents by artificial means after years of infertility will be able to relate, in an emotionally stable manner, to their much-wanted children. It has even been suggested that IVF children will be loved too much and may not be able to live up to their parents' hopes for them. It is only a matter of time before our troubled imagination succeeds in turning IVF into a child safety issue.[1]

The Internet has a remarkable potential to enhance young people's lives by providing educational opportunities. Yet it is widely seen as another new technology that poses new *dangers* to children. Much of the discussion about the World Wide Web has focused on how to protect young people from its perils, to prevent innocents stumbling across 'adult' sites or into the clutches of paedophiles. 'The Internet can be a big and dangerous place for your children, but for the price of a local phone call, it needn't be,' promises a newspaper advertisement for an Internet provider specializing in protecting children in cyberspace. Such manipulative marketing schemes are confident that they can convert parental paranoia into hard cash.

Sadly, virtual reality provides infinite space for the exercise of the anxious imagination, an unknown world where our fear of invisible strangers can run riot. Since children are often more adept at negotiating the net, parental control is forced to confront uncomfortable new challenges. 'You don't know what's out there,' a group of fathers confided in me. One raised the spectre of paedophile rings lurking in the shadows online, ready to pounce on his unsuspecting teenagers by e-mail. Nobody I talked to actually knows of any child who has been damaged, but nevertheless they regarded the Internet as a really big problem. As one parents' guide to the Internet warns: 'You might think you have taken adequate steps to protect your child, but please beware that a determined child might nonetheless be able to circumvent any protective software or security measure.'[2] And apparently there are other risks to worry about. A London conference on parenting in April 2000 was informed by Dr Jane Healy, an American educational psychologist, that computers can also damage children's brain development.[3]

Old-fashioned television is often indicted for its negative impact on children. Parents complain that television is teaching their children to be violent shopaholics. They protest that video games distract children from reading or riding a bike. Even parents who rely on the VCR to keep their children busy feel guilty about their pragmatic embrace of this electronic baby-sitter. The experts encourage these concerns. One American study warns that the impact of the media on children 'should be eliciting serious concern, not just from parents and educators but from physicians, public health advocates, and politicians as well'.[4] Parents are encouraged to blame television because, in a world where they already feel pretty powerless, yet another outside influence on their children is experienced as a threat to their authority.

Parents mistrust the Internet and television because of a more general unease about having to cope with external influences that bear upon their children. Many of these influences – television advertising, consumerism, the Internet – are portrayed as part of a complex new world that is causing parental insecurity. But adult over-reaction to new technology is a symptom, and not the cause of the problem. Many parents now feel so insecure and fearful of what they do not understand that virtually anything can be turned into a potential childcare crisis.

Fear for children's safety has come to dominate the parenting landscape. In 1998 the advocacy group Families for Freedom interviewed 200 parents. The results make frightening reading. Most of these parents paint a picture of a world that is hostile territory for their children. They routinely use words like 'scared' and 'frightened' to describe their feelings about their children, particularly when they are outdoors. When the marketing organization System Three surveyed public opinion on the safety of children in Scotland for the BBC in 1998, the results suggested an overwhelming sense that children were far less safe than 20 years ago. Although the incidence of child murder by a stranger in Scotland is very low and has shown no change in the past 20 years, 76 per cent of respondents thought that there had been an increase in such tragedies, while 38 per cent believed that the increase had been 'dramatic'. A large majority – 83 per cent – also thought that more children were now being knocked down by traffic on the roads of Scotland. In fact the incidence of road injuries to children had *decreased* by 60 per cent during the previous 20 years. The gap between adult perceptions and the reality of the risks faced by children is confirmed by other studies in the Anglo-American world. A survey of US paediatricians carried out in 1995 claimed that parental anxieties were on the rise amongst their patients – and that these anxieties tended to be significantly out of proportion to any real risks. The discrepancy between actual and imagined risks was particularly striking in relation to the dramatic issues of child welfare, such as abduction, environmental poisons and cancer.[5]

A culture of fear has led parents to restrict their children's independent outdoor activities. In 1971, eight out of ten 8-year-olds were allowed to walk to school alone. Now it is fewer than one in ten. At age 11 almost every child used to walk, now it is down to 55 per cent and falling. A report published by the Children's Play Council in 1997 argued that children had become virtual prisoners in their own homes.

Paranoid parenting does not only restrict children's freedom to play. It also diminishes the creative aspect of play. There is considerable evidence that children are more creative when their parents are not around to monitor their behaviour. A study by Dale Grubb and Alicia Snyder concludes that adult supervision turns play into a structured activity and that this weakens youngsters' drive to experiment. Unfortunately, the concept of unsupervised children's activity – what used to be called play – is now defined by parenting professionals as a risk. Restricting children's outdoor activity has predictable consequences for their development, and a sedentary lifestyle is inevitably bad for their health. Research has linked the decline in British children's fitness to the decrease in the amount of time they spend walking and cycling. The First National Travel Survey reported a fall of about 20 per cent in the annual distance walked and 27 per cent in the distance cycled by children between 1985 and 1993.[6] An average British schoolgirl now walks for less than seven minutes a day. Deprived of the opportunity to burn calories by racing around outside, children grow fat. A study published in the *British Medical Journal* in September 1999 found an alarming proportion of pre-school children to be overweight and even obese. Among those aged 2, 15.8 per cent were considered overweight and 6 per cent obese. By the time they reached 5, 18.7 per cent were deemed overweight and 7.2 per cent obese.

The precautionary approach to parenting

Parental paranoia today is more than simply a worse version of past anxieties. For instance, a common target of child-rearing manuals before the Second World War was the over-protective parent, and guilt-ridden parents worried that they might be 'smothering' their children. But how many times do we hear parents criticized for being over-protective today? Indeed, many of the traits associated with the classic over-protective father or mother are likely to be praised by today's child experts as responsible parenting. Parents are continually urged to do even more to protect their children.

Researchers advise parents to supervise children, not only outdoors, but even when they watch television. The term 'coviewing' has been coined to describe the practice of hands-on parents playing the role of a 'media value filter and a media educator'. Other researchers further claim that parental supervision inoculates children from many of the dangers they face. They contend that 'parental monitoring has been inversely associated with antisocial behavior, drug use, tobacco use, and early sexual activity'.[7] There is obviously some truth in this. The more time a child spends in the company of his or her parents the less time is available for smoking, drinking and sex. But to equate the amount of parental supervision directly with behavioural outcomes tells parents that the more time they manage to spend with their children, the better their offspring will be. This raises the question of where to draw the line. How do parents decide how much monitoring is reasonably required, as opposed to optimally possible?

Unfortunately, parental supervision is today always interpreted as a positive virtue – so parents can never spend too much time supervising their youngsters. Child-rearing experts occasionally concede that it is simply impossible to keep children and young teenagers under constant adult supervision. But even then they insist that alternative, indirect, forms of child surveillance are employed. One American expert argues that if a child has to be left under self-care, then parents must do whatever they can to supervise *in absentia*, by liaising with a trusted adult who knows what the youngster is up to. The message is clear: if you are going to shirk your responsibility towards your child even for a few hours, you must at least make sure that somebody else is doing your job for you.[8]

Parents are not just advised to supervise their children. In Britain, such advice contains the implicit threat of legal sanction. Although in England and Wales there is no statutory age at which it is illegal to leave your children unattended, a parent who is deemed to neglect, abandon or expose her children to danger can be liable to prosecution. According to Carolyn Hamilton of the Children's Legal Centre, the general view taken by child protection professionals is that a parent should not leave children under 12 alone for more than 20–30 minutes. What a shock this would have been to the parents of 'latch-key' youngsters in the 1970s. At that time debate about the children of working mothers returning from school to empty homes focused on whether it was right for women to have jobs which deprived their children of a welcoming smile and the smell of home baking. The issue was not seen as one of child safety and certainly not abandonment. Yet today's legal experts advise that, while parents are unlikely to face prosecution for a 30-minute absence, the parent of an 11-year-old left alone for three to four hours might face legal action. Even though very few parents *are* prosecuted in these circumstances, the strict guidelines convey a clear message about what society expects of parents. And that expectation is founded on the premise that parents can never do too much to protect their children.

Twenty or thirty years ago, authors of child-rearing manuals had their own way of making parents feel guilty. But they would have reacted with disbelief to the proposition that it was wrong to leave children under 12 alone for more than 20–30 minutes. Fortunately, there are still some societies where the over-protective parent is not promoted as role model. Children in Norway and Finland 'enjoy being at home without their parents from about seven onwards' records Priscilla Alderson, a Reader in Childhood Studies at the Institute of Education in London. According to Alderson, Finnish children start school at 7 years, and sometimes go home at 11 a.m. where they play with friends until their parents arrive home in the late afternoon.[9] In Anglo-American societies, where a paranoid parenting style prevails, such practices would be condemned as child abuse.

The view that children cannot survive without the constant presence of a responsible adult is continually reinforced by public campaigns designed to frighten parents. 'Only use baby-sitters who are over 16 and responsible enough to look after your children' warned the NSPCC during its August 1999 Safe Open Spaces campaign. Even the time-honoured practice of using 14- or 15-year-olds eager to earn some pocket money through helping parents look after their children is now dismissed as an act of gross irresponsibility.[10]

Today's parenting style sees safety and caution as intrinsic virtues.

Paranoid parenting involves more than exaggerating the dangers facing children. It is driven by the constant expectation that something really bad is likely to happen to your youngster.

Jacqueline Lang, Headmistress of Walthamstow Hall School in Sevenoaks, Kent, has characterized today's parenting style as 'the worst-case scenario approach'. Lang caught the public imagination in 1997 when she remarked to the local media that 'some girls in her school did not own a raincoat because they were ferried everywhere by car'. She identified one of the fundamental principles of paranoid parenting: the fear of taking risks.[11] Her students' parents were simply too scared to allow their girls to walk to school. Children who are strangers to the outdoors do not need raincoats.

Apprehension about child safety, and a morbid expectation that something terrible can happen any moment, mean that many risks that are well worth taking because of their stimulating effect on a child's development are simply avoided. Child-rearing today is not so much about *managing* the risks of everyday life, but *avoiding* them altogether. As child psychologist Jennie Lindon argues, the adult 'pre-occupation with risk can create too much emphasis on removing every conceivable source of even minor risk'. The characteristic feature of such an obsession is, according to Lindon, 'to speculate excessively on what can go wrong rather than on what children may learn'.[12] It is this precautionary approach which defines the parenting culture of contemporary society.

Parents have always been concerned about protecting their children from harm. Asking 'What can go wrong?' is a sensible way of dealing with the many new experiences children encounter. To weigh up probabilities before doing something is an informed way of managing risk. But asking what can go wrong is very different from acting on the assumption that things *will* go wrong. Such a fatalistic outlook reduces the power of parents to make informed, intelligent judgements. A more appropriate approach might be to follow an assessment of what can go wrong with two other questions – 'Does it matter?' and 'What might the child learn from the experience?' The precautionary approach continually encourages adults to adopt the same one-dimensional response: beware!

It is tempting to interpret the precautionary approach to child-rearing as the irrational reaction of individual mothers and fathers. Parenting professionals sometimes point the finger at over-anxious parents and advise them to be more sensible about managing the risks their children face. Jacqueline Lang, who is exceptionally sensitive to the consequences of trying to 'inoculate' children against the risks thrown up by life, blames 'a generation of timid parents' for 'stifling the sense of adventure' of Britain's children. However, it is a mistake to reduce the problem to the personalities of some parents. How individual adults relate to their infants at any time is inseparable from the parenting style encouraged by our culture and society.

Parents today face strong social pressures to adopt a precautionary approach towards child-rearing. Intimidating public campaigns endlessly remind them about the many risks their children face. It is difficult to retain a sense of perspective when the safety of children has become a permanent item of news.

The erosion of adult solidarity

Christina Hardyment, in her excellent study on baby-care advice past and present, is struck by the intensity of parental paranoia today. She senses a climate of permanent panic that invites a guilt-ridden style of parenting. The loss of small children's freedom is one consequence.[13] Children's freedom has never been as restricted as it is today. A study by Dr Mayer Hillman of the Policy Studies Institute indicates that while 80 per cent of 7- and 8-year-olds went to school by themselves in 1970, fewer than 10 per cent are now allowed to do so. In the past, not even the archetypal over-anxious parent would have taken the precautionary approach that is now seen as the norm. Even though children have never been safer or healthier, at no time has so much concern and energy been devoted to protecting youngsters from harm.

A Glasgow researcher, Stuart Waiton, has produced compelling evidence that counters the fear that children are at greater risk than in previous times. According to Waiton, between 1988 and 1999 the number of children murdered between the ages of 5 and 16 decreased in England and Wales from 4 per million to 3 per million. The total murdered under the age of 5 dropped from 12 per million to 9 per million. Cases of abduction in which the offender was found guilty dropped from 26 to 8 over the same period.[14]

Although surveys confirm that paranoid parenting is widespread, there has been little attempt to understand its causes. The most common explanation is that it is all the fault of the sensationalist media. Panics about children's safety are interpreted as 'media-led' and television is accused of making parents unnecessarily apprehensive. 'Increasingly, we are bombarded by the news media with spectacular accounts of violence, illness and health concerns, as well as varied opinions about appropriate diets and child rearing practices', concluded the authors of one study of parental worries in the United States. They certainly have a point. Research into the British media's reporting of the horrific murder of 2-year-old Jamie Bulger by two 10-year-old boys shows that it had a major impact on parents. In a survey of 1,000 parents taken a year later, 97 per cent cited the possible abduction of their children as their greatest fear. *The Times* reported that many of these parents revealed that 'video images of the two-year-old being taken by his killers were still fresh in their minds'.[15]

So yes, the media helps shape adults' perception of the risks faced by children. But it is far too simplistic to blame the media for the problems of parenting. Parents do not need high-profile media horror stories to provoke their insecurities. They worry about all manner of everyday things, all of the time. They can be anxious about Mary's weight on Monday, Tim's refusal to eat vegetables on Tuesday, the poor state of Mary's and Tim's education on Wednesday, and so on. A heightened sense of insecurity can attach itself to relatively mundane experiences such as whether a child is too fat or too thin. The media does not cause paranoid parenting. Its main role is to amplify society's concerns, to give shape to our fears. Confusing the messenger with the bad news is an understandable reaction, but not one that will help illuminate the issues at stake.

So what is the bad news? In the chapters that follow, it should become clear that a variety of influences help to shape contemporary anxieties about parenting. But if one thing above all others has created the conditions for today's parenting crisis, it is *the breakdown of adult solidarity*.

Adult solidarity is one of those unspoken facts of life that people used to take for granted. Most of the time, in most places, adult solidarity is practised by people who have never heard of the term. In most communities throughout the world adults assume a modicum of public responsibility for the welfare of children even if they have no ties to them. When the local newsagent or butcher scolds a child for dropping a chewing-gum wrapper on the road, they are actively assisting that boy's parents in the process of socialization. When a pensioner reprimands a young girl for crossing the road when the light is red, he is backing up her parents' attempt to teach her the ways of the world. These displays of public responsibility teach children that certain behaviour is expected by the entire community, and not just by their mum and dad.

It has long been recognized that the socialization of children relies on a wide network of responsible adults. Parents cannot be expected to act as 24-hour-a-day chaperones. Across cultures and throughout history, mothers and fathers have acted on the assumption that if their children got into trouble, other adults – often strangers – would help out. In many societies adults feel duty-bound to reprimand other people's children who misbehave in public.

As every parent knows, in Britain today, fathers and mothers cannot rely on other adults to take responsibility for looking after their children. British adults are hesitant to engage with other people's youngsters. This reluctance to assume responsibility for the welfare of the young is not simply a matter of selfishness or indifference. Many adults fear that their action would be misunderstood and resented, perhaps even misinterpreted as abuse. Adults feel uncomfortable in the presence of children. They don't want to get involved and, even when confronted by a child in distress, are uncertain about how to behave.

Take the following scene in a primary school in Bristol during the spring of 2000. The teachers have organized a group of 7-year-olds to go outside the schoolyard to count the cars that pass by. Little Henry is bored and proceeds to poke his head through the railings that separate the schoolyard from the street. He gets his head stuck. The teachers are at a loss to know what to do. A crowd gathers around the trapped child. One teacher finds a jar of cream and applies some of it on the railings to help Henry wriggle out of his predicament. It doesn't work. Parents begin to arrive to pick up the children. The teachers are standing around. Not one of them has attempted to pull Henry out. Not one of them has put an arm around the distressed boy in an act of reassurance. They are afraid of touching the child. Finally, Henry's mum arrives. She takes one look at her son, grabs hold of him, gives him a yank and he is out. Henry's 80-minute ordeal is over.

The story was recounted to me in horror by a young teacher, as a statement about the world we live in. When I asked why she hadn't done something to help little Henry, she said that she had already been reprimanded a year earlier for being 'too physical' with one of her pupils.

When we live in a society that warns off teachers, traditionally seen as being *in loco parentis*, it is hardly surprising that strangers hesitate before becoming involved with other people's children. If a teacher is not allowed to cuddle a crying child for fear of the action being misinterpreted, no wonder that passers-by will turn their backs on a weeping infant.

Awkward adults uncomfortable in the company of children represent a serious problem for parents. Mothers and fathers feel that they are on their own. Worse, many parents are convinced that it is best if other adults don't interfere in their children's affairs. Parents regard other people not as allies, but as potentially predatory on their young ones. Clumsy adults inept at relating to children and anxious parents concerned about 'stranger-danger' are two sides of the same coin.

This breakdown in adult solidarity breeds parental paranoia. The fear of the 'other person' is the most tangible expression of parental insecurity. A 1998 survey carried out by Families for Freedom noted that 89.5 per cent of the respondents had a general sense of foreboding about the safety of their children. This general sense of alarm became more focused when other adults were brought into the equation. It was said by 76 per cent that they were 'very worried' about their children's safety in relation to 'other people'. The other person is the stranger. Research carried out by Mary Joshi and Morag Maclean in 1995 found that more parents gave 'stranger-danger' as a reason for using cars for school journeys than any other reason.[16]

Perhaps that is why parents in Britain are more likely to drive their children to school than in Germany, Scandinavia and other parts of Europe where the distance between home and school may be far greater. In societies where neighbours and other adults assume a degree of responsibility for keeping an eye on children, attitudes towards their safety are far less obsessive. A comparative study of children's independent mobility concluded that there is far less parental supervision in Germany than the UK. According to the authors, one reason why German parents are more likely to allow children out on their own is because they expect other adults to keep an eye on them; in turn, German children reported feeling that they were watched over by the adult world. This culture of collaboration creates a sense of security for German parents. The expectation that other adults will do the right thing helps them to take a more relaxed attitude towards letting their children out of the door than might be the case in Britain.[17] One consequence of the erosion of adult solidarity in Britain is that the distance that children are allowed to stray from home has been reduced to one-ninth of what it was in 1970.[18]

A poisonous atmosphere for parenting

The finger points not only at other adults; British parents themselves have also come under suspicion. The public is frequently warned that children are at risk from their own parents. Parents who find it difficult to deal with the pressures of everyday life have been portrayed as potential abusers. In May 2000, the NSPCC launched its Full Stop campaign. Shocking pictures on billboards show a loving mother playing with her baby. The caption reads: 'Later she wanted to hold a pillow over his face.' Another picture highlights a loving father cuddling his baby. The words 'that night he felt like slamming her against the cot' serve as a chilling reminder not to be deceived by appearances. The NSPCC justified its scaremongering tactics on the grounds that it was telling parents that it is normal to snap under pressure, and that they need to learn to handle the strain. But this alleged link between parental incompetence and abusive behaviour has disturbing implications for every father and mother. If anyone can snap and smash the head of their baby against the wall, whom can you trust?

It is easy for a mother or a father to lose control and lash out at their youngster. Regrettably most of us have done it on more than one occasion. Snapping under pressure is a normal if unfortunate fact of life. But when we snap we don't go on to smash our baby's head against the wall. It may be normal for parents to snap, but it is wrong for the NSPCC to suggest that this temporary loss of control 'normally' leads to abuse. The implication that parenting under pressure is an invitation to abuse is an insult to the integrity of millions of hard-working mothers and fathers. It also helps to create a poisonous atmosphere of suspicion and mistrust.

A booklet, *Protecting our Children: A Guide for Parents*, sponsored by Labour MP Dan Norris and with a foreword by Prime Minister Tony Blair, explains that anybody might be a paedophile. 'They live in our communities, in our families and may even be someone we know and love', the booklet informs the reader. 'How can seemingly kind and even respectable people abuse children?' it asks.[19] Anyone reading this book is invited to look at people 'we know and love' with a newly suspicious eye. If it is indeed the case that anyone and everyone in our communities and our families should be treated with caution, then trust and collaboration between adults become impossible.

Family life, once idealized as a haven from a heartless world, is now widely depicted as a site of domestic violence and abuse. Child protection professionals and press commentators are always warning of the dangers that children face from their 'normal' parents. If victimization within the family is pandemic then clearly we are obliged to mistrust even those closest to us. The focus of anxiety can no longer be the alien stranger or criminal, but our closest family relations, neighbours, friends, lovers and workmates. Such a suspicious attitude towards everyday life redefines how people are expected to relate to those closest to them. This culture of fear places parents in a difficult position. Every year some 120,000 parents experience the nightmare of being wrongly accused of child abuse.[20] Since normal parents are now portrayed as potential abusers, it is not surprising that so many face investigation on the basis of hearsay and rumour.

Scare campaigns that target parents represent a body blow to the authority of every mother and father. Here and there, public figures still pay lip service to the 'great job' performed by parents. But the ceaseless reminders of parental failure take their toll. Campaigns which claim that it is normal for parents to snap and abuse permeate the public imagination, and incite us to be suspicious of our neighbours.

When even nice mothers and fathers are potential monsters it is difficult to regard parents in a positive light. Everyone now feels entitled to speculate about what Mary's dad is up to. Under this pressure, parents will openly criticize other mothers and fathers – sometimes in front of the children. A society that expects parents to teach children to avoid strangers and to regard them with dread is storing up big problems for the future. When parents instruct children about stranger-danger these days, they are also communicating a negative statement about the adult world – and, by implication, about themselves.

The code of mistrust

If family life is seen as essentially rotten to the core, which other institution could possibly be perceived as good? If parents, brothers and sisters cannot be entirely trusted, how can we have faith in the integrity of more distant acquaintances? This is the message conveyed on a daily basis through television and popular culture. Not a day goes by without another sordid tale of some professional abusing the trust that has been placed in him or her. The suspicion of abuse that hangs over the family has spread like a disease to infect other institutions from schools to Scout and Guide groups. Where once there would have been an assumption of goodwill, dangers are now seen to lurk.

An editorial in the *British Journal of Sports Medicine* claims that sport is 'the last refuge of child abuse'. 'I know it is going on from hundreds of interviews with athletes but it is difficult to get any statistical evidence', writes Celia Brackenridge.[21] Many sporting bodies have issued guidelines about how to spot potential abusers working in their midst. In December 1998 the Amateur Swimming Association, in conjunction with the NSPCC, set up a helpline for children on the grounds that their sport might be targeted by paedophiles like the Olympic swimming coach jailed for child sex abuse. In 1999, the England and Wales Cricket Board issued child protection guidelines. At least one commentator blamed the collapse of English cricket on paedophiles who made parents reluctant to allow unsupervised children to play the game.[22]

Predatory paedophiles have also become an issue with the St John

Ambulance service, after three of its officers were jailed for the long-term abuse of cadets in 1998. The British Scout Association has been implicated in sex scandals. After a Coventry Scoutmaster was jailed for indecency offences against two boys and a Hampshire Scoutmaster was sentenced to six years for sexually abusing eight boys, the Association adopted a policy to 'safeguard the welfare of all members by protecting them from physical, sexual and emotional harm'.

Even religious organizations have been implicated in this climate of fear. In Australia, Roman Catholic bishops have sought to ban their priests from having any private contact with children. Guidelines drawn up with the approval of the Vatican mean that confessionals have to be fitted with glass viewing panels. Priests are also banned from seeing any child alone with the door closed.[23] Closed doors and private interaction are no longer acceptable to a society fed on a constant diet of mistrust. It is as if by definition the closed door is an invitation to abuse.

Any one-to-one contact between adults and children has effectively been stigmatized. A guideline published by the Salvation Army advises its members to ensure that 'an adult is not left alone with a child or a young person where there is little or no opportunity for the activity to be observed by others'. It adds that this 'may mean groups working within the same large room or working in an adjoining room with the door left open'.[24] Salvation Army members were far from happy with this rule since many of their activities involve musical practice. Since band members play different instruments at various levels of proficiency, a lot of the training took place one-to-one in separate rooms.[25] Nevertheless, the new order dictates that doors should be left open – and, presumably, ears closed.

A guideline issued by the British Home Office to voluntary organizations recommends that activities 'which involve a single child working with an adult' should 'take place in a room which can be observed easily by others in nearby areas, even if this is achieved simply by leaving doors open'.[26] Scout Association guidelines warn scout leaders to avoid one-to-one situations and contact sports. Guidelines issued by the England and Wales Cricket Board tell coaches not to work with a child 'completely unobserved', and suggest that 'parents should take on the responsibility for their children in the changing rooms'.[27]

The return of the medieval chaperone in Britain provides eloquent testimony to the regulation of adult contact with children. In one case a rector at a village church was forced to disband a choir because of new guidelines on child protection. Up to 20 child choristers met weekly for rehearsals and sang every Sunday at St Michael's Church in Northchapel, West Sussex. The Revd Gerald Kirkham had to stop recruiting because, under the new code, at least two adult chaperones were needed at choir practice.[28]

Mistrust of adults, especially of men, has had a destructive impact on working relations between adults and children. Many adults have become wary of volunteering for working with children. The British Scout Association faces a shortage of volunteer leaders. 'If a man says he wants to work with young boys, people jump to one conclusion', reported Jo Tupper, a spokeswoman for the Scout Association.[29] A similar pattern is evident in primary education. Research carried out by Mary Thornton of Hertfordshire University suggests that men are turning away from primary school teaching because of fears that they will be labelled 'perverts'. Thornton claimed that men on teacher training programmes 'felt they had no idea how to deal with physical contact'. Some of the trainees asked, for example, whether they 'should cuddle a distressed child'.[30] When physical contact with children comes with a health warning, teachers face a continual dilemma over how to handle routine issues in the classroom. In August 1998, the Local Government Association even went so far as to advise teachers not to put sun cream on pupils because it could lead to accusations of child abuse. Lord Puttnam, chairman of the General Teaching Council, has warned that when teachers are regarded as potential rapists and paedophiles their authority is seriously undermined.[31]

In November 1999, it was reported that 'Teachers, fearful of accusations of any kind of inappropriate touching, are increasingly wary of direct contact with the children in their charge, even if tears are involved.' One school in Glasgow has responded to this 'affection-phobic culture' by introducing special massage classes for children. The idea is that pupils will stay fully clothed and standing upright while they take turns to massage each other's heads, backs and shoulders. While the teacher reads a story, they will also take turns to massage each other's forearms with plain, unscented oil.[32] A new ritual for an age that dreads physical contact between adult and child.

Fear of adults victimizing children is fuelled by a child protection industry obsessed with the issue of abuse. The NSPCC's Safe Open Spaces for Children, launched in August 1999, advised parents never to make their children 'kiss or hug an adult if they don't want to', and that included grandmothers and aunts. The justification for this proposal was that it would make children confident about refusing the advances of a stranger.[33] From time immemorial, parents have pleaded with their children to kiss or hug grandmothers and aunts. The call to ban this innocent practice is symptomatic of the intense professional mistrust of adult behaviour towards children.

All this hysteria about physical contact actually does little to protect children. By casting the net so wide and expecting child abuse to be a normal occurrence, there is a danger of trivializing this dreadful deed. A climate of suspicion will not deter the child abuser, but it will undermine the confidence of all parents. And at the end of the day, confident parents are best placed to educate their children to deal with risks and danger.

The flight from children

From voluntary organizations to primary education, well-meaning adults are being put off from playing a valuable role in instructing and inspiring young children. At a conference organized by Playlink and Portsmouth City Council in November 1999, the delegates were enthusiastic professionals committed to improving children's lives through outdoor play. But several of the play workers felt that their role was diminished by bureaucratic rules designed to regulate their contact with children. One play worker complained that she often could not do 'what's right' by the children, because if she did not follow the rules it would threaten her career prospects.

Those who work with children are automatically undermined by new conventions that control their behaviour. If it is assumed that professional carers need to be told how to relate to the children in their charge, why should parents – or children – trust them? But it is not only professional carers or volunteers who are affected by this climate of paranoia. Suspicion towards them reflects and reinforces a more general distrust of adults. It is assumed that none of us can be expected to respect the line between childhood and adulthood: that we need to be told what almost all of us know by instinct – children are vulnerable creatures who need protection. This means comforting a distraught child with a cuddle just as much as it means not abusing those young people who have put their trust in you.

The negative image of adulthood enshrined in the new conventions has far-reaching implications. The healthy development of any community depends on the quality of the bond that links different generations. When those bonds are subjected to such intense suspicion, the ensuing confusion can threaten the very future of a community. After all, relations of warmth and affection are inherent in family relationships, and even in relations between children and other carers. If an adult touching a child comes to be regarded with anxiety, how can these relations be sustained?

Is it any surprise that many adults are literally scared of badly behaved children? Take the following scene on the lawn of one of Britain's leading universities. Over 200 law lecturers and students are waiting for an official photograph to be taken. A young girl cycles up to the group and plonks herself down in front of the group and refuses to move. She is asked politely to move, but still refuses to do so. Not a single adult in this large group dares to intervene, reprimand the young girl or physically move her on. Afterwards, the lecturers justify their paralysis on the grounds that they feared accusations of assault or abuse if they had attempted to move her out of the way. In this stand-off the young girl emerges as the winner. Twenty minutes later, bored with her easy victory over the disoriented adults, the girl leaves of her own accord.[34]

It should really come as no surprise that some children have begun to play off this general distrust of adults to make life difficult for those they don't like. Most children are enterprising creatures, for whom adult insecurities provide an opportunity to exercise their power. Every year hundreds of teachers face false allegations of abuse. A teacher wept openly at the April 2000 conference of the Association of Teachers and Lecturers as he recounted his three months of agony after being falsely accused of punching a 12-year-old pupil. Other teachers recounted cases of false accusation and demanded that school staff should not be treated as guilty until proven innocent.[35] It is tempting to blame malicious children for making life hell for some of their teachers. But it is not really their fault. They are merely manipulating a dirty-minded world created by obsessive adults.

The distrust of adult motives has encouraged a flight from children: a distancing between the generations. In some cases it has led to an avoidance of physical contact, in others the reluctance to take responsibility. The flight from children expresses adult confusions about how to relate to younger generations. Elderly people in particular are often unclear about what is expected of them in dealing with children. An 82-year-old man with numerous grandchildren and great-grandchildren provides a classic illustration of this dilemma:

I was in a shop and this woman came in who the wife knew, with her little granddaughter. I was eating a sweet, and this little girl looked up at me, so I said, 'Would you like a sweetie, duck?' She got all scared and jumped back. And I said, 'Well that's the best thing you want to do. Never take a sweetie off nobody.' She done right, but it made me feel cheap, like. It made me feel awful really, to think I was offering a little girl a sweet. And I love kiddies. In the paper you hear there's horrible people about and it's awful, but it made me feel right cheap.[36]

This octogenarian has internalized the new mood of suspicion towards adult motives. His mental retreat from following his well-meaning instincts towards the young girl is part of a general pattern. Sadly, this flight from children means that adult collaboration in raising the young rests on a fragile foundation. Parents, of course, cannot flee from their children. They are left to deal with the damage caused by the erosion of adult solidarity. They are truly on their own. The decline of adult solidarity means that parents must pay the cost for society's estrangement from its children.

Parents on their own

More than ever parents are on their own. According to Professor John Adams of University College London, we live in an age of hypermobility, where the car has facilitated a new level of social dispersal.[37] Adams believes that hypermobility has led to the increased anonymity of individual households, a decline of conviviality towards our neighbours, a less child-friendly environment and the emergence of parental anxieties towards children's outdoor safety. His concerns are echoed by numerous studies that confirm a palpable sense of social isolation. A survey published by the Royal Mail in 1999 revealed that people now live further away from relatives – though the majority still live within an hour's journey. A quarter of respondents aged under 35 rarely or never spoke to their neighbours. Nearly a third of these respondents said that they would only offer to help neighbours if it was absolutely necessary, and did not want to know them any better.[38] This indifference towards the fate of neighbours underlines the absence of communal affinity. We often live in neighbourhoods without neighbours. The absence of an obvious network of support has important implications for the way that adults negotiate the task of child-rearing.

The theme of social isolation is a familiar one to most parents. Mothers and fathers complain about an uneasy sense that they are 'on their own'. Many mothers, especially those who work, are preoccupied with what could go wrong with their childcare arrangements. When there are no relatives near, and you are not on first-name terms with your neighbours, who is to pick up your child when your meeting runs late? Who can stay home and nurse a child off school for two weeks with chickenpox? The absence of an obvious back-up, the tenuous quality of friendship networks and the difficulty of gaining access to quality childcare all help to create the feeling that life is one long struggle, increasing tensions within the household.

The fragmentation of family relations and the diminished sense of community have inevitably helped to make parents feel insecure. Not knowing where to turn in case of trouble can produce an intense sense of vulnerability – especially among lone parents who feel that they are literally on their own. The isolation of parents is not simply physical.

The erosion of adult solidarity transforms parenting into an intensely lonely affair. A climate of suspicion serves to distance mothers and fathers from the world of adults. In turn, this predicament invites parents to be anxious and over-react – not just to the danger they see posed by strangers, but to every problem to do with their youngsters' development. As we shall see, paranoid parenting now embraces almost every aspect of child-rearing.

Two

The Myth of the Vulnerable Child

Paranoid parenting is directly linked to the way society regards children. Babies and infants are seen as both intensely vulnerable and highly impressionable – above all to parental influences. They are said to be both greatly sensitive to the damaging effects of parental incompetence or neglect and responsive to parental nurturing and stimulation. The prevailing opinion conveyed in child-rearing manuals is that the long-term development of children is determined by their early experience, in which parents play a dominant and decisive role. It is claimed that if parental intervention during these early years is positive, children are destined to grow up to become intelligent and emotionally balanced adults. If it is negative, they are fated to become damaged individuals, condemned to personal failure. That is why adult failures are often represented as the consequence of problems encountered by children in their early years.

The interlocking myths of 'infant determinism' (the assumption that infant experience determines the course of future development) and 'parental determinism' (the notion that parental intervention determines the future fate of a youngster) have come to have a major influence on the relations between children and their parents. By grossly underestimating the resilience of children they intensify parental anxiety and encourage excessive interference in children's lives: by grossly exaggerating the degree of parental intervention required to ensure normal development they make the task of being a parent appear impossibly burdensome.

The denial of resilience

Today we find it difficult to accept the fact that youngsters possess a formidable capacity for resilience. Paranoid parenting is continually fuelled by the belief that unless adults continually protect their infants, they will become damaged beyond repair.

Hillary Clinton's folksy book on child-rearing, *It Takes a Village*, begins with the sentence 'Children are not rugged individualists.' This statement on contemporary childhood – backed up by citations from well-known fashionable child experts – elevates vulnerability as its defining condition. The key concept through which this sense of vulnerability is given definition is that of *children at risk*. 'Children at risk' is an expression that we think we understand intuitively even though it is rarely defined. When reporters allude to a child at risk we rarely ask the obvious question, 'at risk of what?' Just being 'at risk' is sufficient to evoke a sense of permanent danger. We don't ask the question 'at risk of what?' because we already suspect that the reply would be 'at risk of everything'.

It is easy to overlook the fact that the concept of children at risk is a relatively recent invention. As I argue elsewhere, this way of imagining the condition of childhood involved a redefinition of both risk and of childhood.[1] Until recent times, risks were not interpreted as by definition bad things. We used to talk about 'good risks' as well as bad ones. Taking risks was seen as a challenging aspect of children's lives. Today, adults who encourage children to take risks are often condemned as irresponsible. Risks are equated with danger and therefore have to be avoided at all costs. We are so scared about children taking risks that we have invented the concept of 'children at risk'. It is a concept that warns parents that children are in constant danger. This outlook continually reminds us that children are intensely vulnerable and require our constant attention. From this perspective parents can never feel too much anxiety for the welfare of their children. A child that is at risk requires constant vigilance and adult supervision.

Childhood is invariably represented as an intensely dangerous period. 'Everywhere we look children are under assault', claims Hillary Clinton. She believes children are under assault from 'violence and neglect, from the break-up of families, from the temptation of alcohol, tobacco, sex and drug abuse, from greed, materialism and spiritual emptiness'. Here is a picture of a society that actively conspires to bring about the downfall of its children. Clinton concedes that these problems are not new but adds that, in our time, they have 'sky-rocketed'.[2] Numerous other authors reaffirm the point that childhood has become more dangerous. Michele Elliot, author of *501 Ways to be a Good Parent*, believes that previous generations of parents did not have to negotiate the worries that haunt mothers and fathers today. 'It is no good asking our own mothers for advice', she writes. Why? Because, 'when they were bringing us up, they didn't seem to be hit by shocking news of yet another child murder.'[3]

Every society has different ideas about the nature of childhood. Views about children change with fashion. Christina Hardyment, in her excellent study of the history of baby-care advice, shows how perceptions fluctuate between viewing children as little things that need hardening and toughening up to regarding them as vulnerable souls in need of constant love and attention. Since the end of the Second World War, the belief that children are fragile and vulnerable creatures has gained considerable strength. And since the 1980s the belief that youngsters are inherently vulnerable and 'at risk' has acquired the character of a cultural dogma. The premise of this dogma is that children lack the coping mechanisms to deal with adverse experiences. The experts have lost faith in children's resilience and believe that they are unlikely ever to recover from early traumatic episodes. Such unpleasant encounters are said to 'scar' children for life.

It is the exaggerated sense of children's vulnerability that justifies contemporary obsessions about their safety. Today, safety is no longer about taking sensible precautions. Parents are bombarded with advice that demands that they create a risk-free world. The transformation of parks and playgrounds provides eloquent testimony to the fact that contemporary obsessions about children's vulnerability are reshaping everyday life. One accident in a playground can lead to the permanent closure of an amenity. In Greenwich, in South-East London, five playgrounds were shut following an incident in which a child was injured.[4]

Helen Brown fumed with rage when she received a letter from the headmaster of her child's school in Canterbury a few years ago. The school had just informed her that the playground for which Helen and other parents had spent months raising money was to be closed down because of concern about its safety. Helen's Parents' and Teachers' Association did not only collect the money; they also designed it and did the physical work of building it. 'This was a carefully constructed playground and the children loved it', observed Helen. She conceded that the wood had rotted in one of the pieces of equipment and that there was the danger that it could splinter. 'But that could have been easily replaced and the playground kept open', she argued.

The experience of Helen Brown's PTA is not at all unusual. Waves of anxiety about children's safety outdoors have engulfed both sides of the Atlantic. In the United States the traditional playground is in danger of becoming a historical relic. California has become the first state to mandate compliance with safety recommendations. That means that many much-loved ground fixtures such as monkey bars and merry-go-rounds are soon to be consigned to the museum. Other fixtures, such as swings, slides and seesaws, have been scaled down and modified. According to playground designer Jay Beckwith, the equipment will be lowered to the ground. 'Swings are going to be very scarce, and high swings are going to be gone.'

In Britain, fixed goalposts have been removed from school playgrounds. Witches' hats and the plank swing have been banished. The big, fast-moving roundabouts have also been removed along with heavy rocking-horses. Newly installed roundabouts are smaller and slower than previously and, of course, the swings are shorter. Playground areas are now covered with rubber to limit the damage when a child does fall.

Despite the fact that there is no evidence that injuries are increasing, the Children's Play Council has noticed that local authorities are increasingly restricting the kinds of activities and equipment in the play areas for which they are responsible. There is no evidence that children face greater dangers outdoors than in the past. There is on average just one child fatality per year in British playgrounds.

Playgrounds are no more dangerous than they were 20 or 40 years ago. What has changed is society's perception of children's resilience.

Physical injury to children is no longer accepted as an unexceptional fact of life of growing up. Contemporary perceptions of childhood regard such injury as 'unnecessary' and a reflection of irresponsible parenting. Leaflets published by the Child Accident Prevention Trust note that in 1996 over half a million children aged under 4 were injured as a result of an accident. It adds, 'many of these could be prevented'. This is probably true, and naturally parents want to prevent as many accidents as possible. But accidents are a fact of life even for children of the most cautious parents and, unfortunately, it is not possible to immunize children from experiencing physical injury. The attempt to construct an injury-free childhood can't prevent pain. It can only serve to inhibit children's development. Societies that still believe in children's resilience understand that the risk of children injuring themselves is a price well worth paying in order to allow them the freedom to explore their environment. Priscilla Alderson has noted that children in Norway have a slightly higher accident rate than other European children, which 'Norwegians consider is worth risking for the benefits of freely enjoying the countryside'.[5]

Every parent must have experienced that nervous grab in the stomach as you watch your child balance to walk along a wall, or struggle to climb a tree. The words 'come down now' are on your lips because you *know* that a fall will hurt, and you also know that a fall is possible. But you also know that if your child doesn't fall, he or she will have demonstrated a new skill in physical agility, learnt a new lesson and gained a new sense of confidence. To let your children continue and stretch the limits of their endurance is not without potential cost, but thwarting their ambition has a cost too. Getting the balance right is as difficult for the parent on the ground as it is for the child on the wall.

We are clearly not getting the balance right. A study written by Dr John McKendrick in conjunction with the University of Manchester found that a growing number of playgrounds are too safe. They are designed for anxious parents rather than for assisting the developmental needs of their cosseted youngsters. This survey of 87 families found that apprehensions about children's safety often had the effect of inhibiting the ability of children to learn for themselves.[6]

Contemporary perceptions of children's fragility directly contradict available evidence. Children were far more vulnerable a century or even 30 years ago than they are today. Child mortality rates have been dropping steadily since the nineteenth century. Stillbirth and infant mortality halved between 1971 and 1991. Deaths due to accident have also been falling, from 12.1 deaths per 100,000 in England and Wales in 1975 to 7.3 in 1991. Even traffic accidents – one of the greatest sources of worry to parents – pose less of a risk to children than they did 25 years ago. In 1995, fewer than 200 cyclists and pedestrians under 15 were killed. The death toll was 773 in 1975, 20 years earlier.[7]

If we compare the life of a child 100 years ago with today, it becomes evident that youngsters are living healthier and safer lives than ever before. A typical British child will never have the horrific experience of polio or spend time in an iron lung. They will not get tuberculosis from milk or rickets from vitamin D deficiency. They can go about their everyday lives without having to face a disease like scurvy from vitamin C deficiency, or smallpox. On average, the expectation of life for children is almost 30 years longer than that of their counterparts a century ago.

The good news about the relative improvement in children's physical health and safety tends to be ignored, since the belief in a child's innate vulnerability has little to do with his or her physical state of being. It is founded on the conviction that the principal zone of danger is to be found in the domain of the emotions. It is a child's emotional state that defines his or her vulnerability. The 'damaged child' has become the symbol of contemporary childhood. Increasingly, children's everyday problems tend to be interpreted as a manifestation of their *emotional damage*. And since a damaged emotion, unlike a broken arm, can never be put right it is assumed to represent a graver danger to children's well-being than physical injury.

The concept of emotional damage contains the implication of a life sentence. It is routinely asserted that children can be scarred for life by a variety of negative experiences and therefore need special protection. Many professionals involved in the field of childcare, education and psychology have an inflated conception of children's vulnerability to emotional damage. Childhood pain is now often redefined as a mental health problem. We have lost sight of the fact that frequently a child develops new strengths in the aftermath of an emotionally difficult encounter. Far from being resilient, children are portrayed as permanently subject to emotional distress. It is claimed that mental illness is a common condition of childhood. This pessimistic view of childhood constitutes the central theme of a 1999 report, *Bright Futures*, published by the British Mental Health Foundation, which claimed that around 20 per cent of children and adolescents experience psychological problems, ranging from anxiety and depression to psychotic and major developmental disorders.[8]

There is something self-serving about the way that adults have adopted childhood emotional problems to excuse their own behaviour. Today, it is common for grown-ups to blame their personal problems on difficult encounters experienced when they were youngsters. For many observers, distressing childhood events explain a variety of adult difficulties. Childhood afflictions are continually mobilized to make sense of the dysfunctional actions of adults. Public figures frequently try to avoid taking responsibility for their misdeeds by blaming distress suffered in childhood. Hillary Clinton, the USA's former first lady, clearly articulated this sentiment when she informed her interviewer that her husband's philandering was the outcome of the psychological abuse that he suffered as a child. 'He was so young, barely 4, when he was scarred by abuse', she insisted during the summer of 1999. British parliamentarian Ron Davis, former Welsh Secretary of State, blamed a run-in with the police over an alleged incident of homosexual blackmail which led to his resignation, on beatings he received from his father in childhood. When he told Parliament that 'We are what we are', the message was clear: negative childhood experiences directly shape the behaviour of adults.

The misconception that negative childhood experience constitutes a life sentence is justified on the ground that youngsters are uniquely vulnerable to damage to their emotions. It is often suggested that the emotional pain incurred is far more destructive than physical pain. Many observers contend that the 'invisible scars' inflicted on the psyche never heal, and damage the victim for life. Unlike physical acts, which have a beginning and an end and are specific in nature, the realm of the emotions knows no boundaries and is often seen to influence our very identity and existence. Emotional damage is invariably presented as an assault on a child's self-esteem. It is perpetually claimed that those children who have faced such an assault are likely to lose their self-confidence, suffer from anxiety and find it difficult to sustain close personal relations. The term *emotional abuse* is sometimes used to convey the warning that even insensitive remarks and criticisms by parents can unwittingly cause damage to their child. What underpins definitions of emotional abuse is the belief that since children are extremely fragile, they are easily traumatized and vulnerable to a wide variety of risks.

An NSPCC guide for protecting children in sports from abuse defines emotional abuse in terms that, in the past, would have been characterized as putting youngsters under pressure. It states that emotional abuse includes situations 'where parents or coaches subject children to constant criticism, bullying or unrealistic pressure to perform to high expectations'. According to child protection guidelines, issued by the Home Office, emotional abuse can refer to virtually every parental failing; from 'failure to meet a child's need for affection' to being so 'over-protective and possessive' that parents prevent their children from experiencing 'normal social contact or normal physical activity'. Anything that has the potential for making another person unhappy can be redefined as an assault on the emotions. Delegates at the 1999 conference of the British Professional Association of Teachers denounced the examination system for the 'sadistic' pressure it placed on children to perform well and called for its abolition on the grounds that it was little more than child abuse. The discovery that the age-old system of school examinations is actually dangerous to children's well-being reflects the tendency to reinterpret difficult or challenging encounters as potentially damaging to the children concerned. It is not merely exams that have been given a health warning. Competition, particularly competitive sports, has been attacked because it is said to strike a blow at children's self-esteem. Pushy parents have been labelled as emotional abusers because they place 'unacceptable' pressure on their children. In March 1998, a World in Action television documentary about the Royal Ballet School alleged that this institution's regime caused widespread anorexia, bulimia and bullying among the young students. It claimed that the dream of becoming a ballerina 'has turned into a nightmare for many children who go to the Royal School'. In the same vein, the demanding training programmes that American coaches impose on young gymnasts have been characterized as a form of child abuse.

Claims about risks to children's emotional well-being require an ever-expanding definition of mental illness. Take *Bright Futures*, the report of the Mental Health Foundation referred to above (p. 30). This report presents a vision of childhood experience that is likely to intensify parental paranoia. According to this report, at any one time, around 20 per cent of children and adolescents are experiencing psychological problems, ranging from anxiety and depression to psychotic and major developmental disorders. It claims that the rate of mental health problems among these young people is on the increase and demands more funds for promoting welfare. But this prediction follows from a definition that literally associates every significant childhood experience with the issue of mental health. 'For a child, mental health means being able to grow and develop emotionally, intellectually and spiritually in ways appropriate for that child's age', argues *Bright Futures*. Given its extremely broad definition of mental health, it is surprising that the proportion of children suffering from mental health problems is not nearer 100 per cent. Dr Jennifer Cunningham, a community paediatrician from Glasgow, and a critic of the methodology used by *Bright Futures*, argues that 'mental health is defined so widely that any child who has a normal reaction to adverse circumstances in their lives is now assumed to have mental health problems'.[9]

Children's mental health problems are often blamed on poor parenting. The association of children's mental illness with the actions of their mothers and fathers implies that they are even at risk from their parents. If there is a problem blame your parents! Experts continually indict poor parenting for the emotional and behavioural disorders of children.[10] Hippies in the 1960s used to declare that your 'parents screw you up'. This flippant remark has now been converted into a significant risk factor afflicting children.

The burden of bonding

Society's exaggerated perception of children's vulnerability is most systematically expressed in the idea that emotional trauma and other negative experiences scar them for life. This fatalistic diagnosis is predicated on the assumption that once children have been emotionally hurt they lack the resilience to repair the damage. Even as adults, they will continue to be haunted by afflictions experienced early in life. This bleak view of the human condition that suggests that children's early experiences mark them for life has been characterized as the doctrine of *infant determinism* by the American psychologist Jerome Kagan.[11] According to Kagan, this doctrine has been around since the eighteenth century. Sigmund Freud is probably the most prominent thinker associated with the idea that the early experiences of an infant determine a child's future. The thesis of infant determinism claims that early experiences have an indelible and, in most cases, irreversible impact on the future life of a child. Although the idea of infant determinism has been around for some time, it has never before been used so widely as an all-purpose diagnosis of every conceivable problem. It is only in recent decades that this argument has been systematically deployed to scare parents.

Child-rearing manuals and parenting magazines regularly convey the impression that since the experiences of the earliest years determine a person's future, the responsibility for an individual's fate lies in her parents' hands. The implication of the thesis of infant determinism is that parenting, specifically parenting in early childhood, is *the* main variable influencing the fate of a child. The corollary of this argument is that incompetent parenting during the early years of children's lives can have long-term devastating outcomes for them.

Contemporary arguments about infant determinism are based on ideas pioneered by psychologists such as John Bowlby and Eric Erikson. Bowlby and Erikson believed that what happened to a child during the first hours, weeks and months of life had a profound influence on the entire course of a child's development. These arguments were further elaborated in the 1960s in Bowlby's theories of how children relate to their parents through 'attachment'. Attachment theory claimed that the constant presence of a loving and responsive attachment figure – usually the mother – was the foundation for lifelong mental health. By the 1980s, it was even argued that a child's development would be put at risk if its mother failed to bond with it immediately after birth. Long-term personality disorders were frequently explained as a consequence of circumstances where accessibility to a responsive attachment figure was denied.[12]

The idea of attachment has had a phenomenal impact on the Western imagination. New mothers who have just gone through painful labour are encouraged to bond with their babies. 'After the umbilical cord is clamped, the nurse quickly lays the new born child on its mother's belly to begin a magical process called *bonding*', comment Sandra Scarr and Judy Dunn, two child development psychologists critical of this ritual. Failure to bond has become one of the anxieties preoccupying expectant mothers. Some psychologists go as far as to state that the failure to bond can lead to a condition they diagnose as attachment disorder. According to one hysterical account, 'the numbers of unbonded children, who may become the victimisers of adults, parents, and other children, are growing and will continue to grow if the bonding problem is not addressed'.[13] It adds, 'if proper bonding does not occur, a child may become a "child without conscience"'.[14] From the standpoint of infant determinism, failure to bond, the provision of substandard parenting, the absence of a stimulating environment and any form of emotional injury will leave an indelible mark on a child for the rest of her life. In recent decades this outlook has come to dominate the popular imagination. When a news reporter informs us that a child has been traumatized through some terrible encounter – we all intuitively suspect that this poor soul will bear the burden of this episode for ever. Happily, infant determinism is more of a cultural myth than a scientific truth.

Popular perceptions regarding children's vulnerability find little support in empirical research. The idea that adverse experiences early in life leave irreversible effects on an individual's life has been questioned by numerous studies. Investigations of children who had been subjected to negative experiences early in life but who subsequently were given an opportunity to thrive through a major change in their upbringing confirm that they possess the resilience to overcome adversity. One well-known study of children reared in institutions from their early weeks in life and who remained there for periods ranging from two to seven years before they were adopted, showed that despite such adverse circumstances, most of them settled well in their new homes. Despite virtually no opportunity to form attachments to any one person during their early years, many of them succeeded in adapting to their new environment.[15] Even proponents of attachment theory are forced to concede that there is little empirical evidence to sustain their thesis. When Bowlby attempted to test his theory he was surprised to discover that youngsters proved to be far more resilient than he suspected. He found that children who were separated from their mothers for a long time tended to behave in ways that were only marginally different from those who did not experience separation. Bowlby and his colleagues were forced to conclude that 'statements implying that children who are brought up in institutions or who suffer other forms of serious privation and deprivation in early life *commonly* develop psychopathic or affectionless characters are seen to be mistaken'.[16]

The plausibility of infant determinism is based on the fact that it appeals to common sense. The proposition that in their early years children are impressionable seems self-evident. The idea that traumatic events impact on children for life has for long been accepted since the writings of Freud. Freud's important contribution has suffered from many distortions. During the past 50 years, his interesting insights have been expanded to an extreme version of the Freudian argument that implies that the childhood experience of trauma or abuse automatically has an irreversible effect on a person's life. Horrific experiences can deeply affect a child, but most youngsters succeed in overcoming them. Parents need not fear that a child's traumatic experience constitutes a life sentence.

It is now commonly believed that the experience of abuse continues to affect not only the abused but also the next generation. According to many proponents of infant determinism, abuse is an intergenerational moral disease. They contend that abusers were themselves abused when they were children and their victims are likely to manifest delinquent behaviour in the future. The belief that abuse is handed down from one generation to the next is widely regarded as beyond question. Yet, like many of the propositions advanced by infant determinists, this too is open to doubt. There is considerable evidence that the best predictor of whether a child is likely to be an abuser is not whether they have been earlier abused but that they have come from a disrupted and disadvantaged family.[17]

A major Danish study that sought to investigate the connection between early life trauma and the quality of life some 30 years later directly contradicts the thesis that children cannot overcome early traumatic experiences. The study found only a very small connection between the quality of life as an adult and traumatic events in connection with pregnancy, birth and the first year of life. The study looked at cases of unwanted children, whose mothers suffered from mental illness and who were placed in children's homes. It even considered cases where children were born despite attempts to abort them. Yet these early adverse circumstances appeared to have a 'very small effect on the child as an adult'. This impressive capacity to handle such adverse circumstances suggests that children's resilience, along with positive support, can help neutralize the negative consequences of early trauma.[18] The ability of youngsters to cope with adverse circumstances was also clearly suggested by an investigation of a group of children each of whom had a parent who had committed suicide. The investigators found that all the children were affected by this tragedy and experienced it as a major trauma. But when the children were followed up several years later, there was a noticeable difference in their longer-term reaction to their traumatic experience. Some of the children were manifestly disturbed, yet others had managed to adapt to their circumstance and showed no symptoms of maladjustment. The investigators concluded that the explanation for this differential reaction was linked to the subsequent stability and quality of life experienced by the children. Studies of young children who had experienced natural disasters such as earthquakes, fires, floods, hurricanes and volcanic eruptions indicate that though these events had caused considerable upheaval at the time, they did not necessarily cause long-term damage.[19]

The American psychologist Emmy Werner studied a group of 689 children born on the Hawaiian Island of Kauai. Information was collected on this sample when they were 2, 10, 18 and 32 years of age. A significant proportion of the children in the sample grew up in conditions of serious adversity. Pre-natal complications, poverty, alcoholism in the family, family instability and parental mental illness were some of the conditions they faced. Not surprisingly, many of these children developed serious behavioural problems. But about a third of these children succeeded in overcoming their adverse circumstances and entered into early adulthood unscathed by their early experiences. What the study suggested was that vulnerability was not a fixed phenomenon. It existed in an open-ended relationship with resilience. The best predictor of long-term psychological problems among these children was prolonged residence in a family of poverty, combined with biological stress surrounding birth. However, even these factors did not possess strong predictive powers. The authors concluded on an optimistic note: 'As we watched these children grow from babyhood to adulthood, we could not help but respect the self-righting tendencies within them that produced normal development under all but the most persistently adverse circumstances.'[20]

From his analysis of studies such as the one carried out in Kauai, Jerome Kagan concludes that it was the mother's social class, and not differences in the treatment of the child, that was the critical factor in influencing the outcome. While the potential impact of poverty on a child's development may be crucial, it is important not to accept a form of social determinism as an alternative to infant determinism. The long-term impact of early experiences is mediated through numerous events and relations. Depending on circumstances, youngsters can be either vulnerable or resilient. Moreover, the reaction to one type of adversity tells us little about how a child might react to a problem in the future. One leading psychologist argues that 'vulnerable children can develop resilience; resilient children may become vulnerable'. However, thankfully, positive experiences with supportive adults can provide a condition for overcoming the problems of early years.[21]

To question the assumptions of infant determinism is not to deny the special significance of early experience. What is at issue is how these early events affect a person. Infant determinism offers a one-sidedly fatalistic outlook that holds that the effects of early negative encounters cannot be altered or eliminated by subsequent experiences. Early experience does not inevitably and directly determine adult life. It provides the point of departure for subsequent experience. For the psychologists Alan and Ann Clarke the significance of early experience is its foundational character in that it sets the tone for future experience. One negative experience may lead to others. It can act as the first link in a chain of destructive forms of behaviour. But the cause cannot be reduced to the initial trauma: the entire chain of events illuminates the outcome. Moreover, there is no inexorable process that leads from one unfortunate event to the other. According to the Clarkes, the chain can even be broken and the effects of early trauma can be neutralized.[22]

Trauma expert Yvonne McEwan claims that children have a fantastic capacity for recovery – 'much better than adults, because they don't understand the implications of what is happening'. McEwan is a robust promoter of the idea that children's powers of recovery are phenomenal – and that includes children who are critically ill in hospital, children involved in disasters, children in conflict zones and socially deprived areas. Her follow-up study on children after the Lockerbie tragedy indicates that children coped remarkably well with the effects of this tragedy. The research showed that there was no difference between these children and others – 'apart from an improvement in educational attainment'.[23]

Proponents of infant determinism require extreme examples of child neglect to sustain their argument. A recent study reported in British newspapers of neglected swaddled babies in a Romanian orphanage, subjected to a life of misery, concluded that a mother's touch is crucial for a baby's development. This study of extreme and, by any standards, exceptional neglect allowed Professor Mary Carlson of the Harvard Medical School to provide the 'first hard evidence' that shows how the lack of physical affection can stunt physical stature and mental abilities.[24] But does this study prove anything? No doubt a child systematically neglected by a brutal regime in an orphanage or raised alone in a dark closet for 36 months is unlikely to emerge a normal, healthy 3-year-old. The effects of such a destructive early experience are unlikely ever to be overcome. However, such extreme examples offer little insight into understanding the general relationship of early experience to subsequent development. More specifically, to associate the tragedies that emerge in extreme settings with the developmental problems confronting ordinary parents is to substitute scare tactics for reasoned argument.

Infant determinism is a powerful idea with which to scare parents. If children are indeed so weak and fragile that they cannot overcome the negative experiences of their early years then parents need to be permanently on guard. Fortunately this powerful idea has little foundation in empirical evidence. Parents would do well to ignore the frequent appeals to what is in fact a display of cultural prejudice.

Three

Parents as Gods

The corollary of the assumption of children's innate vulnerability is the conviction that parenting has an overwhelming impact on the child's development. The tendency to downgrade children's internal resources, their coping skills and resilience has been paralleled by the emergence of 'parent determinism'. The belief that children are hopelessly vulnerable and unlikely to be able to cope with the trials of life encourages the view that their fate is decisively determined by their parents. Time and again, mothers and fathers are informed that their behaviour determines the experience of infancy that in turn determines the child's future. Parenting has become an all-purpose variable that shapes a child's future prospects. The influence of omnipotent parenting is the other side of the coin of child vulnerability. Parental determinism not only diminishes the role of children, but also overlooks the influence that their peers and social circumstances have in the shaping of a child's development. The assumption that so much is at stake with parenting legitimizes a highly interventionist adult role in childhood. The widespread acceptance of this view helps to foster a climate of child protection and parental anxiety. The more we conceive of the child as vulnerable, the more we see her future as depending on the actions of her parents.

The inflation of the impact of parenting

Today, parenting has been transformed into an all-purpose independent variable that seems to have the capacity to explain everything to do with an infant's development. Parenting has been used as a main variable to explain the following childhood problems:

- **Eating disorders.** A study published in the *British Journal of Psychiatry* in February 2000 claims that anorexia nervosa among young girls may be caused by over-protective parents who deny their children independence. Despite being based on a small sample of 40 families of girls with anorexia, the study was widely reported as authoritative by the media.[1]
- **The 'terrible twos'.** An American research team claimed that parents are more to blame than their toddlers for temper tantrums and fits of obstinacy known as the 'terrible twos'. Parents who fail to work as a team and who are inept at managing a child's budding individuality create the conditions for this stage of violent tantrums.[2]
- **Student anxiety.** Don Davies, a British educational psychologist, believes that parents are responsible for the stress that A-level students experience prior to and during their exam periods. He claims that although parents are not entirely to blame, they make a 'substantial contribution' to the problem. It appears that anxiety and panic are like an infectious disease which students catch from their parents. Parents who worry simply transmit their fears to their children.[3]
- **Failure in school.** Numerous newspaper reports and two widely publicized television programmes have claimed that children's academic achievement is compromised if their mother is in full-time employment. One such report stated that such children are twice as likely to fail exams if their mother works than if she stays at home. Mothers who work outside the home are also indicted for risking their child's psychological development.[4]
- **Depression.** Some studies report that a higher incidence of depression occurred in children with a parent or parents who suffered from the illness. Children of depressed parents experienced significant cognitive and emotional delays and problems at school. Children with mothers who suffer from post-natal depression are said to be at a particular disadvantage. According to one account, infants whose mothers are depressed in their first year may not learn to modulate attention and emotion, resulting in permanently impaired cognitive ability.
- **Low IQ.** A controversial study carried out by Dr Susan Pawlby and published in January 2000 argued that the sons of women who

suffered from post-natal depression had notably lower IQs than their schoolmates. The study published in the *Journal of Child Psychology and Psychiatry* stated that babies suffer because of the lack of attention they receive in the first weeks of their new lives.[5]

- **Violent behaviour.** In November 1999, the *Observer* reported on American research that claimed that children who were allowed to play with toy guns were likely to be violent in later life. According to Professor Pamela Orphinas of the University of Georgia, parental attitudes to play fighting and aggression are the most important factors in shaping a child's future behaviour.[6]

- **Psychological damage 1.** A report published by Parentline in April 2000 stated that thousands of parents are psychologically damaging their teenage children because of the way they speak to them.[7]

- **Psychological damage 2.** A report widely publicized in the press claimed that children are damaged by 'quality time'. Researchers claimed that the brains of babies and toddlers could develop at a slower rate if they are 'overstimulated' by parents in snatched moments of quality time.[8]

This sample of child pathologies attributed to parental behaviour represents a very small proportion of the conditions for which mothers and fathers are blamed. Almost any child dysfunction is likely to be presented, at some time or another, as the consequence of some form of parental impact.

At a time when conventional wisdom asserts that parenting determines virtually every aspect of a child's future, it is worth noting that this perception is a recent invention of society's imagination. Even today, many societies in Asia and Africa believe that it is not the action of parents, but of God or fate that determines the future of their children. The idea that adult life was predestined by factors outside parents' control was widely held in European societies until recent times. The belief that parental behaviour exercises the key influence developed alongside the emergence of the nuclear family. One reason for this perception is that a child's reaction to a parent is easy to observe. 'We have seen children cry following a punishment, smile after a kiss, obey a gentle request, but disobey a harsh one', notes Kagan. These experiences appear to confirm a one-sided view of the parent–child relationship. The parent acts and the child merely reacts. Parental initiative shapes the child. Kagan warns that since it is more difficult to imagine a child's interpretation of her interaction with a parent, we mistakenly attribute a relation of cause and effect.[9]

In recent decades the view of extensive child vulnerability has encouraged some people to adopt an absolutist notion of parenting. Today, every childhood problem can be linked to parental deficiencies. Parents are continually warned that if they fail to adopt the latest child-rearing practices they will bear responsibility for grave developmental problems in the future. A child's emotional well-being and psychological and future development are directly linked to the way they are handled by their mothers and fathers. Parents are not only expected to nourish and care for their young ones. They are also warned that unless they follow current advice on numerous practical aspects of parenting they will undermine their child's long-term development. Since the experience of children in their early years is irreversible, parents cannot afford to make any mistakes. The consequences of poor baby-care cannot be corrected in later years.

The moment a child is born, the action of the mother is assumed to have profound long-term significance. Mothers must lovingly hold their baby in order to bond. In recent decades, fathers too have been encouraged to bond at this crucial stage. Failure to bond after birth is deemed to have the potential to damage the mother–infant relationship. An infant's failure to thrive, parental neglect and even child abuse are said to be some of the outcomes when postpartum bonding does not occur. After bonding comes the challenge of providing a baby with the right kind of stimulation and care. According the doctrine of infant determinism, this is a critical period when child-rearing techniques can have a fundamental impact on the baby's long-term development. It is not good enough for parents merely to nourish and play with their babies. There is now an influential body of opinion promoting the message that the earliest years of a child's life are critical for developing their brain. Advocates of this standpoint justify their cause by appealing to new developments in brain research. A special conference organized at the White House in 1997 gave official sanction to the view that the amount of time that carers spent talking, reading and stimulating infants was the principal predictor of their long-term intellectual and psychological development. Proponents of this thesis claim that an adult's potential vocabulary is determined largely by the words filtered through the brain before the age of 3. The publicity surrounding the White House Conference on Early Child Development provided a tremendous boost to advocates of infant determinism. Hillary Clinton offered a classic presentation of this doctrine. Her view was that the experiences of the first three years of a child's life 'can determine whether children will grow up to be peaceful or violent citizens, focused or undisciplined workers, attentive or detached parents themselves'. The message was clear: parenting – especially during the first three years – is the principal variable that determines the outcome of a child's development.[10]

The linkage of child brain development with child-rearing practices greatly expands the significance attached to the impact of parenting. Parents are now advised that everything they do in these crucial early years really matters. Advocates of infant determinism categorically state that a child's brain and intellectual development is linked to how carers love, laugh, stimulate, talk and read to the child. As the lead article in *Newsweek* put it: 'Every lullaby, every giggle and peek-a-boo, triggers a crackling in his neural pathways, laying the groundwork for what could someday be a love of art or a talent for soccer or a gift for making and keeping friends.'[11] Gone are the days when parents can simply love and touch and enjoy their child for its own sake. Loving and stimulating are now mandatory child-rearing practices demanded by the new theory of early learning.

In recent years, there has been an explosion of research and publicity that insists that human behaviour is shaped and determined by the first three years of a child's life. Numerous child experts claim that without proper parenting, emotional nurturing, diet and stimulation, the development of a child's brain will be stunted. This alarmist claim was summed up by the following article title in *Time Magazine*: 'Too many children today live in conditions that threaten their brain development.'[12] According to the argument, the number of synapses between brain cells rapidly expands before a child's third birthday. However, if stimulating parenting does not reinforce these connections, they will shrink and disappear. There is a veritable industry of advice providers who prey on parents' desperate hope that their children will turn out to be intelligent. When mothers and fathers are not lectured about the latest insights of brain research, they are told that breast-feeding makes for smarter babies. Bottle-fed babies will have lower IQs than those who are breast-fed. Advice for parents continually emphasizes the long-term consequences of the ways they go about nurturing their babies. 'Love boosts the brainpower' advises the NSPCC.[13] It also claims that 'Babies who get lots of affection show better problem-solving skills at one year of age.' Reading to babies and playing classical music to infants are promoted as vital measures for guaranteeing children's intellectual development. In the United States parents who fail to properly nurture infants during this vital period are condemned for creating major problems for society. Crime, teenage pregnancy, drug abuse, child abuse, homelessness and welfare dependency are all attributed to parents' failure to nurture their children correctly during the first three years of life.[14]

American child-rearing fads usually have a habit of making their way to Britain before too long. Although Downing Street has not yet organized a conference on brain research or early learning, it is evident that British child professionals and parenting magazines have clearly absorbed the new message. Time and again parents are reminded that their mistakes during the first three years of their toddler's life can have serious negative consequences for the long-term well-being of their offspring. To take a few examples:

Nutritionists claim that many British parents are mistaken in the belief that what is a healthy diet for an adult also applies to children. It is claimed that babies and toddlers who receive normal adult fare are deprived of energy-dense food and therefore lack the right calorie intake. According to Dr Jackie Stordy of the University of Surrey, this impedes children's mental and physical growth, placing them at risk from anaemia, stunted growth, learning difficulties, diabetes and heart disease.[15] Parents not only have to monitor constantly the food they give to their toddler, but also have to be careful to set the right example during eating. The May 2000 issue of *Mother and Baby* is categorical on this point. It notes that: 'With an increasing number of children – some as young as eight or nine years old – falling victim from eating disorders, it is worth considering the messages your own eating habits may be giving to your young baby or toddler.' Parents are advised to desist from behaviour – such as dieting, or not eating with children – that can give negative food messages to the child.[16] Mothers and fathers trying to cut down on their calorie intake now need to diet in secret in case their darling receives the wrong signals about eating.

Parents who allow their children a dummy supposedly risk undermining their intelligence. In the past, the anti-dummy brigade raised the objection 'that it did not look right' and that it exposed a child to dirt and infection. With today's emphasis on early learning, dummies are more likely to be indicted for delaying a child's speech development. A Manchester-based speech therapist, Nadine Arditti, argues that dummies can cause significant speech impediments because they severely obstruct articulation. One study carried out by the Medical Research Council has concluded that the use of a dummy was the strongest predictor of 'reduced' intelligence amongst young children. 'Fact – sucking a dummy could delay her development', stated *Prima Baby* in no uncertain terms.[17]

Parents had better learn to be musical. The April 2000 issue of *Mother and Baby* asked its readers: 'We all know music can soothe your baby, but did you know that it can also help him to grow?' Pity the poor child whose mother and father are tone deaf. New 'research' claims that music helps boost babies' brainpower.[18] But help is on the way. The National Lottery has awarded £1 million to an organization devoted to encouraging pregnant mothers to play and sing to their unborn children.[19]

It is also claimed that children's intelligence is influenced by whether they are breast-fed or not. A number of studies have discovered a 'small but still detectable' increase in cognitive development to an eight-point IQ difference between breast- and bottle-fed babies. In case you remain unconvinced, *Mother and Baby* offers another argument for the 'breast way forward'. It cites an Australian study of 2,000 children, which purports to show that those who were breast-fed exclusively for four months were less likely to have asthma and other allergies by the age of 6. If parents are so irresponsible as to bottle-feed their babies they should use milk supplemented with iron. According to *Parents* magazine, Birmingham Children's Hospital tested 100 children aged up to 24 months and found that remedying iron deficiency led to improved language, motor and social skills.[20]

Parents also have a duty to laugh on demand and stimulate their baby using the 'appropriate' tone. A child expert is quoted in *Prima Baby* as stating that the time when babies first laugh 'really depends entirely on what stimulation your baby is given'. Unsmiling babies provide incontrovertible proof of unstimulating parenting.[21]

Listening is another skill that parents must perfect if they are to avoid damaging their children's well-being. 'You can boost your baby's development and your child's confidence simply by listening to them', advises an expert in *Practical Parenting*. It also helps your baby to talk. The expert advice is to 'practise listening so that it becomes automatic'.

Parents must be constantly attentive to their babies' signals when they talk to them. In April 2000, *Practical Parenting* informed its readers that by the time of her second birthday, your toddler may know more than 200 words, and you can teach her more if you are quick off the mark. Why? Because when your baby points at something she wants you to name, 'you have to be on the ball: even a 10-second delay before hearing the word may mean she'll forget what's being named'. Parents who are slow on the uptake bear responsibility for the restricted vocabulary of their toddler.[22]

Parents must not only be quick off the mark and anticipate their toddler's next signal, but must insulate their children from television. 'Kill your television', warns an expert in *Baby Magazine*. It appears that babies and children under 3 can easily get addicted to the visual aspect of TV and 'this does nothing to help them learn and develop language'.[23]

The supposed educational value of laughing, singing, playing music, listening, anticipating a baby's next signal pales in comparison with the impact that parents can have if they read books to their babies. It appears that it is never too early to read books to a baby for the magic to work. Britain's leading proponent of this thesis, Professor Barrie Wade of Birmingham University, discovered that children whose families read to them from the age of nine months gained a head start in maths when they got to school. Others have suggested that such children were on average 27 per cent ahead in English and 22 per cent ahead in number skills by the time they started school.[24]

The view that certain forms of parental behaviour guarantee the development of certain character traits and educational outcomes has been around for the better part of two centuries. But claims made in the past about the impact of parenting are insignificant in relation to the bloated version of today. What has also changed is the way in which almost every parenting act is correlated with either a negative or a positive outcome. Parenting is now analysed in minute detail and everyday routine practices are endowed with important implications for child development. It is not surprising that parents who are told that they possess this enormous power to do good and to do harm feel anxious and overwhelmed. John Bruer, in his powerful critique of the use of brain research to legitimize the theory of infant determinism, *The Myth of the First Three Years*, is concerned about the way that claims about early years' development evokes a sense of guilt among parents. He cites a parent who stated: 'I have to admit when I first read the research, I felt as though I'd failed my three kids.'[25]

The myth of the Mozart effect

A whole industry has been built around the doctrine of infant and parent determinism. Parents are preyed on by entrepreneurs who offer them all kinds of gadgets to make sure that their children get the maximum amount of stimulation in their early years. The so-called Mozart effect – the idea that musical training and listening to classical music enhance a child's intelligence – has encouraged millions of American parents to purchase special videos or to send their toddlers to music class. A company called Baby Einstein has been particularly successful in the marketing of its series of videos titled 'Baby Einstein', 'Baby Mozart', 'Baby Shakespeare' and 'Baby Bach'. In March 2000, the company announced that the products would be launched in Britain so that babies as young as 1 could gain an intellectual head-start in life. Even the Government has got in on the act. During the summer of 1999, Ofsted announced that it would set early learning goals for nurseries in order to provide a more structured and stimulating environment for toddlers.

Contemporary obsessions with early learning are driven by the cultural myth of infant determinism. Its main effect is to intimidate parents. Well-known child psychologists Sandra Scarr and Judith Dunn believe that this myth provides the rationale for guilt-tripping parents. They argue that 'The baby who needs to be taught and stimulated is, in our opinion, a creation of salesmen who profit from making parents feel that they are not doing enough for their children.'[26]

Numerous researchers question contemporary myths that suggest that infant development will be hindered without systematic parental intervention. For example, the claim made by Francine Rauscher that listening to Mozart's music enhances a child's IQ or spatial-temporal abilities has been undermined by studies that have tried to measure the Mozart effect. Numerous studies have failed to confirm the alleged benefits of children listening to Mozart.[27]

Two leading American child psychologists and a leading authority on speech development have recently published a book that warns that the demand to artificially stimulate children can actually do more harm than good. They question the claims that babies will become smarter if they are stimulated by flash cards, Mozart tapes or other gadgets. They write that 'everything we know about babies suggests that these artificial interventions are at best useless and at worst distractions from the normal interaction between grown-ups and babies'. Their sentiment is informed by a view of child development that understands that babies have important internal resources for interacting and learning from their experience. According to Alison Gopnik, Andrew Meltzoff and Patricia Kuhl, babies are already as smart as they can be, they know what they need to know and are rather good at getting the kinds of information they need. Babies thrive and learn about the real world by playing with things that surround them, and 'most of all by playing with the people who love them'.[28]

The idea that a child's intellectual development is determined during the first three years of his life goes against much of what we know about learning. Children who are slow at learning to read at the age of 6 or 7 often go on to master this skill three or four years later. Indeed, with proper instruction teenagers and adults can pick up reading skills later in life. According to John Bruer, most knowledge and skills are culturally transmitted rather than biologically determined. 'Don't worry about cramming all those music, dance and sports lessons into a child's early years', he advises. Bruer believes that, as far as we know, 'the windows of opportunity stay open much, much longer than that'. Brain research has been misused to argue that parental stimulation during the early years helps the development of the brain of a child. Yet according to the available neuroscientific data, this process of development is mainly under genetic and not environmental control. Bruer argues that the amount and quality of early stimulation 'affects neither the timing nor the rate of synapse formation'. There is nothing wrong with reading, singing, talking to and cuddling your baby. It is a pleasurable experience that is worthwhile in its own right. But don't believe for one minute that these 'stimulating' activities will do anything to boost your child's brainpower.[29]

The good news is that children are hot-wired for developing. As Steve Petersen, a neuroscientist at Washington University, argues, 'at a minimum, development really wants to happen. It takes very impoverished environments to interfere with development.' What does that mean? 'Don't raise your child in a closet, starve them, or hit them on the head with a frying pan.'[30] Children actually play an important role in influencing their development through their experiences in the environment they inhabit. It is only when they are confronted with an abusive and neglectful environment that this development can be compromised. What children require are protective and loving parents, responsible adults and a surrounding community within which the child will be socialized. Within the context of this normal environment, the impact of parenting is far less significant than we suspect. Child psychologist Sandra Scarr goes as far as to argue that 'good enough' ordinary parents probably have the same effect on their child's development as 'culturally defined super-parents'.[31]

Parents know only too well that their children do not turn out according to their big plan. Parents do have an important role to play in nurturing, stimulating and socializing their children. And no doubt distinct parenting styles influence a child's subsequent development. Judith Rich Harris is the author of *The Nurture Assumption*, a stimulating critique of parent determinism. She believes that the impact of parenting is mainly restricted to how children behave at home. Harris adds that parents also supply knowledge and training that their children can take with them to the outside world. However, she contends that parents have little power to determine how their children will behave when they are not at home. According to Harris, children's behaviour in the outside world is learnt in their peer group.[32]

Arguments about what influences a child's development are far from resolved. There can be little doubt that important aspects of a child's personality are inherited. There is also considerable evidence that shows that social circumstances and environment play a crucial role in the shaping of a child's development. No doubt Harris's thesis of peer influence also has considerable significance in illuminating the process of child development. The relationship of parenting to any particular outcomes is, if anything, much more difficult to grasp. Parenting and family make an important contribution to a child's development – but they do *not* determine any particular outcome. As we argue in Chapter Seven, we actually know very little about the impact of parenting. Serious research, unlike the plethora of parenting advice available through child-rearing manuals and parenting magazines, is very hesitant on this subject. Why? Because the contribution of parental practices to the development of a child's personality cannot be viewed in isolation from the wider social and cultural setting. Moreover, in some sense parental behaviour is closely linked to that of the child and, through a complex process of interaction, a unique parent–child relationship is forged.

So it is culture and not science that encourages parents to acquire an inflated sense of power over their children's destiny. It is culture and not science that stirs the public imagination to panic about children's vulnerability. Inflating the public's perception of parental impact promises the potential of influence and power but inevitably delivers disappointing results. Unfortunately, when this happens we don't discard the doctrine of parent determinism, we insist instead that mothers and fathers learn and adopt new parenting skills. Such pressures have led and continue to lead to a major redefinition of parenting. This redefinition of parenting, which is an important source of parental paranoia, is examined in the next chapter.

Parenting before children

Proponents of parent determinism continually expand the range of tasks demanded of fathers and mothers. There is a relentless pressure on parents to reflect continually on how their actions influence their infant's life. With so much power attributed to parenting, mothers and fathers are continually forced to calculate the effect of their actions on their child's development. Parents are under pressure to adopt this approach way before the child is born. The idea that experiences of early life are decisive in influencing what happens in later years is increasingly interpreted to include the experience of pregnancy. Parent determinism encourages a form of thought that continually moves back into the deep past. Parents' actions during pregnancy are portrayed as crucially important for the healthy development of a child. Indeed there is even a tendency to accord potential parents' action before pregnancy as deeply significant for the future well-being of the child. Consequently experts now instruct and warn parents to be vigilant about what they should and should not do during the period in which they are thinking of starting a family. Parent determinism puts pressure on mothers and fathers to alter their behaviour before their child is born – even before its conception.

Ante-natal care is not a new concept. It has been a part of medicine from the turn of the century. As early as 1901, the Scottish obstetrician J. W. Ballantyne proposed a 'pre-maternity' hospital where women could be cared for and doctors could study the pregnant state. Over the next three decades ante-natal care became increasingly widespread, with 80 per cent of women receiving some kind of care by 1935.[33] However, at that time and until recent decades, ante-natal care concentrated on the health of the woman, rather than on the developing foetus. Little was known about what could and could not influence foetal development. In fact, it was not until the thalidomide tragedy in the late 1950s and early 1960s, when hundreds of women gave birth to severely disabled babies after taking the anti-sickness drug Distaval, that the medical profession realized that substances taken in medicine could harm the developing foetus. Until then it had been assumed that the placenta acted as a protective barrier between the maternal and foetal systems.

Since the 1960s, much attention has been devoted to what is and is not harmful to a developing pregnancy. Medical science has demonstrated that the health of a baby is not only affected by the actions of the mother while pregnant, but even in some circumstances by what she does before she conceives. Parenting determinism has attached itself to this discovery, leading to a reorientation of the focus of modern ante-natal and pre-conception care.

The modern pregnant woman is expected to adopt the lifestyle and behaviour of a 'putative parent' while she is pregnant and before she becomes pregnant. There are some sound reasons why women might want to modify their behaviour to maximize the chances of a healthy pregnancy and healthy child. A summary of expert evidence considered by the Parliamentary Health Committee in 1991 identified certain factors that were known to influence the outcome of a pregnancy: smoking, alcohol intake, certain medicines and recreational drugs, diet, infections such as rubella, toxoplasmosis and sexually transmitted diseases, and exposure to environmental factors such as radiation and chemicals.[34]

Consequently women trying to conceive are advised to:

- cut down on caffeine as it is associated with a slight increase in the risk of early miscarriage;
- ensure a balanced diet, with supplements of folic acid from three months before attempted conception to three months after, to reduce risk of neural tube defects such as spina bifida;
- quit smoking as smokers tend to have babies of lower birth weight, and smoking can affect the functioning of the placenta;
- reduce alcohol intake, as alcohol is thought to increase risk of miscarriage and the intake of large quantities of alcohol have been linked to foetal malformation;
- take a blood test to ensure immunity to rubella and, if necessary, be vaccinated against it before conception;
- be tested for infections such as chlamydia.

This advice is pretty much common sense and it would be rash to take issue with it. But zealous health promoters turn sensible advice into an obsessive concern with the lifestyles of pregnant women. Potential parents now have to watch what they do, since even a mistake committed some time before a child is born could have grave consequences in the future.

Pregnant women, in particular, are obliged to demonstrate that they are responsible by following practices prescribed by the parenting lobby. Visibly pregnant women who flout 'healthy pregnancy' advice by smoking or drinking, or fail to attend ante-natal hospital checks, are subject to disapproval and admonishment. This has reached absurd proportions in the USA where it is common for bartenders to refuse to serve alcohol to pregnant women in bars and restaurants, and users of recreational drugs have been subject to restraining orders.

Couples trying to conceive and parents-to-be are intensely vulnerable to the pressure they face from their professional advisers. Hints that their actions may compromise the health and development of their child-to-be are difficult to disregard. The insecure position of parents-to-be is regularly exploited by experts who propose a variety of measures that can help babies become smarter or healthier. 'Some babies will be brainier than others just because of their genes, but there are other ways to add extra points to your baby's IQ long before he is born', is the opinion of an expert in *Prima Baby*.[35] How this feat is to be achieved is not explained, but instead mothers-to-be are instructed to 'start talking' to their tummy, so that the baby-to-be learns to recognize her mum's voice. Getting parents used to the idea that what they do is decisive is the hidden agenda behind a lot of the advice. Fathers too are advised to talk to the 'baby' in the womb by the Government-endorsed *The Bounty Guide to Fatherhood*.[36] Such advice has no scientific merit. Its main purpose is to inculcate in its readers the thesis of parent determinism. Getting parents to listen to the baby in the womb is a way of training them for their future role.

Here in the UK a climate of fear has been created that leads many pregnant women to be neurotic about their behaviour lest they inadvertently place their child at risk. David Paintin, Fellow of the Royal College of Obstetricians and Gynaecologists and board member of the British Pregnancy Advisory Service, tells of how he has counselled women who have sought abortion advice because they are terrified that they have damaged their children-to-be by some action taken before they knew they were pregnant.

Advice to pregnant and pre-pregnant women stretches far beyond the boundaries of what has been proven. There is a growth industry in books, magazines, videos and health promotion advice about how to ensure your child has the best possible start in life. And it is consumed eagerly by pregnant women and their partners. When Francesca Naish and Janette Roberts published their book *Healthy Parents, Better Babies: A Couple's Guide to Natural Preconception Care*, it took Australia by storm. The authors assert that, by following their bible, women can maximize their chances of a 'better' baby. The prologue contains two cautionary tales – examples of babies, one whose mother followed their regimen and one who did not. Predictably, the mother whose child was conceived before the mother had a chance to adopt the 'healthy lifestyle' suffers a nightmare pregnancy, and after the birth suffers all manner of infections and depression. The child is physically unhealthy, developing nappy rash and eczema, and the problems go on. 'When he starts school he finds it difficult to sit still, his attention span is short, he is disruptive and is diagnosed as having a learning problem. He has constant colds and develops glue ear. He continues to wet the bed.' This sad creature is compared with the 'better baby' born following a pre-conception care regimen: 'He is particularly handsome and has a large perfectly shaped head, with broad, evenly spaced features. His skin glows with good health. He is alert but content . . . He never cries for longer than it takes his mother to attend to his needs. She seems to know instinctively what he wants and when he wants it.' Much of the advice issued by Naish and Roberts flies in the face of published evidence – such as their assertion that the contraceptive pill damages fertility. Other advice is simply bizarre, such as instructions to sit well back from the TV, avoid electrical gadgets in the bedroom and avoid an over-acidic diet (as this supposedly 'increases your susceptibility to radiation and heavy metal toxicity)'.[37] However cynical we are about such advice, it is difficult to reject it out of hand. It is a strange parent who does not want a 'better baby'.

In truth, from a health point of view it is doubtful that there is any particular advice necessary for pregnant women. For thousands of years women have been giving birth to healthy babies without taking special precautions either before or after they conceived. Embryos and foetuses are remarkably well protected, as women who have tried to end their own pregnancies have found to their cost. Before the legalization of abortion women frequently damaged their own health with instruments or by taking substances thought to have abortion-inducing properties, only to be delivered, eventually, of a perfectly healthy baby.

The resilience of pregnancies is illustrated by the fact that things that are considered hazardous to pregnancy in our culture are considered to be perfectly acceptable, even recommended, in others. Sociologist Jacqueline Vincent Priya describes in her study of different birth traditions how different societies recommend different diets to pregnant women.[38] For instance, pregnant Yoruba women in Africa are not encouraged to eat protein-rich foods such as meat or fish, which is the opposite of advice given to women in developed societies. In places such as rural Bangladesh, pregnant women are encouraged not to eat too much so that their babies will be small and born without difficulty. A large 'bonny' baby that we would regard as healthy could spell disaster in a society without an obstetric service.

Even addictive drugs seem to pose less of a risk to the unborn than we tend to assume. For the past decade, researchers in the US have tracked the neurological development of 200 children from some of Philadelphia's poorest neighbourhoods; half had been exposed to cocaine during their mother's pregnancy, and half had not. But, despite fears in the late 1980s that a surge in 'crack babies' – one in six born in city hospitals in 1989 had cocaine-using mothers – would lead to a whole class of children destined for neurological problems, the study turned up no evidence of a devastating cocaine effect. What it did turn up was that all the youngsters at aged 4, in both the crack and the control group, had under-developed intellectual performance compared to the US average. The project concluded that social deprivation is the key indicator of children's performance – and that is not something that parents can resolve through good behaviour and a pregnancy preparation plan.

An insidious effect of pre-conception care and ante-natal advice is that many women take to heart its message that they are responsible for the healthy outcome of a pregnancy, even if they reject the more bizarre lifestyle instructions. Few women feel sufficiently confident to shrug it all off. Most, during those endless, uncomfortable wakeful nights, worry about whether the baby will be OK. When a child arrives that is less than perfect – and around 2 per cent of newborns are affected with an abnormality – most parents scrutinize their lives to discover if they could have 'done anything' to cause the problem.

A fundamental problem with pre-conception care advice is that it rests on the assumption, an urban myth in itself, that it is possible for couples to plan and prepare for conception. When medical sociologist Anne Fleissig asked a number of women who had given birth six weeks earlier if their pregnancy had been planned, she found that 31 per cent of pregnancies were not, and subsequently concluded in a paper published in the *British Medical Journal* that almost a third of births in Britain could be the consequence of accidental pregnancy.[39] In such circumstances there is no chance for pre-conception care and limited chance for ante-natal care, yet there is little evidence that birth outcomes of unintended pregnancies are significantly different from those of wanted, planned pregnancies.

Furthermore, it seems that, despite all the public health advice, even when babies are planned, they are rarely conceived in circumstances that would please experts on maternal and child health. A 1999 survey for *Pregnancy and Birth* magazine horrified health correspondents by discovering that 73 per cent of couples make no effort to get healthy before trying to conceive, and almost half of all babies are conceived while both 'parents' have a blood alcohol level that, if they were breathalysed, would probably earn them a driving ban. Healthy babies, it seems, are born despite our behaviour rather than because of it.

It is difficult to resist professional advice during pregnancy. This is a time when parents feel singularly dependent on professional support. That is why pregnant women are so frequently targeted by health professionals. It is during this period that the present generation of parents is trained to become dependent on the expert. By the time the baby is born, the new fathers and mothers have already internalized the contemporary culture of parenting. If they believe that by singing and talking to the embryo they can help produce a clever baby, then they will believe just about anything that experts will throw at them in subsequent years.

Four

Parenting on Demand – the New Concept of Child-rearing

Many of the anxieties that parents have about their children are shaped by the changing expectations of society about parenting. The parenting role is no longer restricted to simply *raising* children. Parents are expected to do far more than that. Today's parents must pay attention to every moment of their child's day – ensuring that their lives are filled with appropriate activities. The roles of the modern parent stretch from that of a chauffeur, who transports the child from one activity to another, to an educator, who supplements formal schooling.

It is notable that parents used to be deliberately excluded from some of the functions they are now expected to embrace. For example, in the past, teachers were often suspicious of the intrusion of parents into their children's education. Parents who took too close an interest in what went on during the school day were regarded as interfering. Teaching your child to read was as likely to be treated with opprobrium as with praise. The parent was seen as the bumbling amateur teacher who got in the way of the education professional. Today parents are exhorted to play an active role in this field. Those who fail to get involved are stigmatized for letting their children down and for abandoning their young ones to a life of failure. The cumulative effect of all these pressures is to *expand* the meaning of parenting. Parents are burdened with new and often unreasonable expectations of how they should perform their role.

Parent determinism expands the concept of parenting to the extent that it becomes an impossibly burdensome task – one that normal human beings could not possibly undertake. No normal father or mother could take on responsibility for everything that affects their child. Moreover, even it were possible, it would not be desirable. It complicates the task of child-rearing and places an intolerable emotional load on the entire family. With so much at stake, no one could be a 'good enough' parent.

It is, arguably, already the case that society has so many expectations of what parents should do that the function of parenting can no longer be carried out by two individuals – however hard they try. This is particularly the case if both parents are in paid employment. For a lone parent, the weight of all the additional responsibilities is even more difficult to bear. Parent determinism sets all parents up to fail by setting goals that cannot possibly be attained.

Contemporary ideas of children's vulnerability and infant determinism continually reinforce the notion that your child needs you. Consequently, what is often defined as child-centred parenting becomes in practice *parenting on demand*. Dr Benjamin Spock's widely read *Baby and Child Care*, first published in 1946, played an important role in popularizing a child-centred view of parenting. His book was the most influential one to advise parents to be child-oriented. Demand feeding, lenient toilet training and constant attentiveness to a child's emotional development were the hallmark of this approach. It is ironic that, although during the 1950s and 1960s Spock's approach was generally regarded as permissive, today his version of child-centred parenting appears to be positively authoritarian. His famous manual comes across as distinctly parent-centred when compared with the child-obsessed advice of modern parenting handbooks. Consider the controversial issue of punishment and discipline. Most sources of contemporary advice are opposed to physical punishment of any sort. Many influential parenting professionals and advice-givers are hostile to punishment as such. Jan Parker and Jan Stimpson in *Raising Happy Children* believe that punishment is essentially a negative act because it involves making children suffer for their misbehaviour. They distinguish discipline from punishment, defining discipline as a term to describe teaching children what they have done wrong. From this perspective Spock's approach to punishment appears unacceptable, as callous if not brutal.

Spock advised that the everyday job of the parent was to 'keep the child on the right track by means of firmness'. He believed that when this system of firmness broke down, it was appropriate for parents to use some form of punishment. Spock was far more worried about forms of emotional punishment that led a child to develop a heavy sense of guilt, than about spanking. 'I'm not particularly advocating spanking but I think it is less poisonous than lengthy disapproval, because it clears the air, for parent and child', he noted.[1] Today's advice is hostile to punishment as such because of the doctrine that the problem is almost never bad children but bad parenting. Consequently, children are not so much acting 'naughty' but displaying negative attention seeking. The proposed solution for this is to ignore it rather than to punish. Instead of using firmness, parents are advised that they can never do too much for a child. This approach is advocated on the ground that punishment merely rewards negative attention seeking.

Although there is no longer a dominant individual child guru who exercises an influence comparable to that of Spock in the 1960s, Penelope Leach probably comes closest to playing that role in Britain. She believes that a 'gradual and gentle exposing of the child to the results of his own ill-advised actions is the only ultimate sanction you need'. From this perspective parents are assigned the role of listening to the child and adapting their lives accordingly. Parents worried about spoiling a child are advised that, 'In fact there's no such thing as too much attention and comforting, play, talk and laughter; too many smiles and hugs.'

Listening to a child and responding to her signals is based on a one-sided conception of child-rearing that transforms parents into 24-hour-a-day servants. Parenting on demand is based on an intensely deterministic view of the child–parent relationship. Leach warns parents that every aspect of a baby's development is in their hands. 'You can help him develop and learn or you can hinder him by holding yourself aloof', she writes. And that's not all. Leach raises the stakes: 'You can keep him happy and busy and learning fast, or leave him to be discontented, bored and learning more slowly.'[2]

Listening to children is something that sensible and sensitive parents do in any case. But the way that listening is defined by child professionals gives this act a very different meaning. It assumes that a toddler's every signal has an intrinsically profound significance, which, if overlooked, can have a potentially negative consequence on her development. From this standpoint, contemporary advice dismisses

Spock for being far too parent-centred. In her book, *Three in a Bed: The Benefits of Sleeping with Your Baby*, Deborah Jackson takes issue with Spock's advice to mothers to leave their baby to cry. According to Jackson, a baby left to cry at night is one who is forced to learn the 'cruel lesson' that suffering is the human condition. She claims that, by ignoring a baby's cry, we are missing out on the potential 'for small, subtle, positive communication' between parent and child.[3] Since so much value is invested in communication, the refusal to engage with a child's cry becomes defined as irresponsible parenting.

Parenting on demand is not confined to the interaction between mothers and fathers and their babies. The expansion of the terrain of parenting continues from childhood through to adolescence. These sentiments are further reinforced by cultural and social norms, which increasingly demand an ever-widening role for parents. As noted in Chapter 11 below, improved parenting is even seen by policy makers and politicians of all parties as the one obvious solution to society's ills. The New Labour Government's consultation document, *Supporting Families*, explicitly spells this out. It claims that 'better parenting can bring down the number of children looked after by local authorities, as well as alleviate problems of discipline at school or youth offending'. Better parenting today means not only parenting on demand but also the assumption of new responsibilities. So what do we expect of the new parent? What are some of their new duties?

Parents as full-time lovers

The principal role which society today allocates to the parent is to love their child. At first sight this seems like an entirely unexceptionable request. The love that mothers and fathers have for their children is one of the enduring themes of the human experience. Our culture and history is full of examples of the tremendous sacrifices that parents have made for their children. Mothers and fathers have been prepared to undergo great hardships in order to protect and improve the lives of their offspring. Of course, there are also stories of cold, aloof mothers and of uncaring, neglectful fathers. But such instances were seen as exceptions to the norm of parental love. Paradoxically, until recently child-rearing manuals were concerned that parents were spoiling their children with too much love. Child-rearing books produced during the early part of the twentieth century chided mothers who over-indulged their children with too much love. A survey of child-rearing manuals published in the USA from 1915 to 1980 reveals that mothers were continually portrayed as having a tendency to 'over-react' emotionally and their unrestrained passion was pathologized as harmful to both daughters and sons. Paradoxically, the very expressiveness that was the socially sanctioned form of appropriate maternal behaviour was believed to jeopardize a child's healthy development. Such ideas were constantly promoted up to the 1970s.[4] So why do child-rearing manuals insist on instructing parents on the art of loving their children today?

It is worth noting that the contemporary version of parental love is an affectation that has little to do with the intense, albeit undefinable, passion usually associated with the term. Love has many dimensions. But as a state of feeling that arises from natural ties and which manifests itself in warm affection, love was rarely presented in the instrumental manner in which it is conceived of nowadays. Today, loving is rarely perceived as a spontaneous sentiment. It has been transformed into a parental function or a skill. It has become *the* principal parenting skill, for the very pragmatic reason that the possession of such a sentiment is seen to be the precondition for 'parenting on demand'. That is why mothers and fathers are routinely advised to 'enjoy their baby' and to give him 'unconditional love'. Penelope Leach goes as far as to state that if a working mother has only a limited time for her child, then her time would be better spent playing with her daughter than attending to her physical needs. 'If you had to share your baby's total care with one other person and you handed over all the physical tasks, using your limited time for loving and play, you would keep your prime role in the baby's life.'[5] That loving and playing are elevated above, and separated from, the tasks of feeding and providing for the physical needs of a child is a testimony to the significance attached to the emotional side of parenting. This conception of love transforms the emotional outcome of an intimate relationship to a mechanical function that can be exercised at will.

The separation of love into an independent activity and its association with play is a defining feature of a sentiment that actually means a call for unrestrained parental responsiveness to a child's emotional need. 'Love' is often used interchangeably with the term 'attention'. Whereas parental love is defined as meaning giving attention to children, a child's love is equated with a demand for attention. 'Babies are born wanting to love their parents', writes the child psychologist Dr Dorothy Rowe. To state that infants, as yet unable to conceptualize, could be wanting to love is to equate this sentiment with the instinctual drive for security. From this instrumental adult point of view, this one-sided definition of love in effect means being nice to a child. According to Leach, playing and showing new things to babies is really what matters to them. 'These are the things which make for love', she argues. Not surprisingly, the demand for nice things is unrestrained. Or, to put it in Leach's words, 'love creates love'. Love creates its own demand for the greater expenditure of loving. To ration love is dysfunctional since, through loving, parents discover a baby's need for . . . you guessed it, more love. In turn, loving programmes parents to love even more. Deborah Jackson claims that 'the more you hold a baby, the more you want to hold him'.[6]

Advocates of unconditional loving ascribe to it powers that are almost magical. The authors of *Raising Happy Children*, Jan Parker and Jan Stimpson, claim that if we 'show our children that we love them unconditionally, that they and their feelings and wishes matter and that we value, acknowledge and care for them, we will boost their sense of self-worth'. This in turn will set children 'up for life' and they will become confident adults able to cope with everything that life can throw at them. There would be something endearing in this naïve belief in the power of love if it was not promoted with the fervour of an intolerant ideology. The sentiment 'love or pay the consequences' always lurks in the background of the discussion. That is why lectures on parental love have both a patronizing and intimidating quality. They are patronizing because parents do not have to be told to enjoy their children. They are intimidating because the failure to love on a child's terms is condemned as an act of parental malevolence. 'Many parents do succeed in withering their children's love', writes Dorothy Rowe on an ominous note. Rowe seems to divide the world of parents into two types: those who love and those who try to control their children through fear. It is interesting to note that Rowe associates the failure to love with tragedies and dysfunctional behaviour. There is always an underlying implication that the failure to love on demand is a precursor to abuse. These arbitrarily counterpoised parenting styles feature in the NSPCC's recently published manual, *Baby's First Year*. This booklet advises its assumed cold-blooded readership to 'enjoy' their babies. Mothers are told to 'use loving positive words'. *Baby's First Year* even instructs parents in how they can help love grow. The four-point plan consists of the following instructions:

early sucking at the breast
skin-to-skin cuddles
holding and stroking
watching what your baby does.

This advice is then followed up with a carrot and a stick. The carrot is that your baby 'is crazy about you', the stick is that therefore she needs to feel that she is in the centre of your life – whether you like it or not.[7]

The exhortation to love on demand encourages the organization of parenting around the demand of children for attention. With all the earnest appeal for love, it is worth noting that most parents today actually spend far more time paying attention to their children than at any time in human history. Parents have internalized the repeated exhortation to love and stimulate. In fact, the problem that many mothers and fathers face is that they can never meet the ever-increasing demand for their attention. Parental attentiveness is quite habit-forming. Which is why many parents actually feel that they have become hostages to circumstances beyond their control. 'My child has my undivided attention when I am at home', is a culturally sanctioned statement often repeated by working mothers. Such sentiments express the idea that there is something intrinsically worthwhile in routine attentiveness to a child. Child professionals encourage this approach since they insist that listening, analysing a child's words and signals, together with stimulation, will directly contribute to a child's development.

It is far from evident that loving and giving attention for its own sake provides any real benefits for children. Children who are provided with attention on demand have little motivation for confronting problems on their own. In particular, they have little incentive to learn to share their parents with others. They do not have much stimulus to explore the world by themselves, to learn to reflect on their experience or to engage in solitary play. Learning to be alone, away from the intrusive world of adults, is itself essential for the development of a child's imagination. These private experiences are critical for the development of the self. Constant adult attentiveness tends to promote the self-centred child. Children, too, can become addicted to parental attention. Youngsters who are trained to believe that parental attention and love on demand is their birthright are likely to find it difficult to cope with circumstances where they are not the focal point of everyone's attention.

Parents who provide attention on demand are not doing their youngster a favour. Constant attention is impossible to sustain, and mothers and fathers who go down this road are likely to become too exhausted to do much good. As with any habit, attention on demand is likely to turn into an undiscriminating routine. Instead of leading, guiding and inspiring, such parents are likely to spend too much of their time responding to the latest demand of their child. This ethos has probably the worst consequences for the working father and working mother. Such parents often report that they spend most of their time at home doing things for their child. Such a reaction is a quite understandable expression of the anxiety that one is not doing enough for the child. The downside of this approach is that the child who only sees her parents doing things for her and with her rarely experiences her mother and father engaged in doing adult things. Yet exposure to adult-oriented activities are experiences which are no less important for a child's development than the undivided attention of a parent.

Do parents always have to know what their children are feeling and thinking? Probably not. Sensitive mothers and fathers can strike a balance between seeking to understand their children and routinely responding to them. If everything that a child does is analysed and re-analysed there is the danger of not seeing the wood for the trees. Not every signal is a portent of great significance and not every word uttered by a child contains a profound hidden meaning. A child's development is not doomed if she is the daughter of an adult who has to divide her attention among many children. There is no evidence that parenting on demand does any good for children. But there is little doubt that the re-ordering of adult life around the child creates impossible expectations that can never be fully realized. It fosters an atmosphere in which parents – especially the ones who conscientiously try to act on contemporary advice – become doomed to a life of continual anxiety about the emotional welfare of their children. Despite good intentions, some parents actually end up trying to live their child's life in order to avoid failing to carry out the required duties.

Parents have attempted to avoid failure by dragging their child from one source of stimulation to the next. Those who can afford it chauffeur their children to the music class before picking them up and taking them to a specially designed activity centre. But still parents feel they are falling short. Unable to devote even more time to their task, they seek to assuage their guilt by spending more money on children's gifts. Reports indicate that even relatively poor parents spend a disproportionate amount of their income on buying presents for a child.

But in any case, what is love? And why should love be associated with particular actions such as cuddling or singing to a child? As Jerome Kagan notes, the 'invisible belief or feeling that one is loved is not dictated by any particular actions on the part of parent or child'.[8] It is not at all clear what sorts of acts convince children that they are recipients of this highly prized sentiment. Children of authoritarian parents often acknowledge that they are certain that their mothers and fathers love them. And some children, whose parents overdosed them with non-stop attention, indicate that they are ambivalent about their parents' attitude towards them.

Love on demand becomes a parody of itself. The appeal that child professionals make for *unconditional* love superficially seems to make sense. After all, we quite rightly do not expect mothers and fathers to set conditions for the exercise of affection. However, the term 'unconditional love' means more than the setting of conditions. It implies a sentiment that has no reference to anything outside itself. Parental love, however, cannot be reduced to repeating the phrase 'I love you.' Love and affection are mediated through distinct actions. We express love through the way we nourish our child, through the way we reward or praise or question different forms of his behaviour. Children become aware of their parents' love through the way that mothers and fathers encourage certain activities, discourage others, draw lines and, yes, even through the exercise of authority. Loving a child is a wonderful, fulfilling experience. But loving on demand is an incitement to the display of an empty gesture. It introduces a dishonest ritual into the conduct of family life. Worse still, the compulsion to love actually serves to trivialize authentic expressions of this noble sentiment.

Parents as therapists and healers

In part, today's fad of celebrating parental love is linked to the growth of a one-sided concern with children's emotions. As noted in the previous chapter, the all-pervasive sense of children's vulnerability is rooted in the domain of emotion. The advocacy of unconditional parental love is in part seen as a way of bringing parents emotionally closer to their children. This is considered to be the precondition for adults gaining emotional literacy, one of the essential skills demanded of today's parents.

Proponents of the doctrine of emotional literacy believe that lack of self-awareness and a reluctance to acknowledge one's true feelings are responsible both for individual distress and for the problems facing society. Those who are emotionally illiterate are potentially destructive personalities, who bear responsibility for many of the problems facing children. This is most eloquently expressed in Daniel Goleman's best-seller, *Emotional Intelligence: Why it Can Matter More than IQ*. Goleman takes the view that society faces a 'collective emotional crisis'. He sees a 'growing calamity in our shared emotional life', which is expressed in marital violence, child abuse, rising juvenile delinquency and the growing incidence of depression and post-traumatic stress. The problems associated with emotional illiteracy are alarming, according to Goleman. The shooting of classmates by American schoolchildren, teenage pregnancy, bullying, drug abuse and mental illness are some of the consequences of the public's refusal to attend to its emotional needs. The solution offered by Goleman is more emotional education, which provides strategies for managing emotions and recognizing feelings.[9]

Texts on emotional intelligence and emotional literacy tend to be lightweight, both theoretically and empirically. Most offer little more than homespun assertions in the language of psychobabble. In a round-about way, what they describe is what was once represented as the quality of being sensitive. Parental sensitivity is not, of course, in and of itself objectionable. It is the obsession with, and the problem-atization of, emotional relations between parent and child that create potential difficulties.

It is no longer considered sufficient for parents to be able childcarers. They need to be skilled therapists capable of getting in touch with their children's feelings. One of the most vociferous advocates of emotional parenting is Professor John Gottman. His manual, *The Heart of Parenting*, which received considerable publicity in the British press, insists that good parenting requires more than intellect, involving emotion as well. In the real world, parents are all too aware that the management of emotion is an important component of their job. However, it is not the normal emotional engagements of family life that Gottman has in mind. He believes that parents have to be 'emotional trainers' who use 'emotional moments' to educate their youngsters in the art of emotional literacy. According to Gottman, love and positive parenting are insufficient by themselves for dealing with a child's negative emotions. It is a start, but mothers and fathers require additional skills in order to carry out their role as parents.[10]

There is considerable pressure on parents to fall in line with the worldview of therapy. Most British parents have probably never heard of Gottman and are unlikely to have submitted themselves to his 'good-parent test'. But they might have heard Government policy makers insist that the 'quality of the emotional bond between parent and child is the key variable in the causation of delinquency'. British parents are also continually reminded that successful child-rearing requires what are in fact distinct therapeutic skills. Child-rearing advice today, in all its forms, is saturated with the language of emotion and therapy. The management of feelings, learning how to interpret a child's emotions and the art of listening feature prominently in manuals and advice columns. Tutors of parenting classes are trained to promote the therapeutic approach. A manual designed for such tutors by the NSPCC, titled *Positive Ways of Managing Children's Behaviour*, informs group leaders that 'most of the activities are designed to allow participants to think about their own feelings and the feelings of their children'. Parenting magazines and manuals continually admonish parents that unless they learn communication and listening skills they will lose touch with their children. 'Without them, communication channels may begin to close – which is when problems can escalate beyond an easy point of return' warns *Raising Happy Children*.[11]

Therapeutic advice on parenting insists on continually complicating a child's feelings. Mothers and fathers are offered detailed advice about how to decode their baby's emotions. They are told how to go about praising their child and what words to use in response to negative behaviour. Manuals explain in intricate detail how to acknowledge a child's emotions and provide practical tips on how to raise infants' self-esteem. It is not surprising that many parents who are daily bombarded by such advice agonize over the words they use to reprimand a son or daughter. 'Is this going to undermine his confidence?' asked a friend, after showing disappointment at her son's refusal to go down the slide at the swimming pool. She must have been reading Dr Michael Boulton, who informed the readership of *Mother and Baby*, that reacting negatively to failure 'could actually hinder your child's self-confidence'.[12]

Therapeutic advice presumes that parents can be on constant alert to interpret shifts and fluctuations in their child's feelings. And if they are not available for providing what child professionals call 'positive attention', then at the very least they can expect a gentle reprimand. 'It's so tempting to carry on doing something with only half an ear to what your child is saying but the fact is you're supposed to listen to her', insists Eileen Hayes in *Practical Parenting*. Hayes justifies mandatory listening on the grounds that you, the parent, are leading your child to the next stage of her development. The pressure to listen and to show emotion is intense. A *BabyPower* article titled 'Give your child real learning power' tells busy parents that book-sharing is 'necessary' for their children's intellectual and emotional development. And if you are busy with housework – tough! 'It's better to help build your child's future than to worry about chores all the time', counsel the authors.[13]

Parents are actually quite vulnerable to the charge that they lack the ability to understand their children. Many mothers and fathers are haunted by the fear that they might not be able to communicate with their children and might lose their love. Others are apprehensive about their ability to do what the books require at a particular stage of a child's development. Consequently, parents become captive to whatever is offered as the latest advice about how to get near to your child. Massaging your child is the latest fad offered to parents who are concerned about getting close to their children.

The parent as masseur is yet another new role expected of the enlightened mother and father. Massage is now regularly advocated for its alleged healing and therapeutic value. 'Did you know', asks *Practical Parenting*, that 'baby massage is a wonderful way for you to get to know and bond with your baby, as well as helping with colic and sleeping?' According to *Prima Baby*, massaging your baby has numerous benefits: it speeds up a baby's development, it prevents skin problems, it reduces stress, it helps digestion and it boosts bonding. Apparently massaging also has therapeutic value for the parent as well. Deborah Jackson, who believes that the 'importance of sensory stimulation to the child may never be fully measured and appreciated', states that human contact has a 'soothing effect on the adult as well as a child'. And there are even more benefits according to the video, *In Your Hands: Baby Massage Therapy Techniques*. This video claims that baby massage benefits both parents and infants. It improves sleeping, breathing and digestive rhythms and provides enhanced physical and emotional development, the alleviation of postpartum depression and a boost to parental self-confidence.[14]

During the past three years, baby massage has emerged as the latest parenting fad in the USA. According to *Time Magazine*, 'For today's upwardly mobile parents baby massage is becoming what Lamaze was to the previous generation.' The University of Miami's Touch Research Institute – coincidentally funded by Johnson and Johnson – regularly publishes research that promotes the therapeutic value of baby massage. Johnson's baby oil also sponsors a web site that offers parents tips on how to massage their baby. It informs the reader that 'babies need to know they're adored' – not just loved but adored – and reassures parents that if they follow the instructions the baby will know that 'she means the world to you'. Parents desperate to get close to their child are more than willing to have a go.[15]

Physical contact between parent and child is a worthwhile enjoyable experience in its own right. However, by assigning an all-powerful therapeutic significance to the power of touching, the fad of baby massage provides a convenient pretext for mystifying yet another aspect of the parent–infant relationship. Like loving, talking and listening, touching is transformed into a complicated skill that parents need to learn in order to perform their function. When parental touching is transformed into the ritual of baby massage it turns physical contact into an instrumental act devoid of spontaneity.

Ironically, the compulsion on parents to adopt the role of a therapist actually undermines the expression of genuine emotions. Parents, who feel obliged to feign constant interest in their child's every word, are likely to become desensitized about new developments. When nothing is obvious and every act contains a hidden meaning, it is easy to lose one's grip. During the 1980s, the psychiatrist Stella Chess warned about the constant pressure on mothers to 'woo' their babies. She was alarmed by the tendency of paediatric psychiatrists 'to pressure mothers to be constantly on the alert for any sign that they or their babies are deviating from the prescribed ideal'. During the time that has elapsed since this warning, the pressure to which Chess alludes has become far more intrusive on parental life. Tragically, the very obsession with a child's feelings and emotions has fostered a climate where mothers and fathers feel less able to handle many aspects of their relationship with their children.[16]

Back in 1977, in a prescient study of family life, the American social commentator Christopher Lasch warned about the emotional overloading of the parent–child connection. A quarter of a century later the emotional load has become far more onerous. An exaggerated perception of an infant's emotional vulnerability has helped to reinforce the view that children are by definition at risk. In the realm of emotion, certainties give way to doubt and confusion. Parents have tried to respond to this state of affairs by spending more 'quality' time with their children. But, as we shall see in the next chapter, they still get criticized for not giving enough quality time to their children.[17]

The problem with the celebration of therapeutic parenting is not that it focuses attention on emotion. In modern societies, successful child-rearing is invariably founded on the establishment of a firm emotional relationship of intimacy. Effective mothers and fathers need to show sensitivity and flexibility in response to a child's development. The real problem with the privileged status accorded to emotional parenting is that it has the effect of complicating family relations and of undermining the effectiveness of mothers and fathers. Why? *Because the imperative of emotionalism promotes parental obsession about a child's momentary feelings.* Such a strategy is likely to unleash a process in which parents are unlikely to be able to intervene in children's emotional life in a discriminating and decisive manner. Worse still, the preoccupation with a child's momentary feelings is likely to provide an incentive for attention-seeking behaviour. It is also likely to distract children from the effort that is required to deal with their own emotions.

Promoters of emotional child-rearing continually treat mothers and fathers as insensitive people who lack the capacity to understand children's feelings. It is often argued that parents are uniquely illiterate when it comes to their emotional relationship with their children. 'We find children's emotional lives difficult to respond to because we are habituated to ignoring, suppressing, disregarding our own', stated the psychotherapist Susie Orbach. Orbach believes that British culture is terrified of emotions.[18] In fact, what terrifies parents is not emotions, but the obligation to deal with children's momentary feelings. A parent's relationship to a child is more complex than the way it is depicted by advocates of emotional literacy. Most parents are able to show a remarkable degree of flexibility in responding to the individual needs of their infants. Parents spend a lot of time trying to figure out their children and reflecting on their own motives. But these emotional encounters which are mediated through intimacy appear very different when placed under public scrutiny. Emotions that are bound up with intimacy are not designed for public display. It is the exposure of parenting to this scrutiny that puts fathers and mothers on the defensive. The perception of being judged on personal and intimate detail is unlikely to make a contribution to confident parenting.

Parents as teachers

The truth is that the main consequence of the psychologizing of child-rearing is that it puts tremendous emotional pressure on parents. The new roles imposed on mothers and fathers by society guarantee that parents can never feel that they are good enough. 'I always worry that I am not doing nearly enough for Jessica and Angus', was how one father echoed the opinion widely held by parents. John works as a software designer. He spends most of his free time with his two children and outwardly presents the image of a confident father. Yet, after a short conversation about fatherhood, it becomes evident that he harbours profound anxieties about letting his two children down. Like many other fathers, he worries about disappointing his children and not doing enough to give them a good start in this world. Nor are these concerns confined to the comfortably off, university educated, middle-class parent who has carefully studied child-rearing literature.

I was talking to a group of fathers at Faversham swimming pool. They had brought their children for their regular Sunday swim, and while they kept one eye on the pool the conversation soon turned to an exchange of opinion about parenting. Most of them were worried about money and about their own ability to manage their children's lives in what they perceived to be a challenging and complex world. Money was a problem because they felt obliged to provide their offspring with the latest toys and clothes regardless of whether they could afford it. But their main preoccupation was not family finance. Pete, a mechanic, expressed the common dilemma most clearly: 'I know that there is nothing I can do to make sure that my son is going to get a decent education.'

Words of doubt exchanged over a quick cup of tea at Faversham swimming pool are repeated time and again when you talk to parents. Parents, who feel insecure about whether they're doing enough to stimulate their children, are particularly exposed to new social pressures to do more for their children's education. These reactions are not surprising, since society attaches an unprecedented importance to the educational role of the mother and father. Parental responsibility for child development has been expanded so that mothers and fathers are expected to play a direct role in their children's education. As far as parents are concerned, it is not only the children who are judged and assessed by school authorities.

Parents are now expected to play an active role in the schooling of their children. Since the 1980s there has been a steady expansion of the different claims that schools make on parents' time. No one can assume the title of a good parent unless he or she takes an active interest, not just in the education of their child, but in the affairs of their child's school. It is no longer simply the ambitious mother and father who regularly attend teachers' and parents' meetings. A MORI poll of 1,000 parents of 5- to 11-year-olds, conducted in December 1999, indicated that 40 per cent of the respondents spoke to teachers at least once a week. Many parents now accept invitations to help out in the school. School and peer pressure ensures that the responsible parent does her bit by helping out on a field trip or by organizing a fund-raising initiative. According to a survey in a report by Abbey National/Future Foundation in June 2000, changing attitudes to parenting 'came through strongly in relation to schooling'.[19]

It is assumed that mothers and fathers have an obligation to play a direct role in their children's education. Politicians, educators and child-rearing professionals constantly pile on the pressure. Since parents are intensely sensitive about the charge that they are not doing enough for their children, the relentless expansion of their new role as educators has gone unchecked. Expanding the role of parents in education has been a key policy of recent governments in Britain. Schools now regularly produce home–school agreements that set out the new role of parents in monitoring their children's attendance, discipline and homework. Nor is this role simply restricted to a monitoring function. The vogue term is 'supporting a child's learning'. This means that parents play an active pedagogic role in the educational life of their children. Numerous schemes have been introduced to train parents to participate directly in the homework of their children.

The assumption of the new role of parent as teacher is a particularly burdensome one. Unlike many of the new functions assigned to mothers and fathers, this one is directly exposed to continuous public scrutiny. The behaviour and performance of schoolchildren is now seen to be a direct reflection of the quality of support they receive from their fathers and mothers. This is not surprising, since homework is no longer what schoolchildren do when they get home – it has become a joint enterprise with their parents. Thus homework has become an instrument for assessing parental behaviour.

Parental responsibility for homework and their children's progress in school is a source of tremendous consternation to many mothers and fathers. Since the contemporary definition of what constitutes a 'good' parent depends so much on effectively managing this responsibility, mothers and fathers feel powerless to complain. A survey published in March 2000 indicated that instead of complaining, many mothers and fathers are struggling to live up to the expectation that society has of them. The survey of 1,200 parents reported that many were experiencing great difficulty in trying to assist their children – especially in subjects such as maths and science. Since these subjects are now taught differently, many of the respondents were confused about how to guide their children. As a result, parents sought to compensate for this problem by putting in long hours helping with homework. The survey claimed that on average parents spent seven hours a week on their homework duties. In effect, parents were spending more time on after-school studies than the official guideline of five hours a week for 11-year-old children.[20]

Obviously not every parent has seven hours a week to spend on homework. Some have the confidence to draw a line and not accept that it is their responsibility to play the role of surrogate teacher. However, the normalization of this new parental role has been accomplished. There has been virtually no public debate on the implications of this development for parent and child alike. And parents struggling over their children's maths assignment have internalized this role to such an extent that their problem is experienced as a reflection on their own weaknesses.

Not so long ago it was sufficient to send children to school clean, well-fed and well-clothed. The teaching profession actively resented busy-body parents who tried to curry favour or asked too many questions about what was going on in school. The best teachers assumed that they would do their job and the parents would do theirs. They and not parents were responsible for the educational progress of students. School was for children and children alone. Homework was seen as what children did out of school and not the direct or indirect product of a parent's output. And parents who 'helped' their children with homework sometimes felt ambivalent about where to draw the line between helping and cheating.

Today the situation has changed. In a desperate attempt to improve standards of education, parents' concern for their children is manipulated to draw them in as unpaid teachers. In the process schooling has become an informal instrument for monitoring parental behaviour. Parents are going back to school – whether they like it or not. One Further Education College I visited offered at least five evening classes concerned with 'Helping your child to read' or 'Helping your child with GCSE maths' or 'Helping your child through GCSE English'. In the United States some schools provide special classes for parents to train them for their new role. How long before pressure is placed on British parents to go back to school?

The expansion of parental responsibility in children's schooling represents a major claim on parents' time and energies. But the addition of yet another load on the backs of parents is unlikely to improve the quality of education of their children. Parents can play a valuable role by providing a stimulating environment for their children. The best form of parental involvement in a child's education is the provision of positive encouragement. Sometimes this involves discussions of issues and problems raised in school. But too much involvement discourages children to make the effort to stretch themselves. The extension of parental involvement in yet another part of the child's life can act as an obstacle to the development of a sense of self-sufficiency and maturity. Nor do parents make the best teachers for their own children. As Elizabeth Newson noted in her study of the parental role, 'a good parent–child relationship is in fact very unlike a good teacher–child relationship'.[21] The deep and intimate emotional ties between parent and child make it difficult for mothers and fathers to have the distance necessary for effective teaching. That is why so many parents have so naturally adopted the role of their child's advocate in their dealings with teachers. Predictably, teachers have reacted with the complaint that greater parental involvement has led to an increase in violent and abusive behaviour towards school staff. A survey published by the National Association of Head Teachers in April 2000 indicated that problems over angry parents were fourth on the list of factors causing head teachers most stress. The erosion of the line of demarcation between parent and teacher opens the way to conflict and mutual recrimination. Not good for the parent, not good for the teacher and certainly not good for schoolchildren.[22]

Five

Parenting Turned into an Ordeal

The expanding definition of parenting in relation to child-rearing at home is more than matched by the increase in the amount of time fathers and mothers spend monitoring the activities of their children out of doors. To a considerable extent the increase in the amount of time adults devote to accompanying their children outdoors is motivated by concern for their physical safety. Parents are not only worried about not doing enough for their child's education, but they also feel the need to do more to protect their child from a world they perceive as threatening. However, the reason parents spend more and more time accompanying children outdoors is not simply their perceptions of physical dangers such as drugs, bullies, drunk drivers or child-abductors. Parents are expected to stimulate and educate their children not only when they are at home but also outdoors. This pressure means that they can never have enough time to do what is expected of them.

Is there a parenting time famine?

In recent years numerous commentators have claimed that mothers and fathers are disabled by the heavy demands made on their time by their employers. According to this argument, since the 1980s there has been an increase in work pressure. It is claimed that men and women are expected to work longer than previously and as a result they have little time to devote to their family responsibilities. Hewlett and West (1998) have characterized this process as a 'parental time famine'. A report published in March 2000 was critical of what it described as

Britain's 'long hours culture'. The author, Shirley Conran, chairwoman of Mothers in Management, claimed that one in five children suffered from stress-related health problems due to their parents' long working hours. Sarah Jackson, chief executive of Parents at Work, echoed her sentiments: 'working parents and their children bear the brunt of the long hours culture'. The view that long hours of work have made parenting a difficult, if not impossible, task has become a regular subject of discussion in the pages of parenting magazines. Calls for flexible work arrangements are often presented as a potential solution to the crisis of parenting.

Parents are indeed busy and, in some cases, *really* busy. The entry of millions of mothers into the labour market has placed new strains on the management of family life. The association of the 'time famine' that confronts many parents with the demands placed on them by work is understandable. It is easy to draw the conclusion that time spent at work is directly responsible for the pressure that parents face in managing their family life. After all, the expansion of maternal employment is a highly visible process. In contrast, the expansion of parenting time takes place behind the scenes and is rarely debated in public. Yet it is this invisible increase in the demands placed on parents' time that represents the greatest pressure on their lives.

The pressure of time is experienced as a relentless everyday problem for millions of mothers and fathers. Many parents who feel that they do not have adequate time to spend with their children feel guilty and anxious about this state of affairs. The time famine helps to intensify and shape parental paranoia. But is it really the case that our problems are caused by an impossibly long working week? The discussion about the long-hours culture and its impact on parenting actually says more about what is expected of parents than about a loss of time. True, we all seem to have little control over our time and many parents feel that they never have enough time to devote to their youngsters. But our perception of living through a unique stage of a parental time famine may well be influenced by the new burden of responsibilities imposed on child-carers. Long working hours may help explain a source of unwelcome pressure on parents but not the ascendancy of the contemporary condition of parental paranoia. The working week in Britain today is not much more onerous than the norm of recent decades.

International Labour Organization figures published in 1999 indicate that the annual hours worked by British full-time workers increased by only six hours between 1980 and 1997. This increase of 1.7 minutes per working day cannot account for the intense time pressures experienced by parents. Mothers and fathers worked long hours before and during the Second World War. They certainly did not like it but they experienced their condition as a general problem of lack of time rather than as a parental time famine. They not only managed to raise their offspring in difficult circumstances, but did it surprisingly well.

It is far from evident why the amount of time men and women spend at work should, in and of itself, have such catastrophic outcomes for child-rearing. In the course of both world wars there were dramatic shifts by women into and out of the labour force, but these did not result in fears of damaging consequences for children. Some claim that the problem is men's long working day. It is suggested that they come home too exhausted to perform their fathering role adequately. However, the relatively small increase in working hours follows more than half a century of reductions. Up to the First World War, the average working week was 54 hours – and for most that meant the sort of arduous manual labour that few now have to endure. It is difficult to believe that when our grandfathers staggered home from 12-hour shifts in factories they were any less exhausted than the computer programmer when he gets in from the office. Yet with far less time available to them, parents managed to raise their children.

It is difficult not to avoid the conclusion that the problem is not to be found in the place of work. It is not the culture of long working hours but the culture of parenting on demand that exacerbates many of the problems faced by mothers and fathers. As long as society continues to expand the role of parenting, mothers and fathers will never have enough time to be good enough parents. Parental paranoia is not simply a symptom of excessive worry about the well-being of a child, but is also fuelled by a profound doubt about even having the time to perform the job expected of mothers and fathers.

The fact that the pressure of time is experienced through the prism of child-rearing suggests that the real issue is the way that society regards parenting. As noted elsewhere, the contemporary version of parenting demands an endless amount of time from adults. The ever-widening definition of parenting has important implications for the way that fathers and mothers manage their time. The recent invention of the concept of 'quality time' is based on the belief that children need a specific period of undivided attention from their parents. The notion of quality time is founded on the conviction that it is not good enough for children to be around their parents or other adults, but that their development requires special treatment. Today, some experts claim that even the regular expenditure of quality time does not meet the needs of children. 'Millions of working parents cling to the belief that "quality time" with their children makes up for frequent absences from home', warns a headline in the *Sunday Times*, before adding that 'research suggests this is a myth'.[1] Numerous parenting professionals claim that parents' devotion to their careers means that they are neglecting the welfare of their children. 'I think quality time is just a way of deluding ourselves into shortchanging our children', says Ronal Levant, a psychologist at Harvard Medical School. He claims that children need 'vast amounts of parental time and attention'.[2]

It is the continual pressure to expand energies and time on child-rearing that accounts for the widely held view that employment today imposes a singular burden upon working mothers and fathers. It is always legitimate to raise questions about whether there are more creative ways of organizing the world of work. There is always room for introducing more flexible arrangements that could help make life easier for parents. But just as it is legitimate to raise queries about the culture of work, so too is it worth asking questions about the long hours that society expects mothers and fathers to devote to their children.

Lack of time is not the cause but a symptom of parental paranoia. Concern about children's safety, welfare and development requires that parents spend more time on the specific job of childcare than at any other time in history. Blaming a new ethos of long working hours overlooks the significant expansion of energy devoted by mothers and fathers to child-rearing. As long as parents feel that they can never devote enough time to their children, any claim on their time by their employer can be experienced as unreasonable. Men and women today do not need to work long hours to feel an intense level of anxiety about the well-being of their offspring. Conversations with full-time mothers indicate that the extra time does not buy them immunity from the fears and anxieties that haunt working parents. Anthea, a 29-year-old full-time mother, gave up her job as a graphic designer in order to have 'enough' time with Maddie, her 4-year-old daughter. Far from being relaxed, she is intensely concerned about Maddie's development. She is an only child and Anthea is worried because Maddie is shy and does not make friends easily. Because of this anxiety Anthea has embarked on a mission to find friends for Maddie. She takes her child to play-groups, swimming, adventure playgrounds and the houses of other parents of potential friends for her daughter. Anthea is entirely sincere when she reports that she is rushed off her feet.

Can never do enough

Child-rearing advice continually insists that parents should not lose any opportunity to communicate with and to stimulate their children. The advice that it is 'never too early to start' is repeated with monot-onous regularity. 'If you want your child to speak another language fluently, start early', advises one educationalist. For the enlightened, upwardly mobile parent non-purposeful children's activity is wasted time. In the United States, the phenomenon of 'hyper-parenting' has become a way of life for many middle-class parents. Books such as *Baby Signs: How to Talk to Your Baby Before Your Baby Can Talk*, *Super Baby*, *Brain Games for Toddlers and Twos* and *Releasing Your Child's Potential* are readily embraced by carers committed to parent determinism. Parents who are trained by a manual titled *How to Multiply Your Baby's Intelligence* are unlikely to abandon this crusade when their children turn 4 or 5. At this stage, many parents are eager to get their infants started on music and language lessons, sports and other stimulating activities in order to get them ready for the next stage of development.

Hothousing children is the inevitable outcome of contemporary culture's preoccupation with the virtue of constant infant stimulation. Many parents who intuitively draw back from this obsessive behaviour nevertheless feel pressure from family and friends to keep up with the super-dads and super-mums in the amount of enrichment they provide for their children. Clever entrepreneurs have realized that there is money to be made from parents desperate to give their children a headstart. In April 2000, a private tutorial college in Watford launched a computer skills course for children as young as 18 months old. After I called up the college and finally put down the receiver, the words 'It is never too early to start' kept ringing in my ear. In the same month, a company called Pushyparent.co.uk announced that it would float on the Alternative Investment Market. Organized activities for children have become a boom industry. It has also turned parents into permanent chaperones forced to spend even more time accompanying their children to numerous activities.[3]

Not surprisingly the constant demand on parents to entertain and supervise children takes its toll. A survey carried out by Nestlé in 1998 showed that nearly half of parents with school-age children felt that the summer holiday was too long – 60 per cent of fathers and 43 per cent of mothers wanted it shorter, even though 85 per cent of adults had fond memories of their own summer holidays. Those interviewed stated that they felt under pressure to organize events to distract or entertain their children. They believed that their children had to have something to do, since they could not be left on their own to play outside or simply mess about. Many parents, whose carefully balanced childcare arrangements can easily come unstuck by the extra claim on their time during school breaks, dread holidays.[4] Amanda, a 36-year-old physiotherapist, went part-time when her daughter Nicky started her school holiday last year. She loves her job and is angry about having to give up a promising career. 'I could not face another summer of begging people to help me with childcare', she told me.

According to one study, parents spend twice as much time looking after children today as in 1961. In the last 30 years the time spent on childcare has increased fourfold for men and two-and-a-half times for women. This change seems to have affected all social classes. Jonathan Gershuny, a sociologist based at the University of Essex, found that even full-time employed women with children in 1995 appeared to devote more time to childcare than non-employed mothers did in 1961. Today's American father spends far more time with his children than did his father and grandfather. The New York based Families and Work Institute estimates that fathers spend 75 per cent of the time that their wives spend on domestic chores, whereas in the 1970s this figure was only 30 per cent.[5]

One consequence of parents spending more time with their children is that the time spent by children together, or alone without the company of adults, has fallen. This is particularly true of free time outdoors. A major study carried out by the University of Michigan showed that between 1981 and 1997 the amount of free time available to children dropped by 16 per cent. Time spent playing fell by 25 per cent and outdoor activities such as walking and hiking declined by a staggering 50 per cent. Conversely, children's involvement in organized adult supervised activities has shot up.[6]

This survey suggests that there has been a noticeable increase in the amount of time that children spend on scheduled activities. It points to two important findings: children's free time has declined, and free time is increasingly structured. The major cause of this change has been the increased amount of time children spend in school, which rose from 21 to 29 hours per week. Children spend less time playing and more time 'going places'. Sadly, this development encroaches on children's freedom to play. It also reduces the amount of time family members spend just sitting around, talking and not doing anything in particular. In turn, parents spend more time organizing and driving children from one stimulating activity to the next.[7]

It is the belief that mothers and fathers can never spend too much time with their children that fuels the belief that society faces an exceptional era of a parental time famine. Some individual parents do face special difficulties and are therefore unable to spend enough time with their children. But, paradoxically, despite the claim that working mothers and fathers are short-changing their children, they are spending more time looking after their children than ever before. Most recent sociological surveys testify to the fact that mothers and fathers spend more time with their children than those of previous generations. A recent survey published for the Future Foundation in March 2000 confirmed that the amount of time invested by parents in their children's upbringing has more than trebled over the past three decades. According to this study, British parents are now devoting an average of 85 minutes per day to each child compared with a mere 25 minutes a day in the mid-1970s. Interviewers talked to three generations of families to find out the difference in time each cohort spent on child-rearing. In every key aspect of parenting and family life investigated by the researchers, the vast majority of the respondents indicated that they spent more time with their children than their parents did. On the basis of this study, the Future Foundation predicted that by 2010 the amount of time that parents spend with their children would increase from 85 minutes to 100 minutes a day.[8]

The Future Foundation report provides compelling evidence of a fundamental reorganization of parenting time. It notes that a variety of developments, some negative (growing concerns about children's safety and well-being) and some positive (increasing desire for creative involvement in children's lives), means that 'parenting takes more time, more consideration and more emotional energy'. This augmentation of the time parents spend on parenting is driven by the belief that children need to be supervised more extensively than was the case in the past. That is why parents interviewed in *Complicated Lives* felt that they spent more time with their children than their parents did with them. The conclusion of the report was that 'Parenting is going to take up even more time and energy in the future as the desire to be an accomplished parent increases.' Michael Willmott of the Future Foundation predicts that 'If society continues to blame a range of problems on the perceived failings of parents, parental neurosis and stress could increase.'[9]

Complicated Lives is one of the few authoritative sources to acknowledge how the redefinition of parenting has led to a massive increase in the amount of time parents concentrate on childcare. This rise from a mere 25 minutes a day in the mid-1970s to 85 minutes a day in the 1990s represents a dramatic statement about the changing character of child-rearing. Sadly, the pressure of time is compounded by strong cultural forces that continually insist that the time that parents spend with their children is simply not enough. The redefinition of parenting time and the perception that self-centred mothers and fathers short-change children constitute an important influence in the shaping of parental anxieties.

The relentless pressure to expand parenting time inevitably forces mothers and fathers on the defensive. Almost every parent I talked to intimated that they believed that they should do more for their children.

Even outwardly confident career women spoke about their guilt. Tracey, who works as a consultant, told of a lecture she received from her son's teacher, after she was 10 minutes late picking up her child from after-school care. 'It was one of the most humiliating experiences in my life', she stated. 'No one in my line of work would dare use that tone of voice with me – but everyone believes they have the authority to lecture working mothers', she said with indignation.

No matter how parents organize their time, there is always an expert to remind them of the inadequacy of their arrangements. So-called quality time is the latest target of expert criticism. Numerous experts have lined up to criticize parents for trying to pack their child-rearing duties into quality time. Mothers who work in paid employment come in for special criticism. A controversial study by the American sociologist Arlie Russell Hochschild accuses parents of deliberately staying behind in the office because they would rather be there than at home.[10] Some studies place the onus on errant fathers who refuse to play an equal role in childcare. Others criticize not so much the parents but a long-hours work culture for the alleged neglect of Britain's children. Hundreds of articles have been written advocating just about anything – from a revolution in work culture to more involvement from fathers and more support for parents to stay at home. Advice on how to balance home and work is liberally offered by what-to-do columns. What the debate about The Great Balancing Act overlooks is that the real issue is not time in the abstract but the culturally endorsed redefinition of parenting time.

Parenting as an ordeal

Mothers and fathers never had an easy time. The demands of family life have always posed difficult challenges for parents. Although in the past most sensible people realized that child-rearing involved a lot of grind and hard work, it was a role that was embraced by most, if with various degrees of enthusiasm. One reason why people were prepared to make sacrifices for the sake of their children was because that was what society expected of them. But it wasn't seen merely as a duty. Until recently, most Western societies were subject to cultural influences that represented family life in glowing terms as the institution through which self-realization took place. The family was hyped up, celebrated and romanticized. Probably many adults who had bought into this dream of family were disappointed and left wondering what they were missing out on.

Today, when parenting is continually linked to a perception of crisis, it is difficult to sustain the promise of family bliss. If anything, society insists on inflating the problem of child-rearing so much that the vision of family life that prevails is most likely to deter the prospective candidate from starting down the road of parenting. Society has rightly rejected the myth of domestic bliss of the 1950s but in so doing it has swung in the opposite direction. The myth of the naturally competent parent who finds complete fulfilment in family life, has given way to a myth of parenting as an ordeal. The same trends towards parent determinism and the expansion of the role of mother and father also give rise to the view that child-rearing is an extremely complicated and difficult job. Parenting is no longer assumed to be an activity that adults can spontaneously carry out. On the contrary, there is an assumption that many people are simply not up to the job and that society would be better off if they did not have babies. Some authoritarian experts in the United States have even proposed a system of licensing parents. Jack Westman, Professor of Psychiatry at the University of Wisconsin, the author of this scheme, claims that since 'incompetent parents gravely endanger society' they need to be weeded out through a system of screening. In Britain, too, the assumption that adults require special training for the job is widely held by child-rearing experts.

Parenting programmes go out of their way to prepare prospective parents for the ordeals they are likely to face – such as toddlers' temper tantrums – because many experts believe that situations parents inevitably face are enough to send them flying out of control. A guide published by the recently decommissioned Health Education Authority observes that 'sometimes, whatever you do, feelings of anger and frustration get out of control', and advises 'then it's vital to get support'. Other official and semi-official guides concur and routinely call upon parents 'not to take it out on the children'.[11]

Child-rearing advice has also adopted a sombre downbeat character.

It often has the character of a letter written by someone who has been through hell and who now wants to share this with the soon-to-be-defeated reader. Christina Hardyment's study of the changing emphasis of baby-care advice draws attention to this new trend. 'Researchers are now saying that the advent of a baby is likely to be the most disruptive thing that can happen to a marriage.' Susan Maushart's *The Mask of Motherhood* is devoted to exposing past myths about the unproblematic joys of this experience. Unfortunately she not only succeeds in acknowledging the difficulties of motherhood but also turns it into a pathological experience. According to Maushart, motherhood 'can be and often is dangerous' to women's mental health. The bearing of a first child is represented as the source of a 'psychic crisis' to the mother. The blurb on the back of Susan Jeffers's *I'm Okay . . . You're a Brat*' claims that this 'fearlessly honest book' breaks 'the conspiracy of silence' and pulls no punches about how 'difficult parenthood is for many'. It seems that virtually the entire child advice industry is in the business of 'fearlessly' breaking the conspiracy of silence. Anyone leafing through recently published child-rearing manuals is unlikely to find any examples of a conspiracy of silence. On the contrary, they will encounter advice that is realistic in its portrayal of the difficulties faced by parents, sometimes brutally so. They will also find material on the bookshelves that is downright scary. Jeffers's fearless exposé of the 'perils of parenthood' actually represents a new genre of advice designed to reconcile parents to the lowest possible expectations.[12]

The representation of parenting as an ordeal is fuelled by strong social pressures that continually inflate the problems associated with it. Parent-scaring has become so deeply embedded in our culture that sometimes commentators wonder why anyone can still enjoy the experience of child-rearing. A report published in December 1999 by Johnson and Johnson promotes the message of sombre realism. Commenting on the report, Maureen Marks, a psychologist, remarked that given 'the inherent difficulties of childbearing and child rearing [it is] surprising that the euphoria and immense joy of becoming a mother, and the sense of achievement and fulfilment it brings, is so widely reported'.[13] Other reports paint a far more dismal picture. A survey carried out by ICM for Mothercare in November 1999 reports that the words used to describe child-rearing by the overwhelming majority of parents were 'demanding, thankless and exhausting'. Of the respondents, 61 per cent found caring for their children difficult or very difficult, and 71 per cent stated that they were 'rushed off their feet'.[14]

Negative perceptions about child-rearing mean that a significant and growing proportion of the adult population is opting not to have children. A study carried out by the Joseph Rowntree Foundation in 1998 claims that one in five women now of childbearing age will not have children. In contrast, only one in ten women born in 1945 did not have a child. One reason why some women have decided not to have children is the perception that parenthood is an intolerable responsibility, a life of sacrifice and of risk. According to the study, 'parenthood was viewed as total responsibility, total commitment and sacrifice – social, emotional and financial'. The inflation of parenting time is one significant factor shaping this perception. Although there are many good reasons why adults take sensible decisions about not having children, it seems that paranoia about parenting has also become a factor influencing some people's calculations.[15]

The transformation of parenting into an ordeal is inseparable from the culture of parent-scaring. It is not child-rearing as such, but the tendency to continually expand parental responsibility that distorts and destabilizes the lives of mothers and fathers. The more we complicate child-rearing, and the more we insist on inflating the tasks facing mothers and fathers, the more we ensure that paranoia dominates the style of contemporary parenting.

Six

Why Parents Confuse Their Problems with Those of Their Children

Policy debates about children are dominated by individuals claiming to give voice to children's needs. We frequently hear the appeal, 'children need this' or 'children want that'. Invariably, these claims – however well-meaning – are based on a grown-up interpretation of children's minds. It is easy to forget that the way we regard childhood depends on adults' perception of that experience. It is not children who write books and newspaper articles about the meaning of childhood. It is not children who produce television programmes about their requirements or who make pronouncements about their emotional needs. Even the demand for 'children's rights' has been formulated by adults. Today, it is not children who are desperately shouting that they are scared of the risks they face. The image of a 'child at risk' is the product of current adult sensibilities and imagination. Ideas about childhood are invariably filtered through the adult imagination and say as much about the world of grown-ups as about that of children.

Throughout history, children have been portrayed in many different ways – as little savages, selfish little animals, objects of spiritual veneration, as resilient or, today, as permanently at risk. Views about children fluctuate not because babies or infants have changed. What has altered is the way that grown-ups regard the world of children. This change in perception is primarily the outcome of tensions that permeate the adult imagination. These perceptions have had a great impact on the way that children experience their lives and continue to do so today. Indeed, the way that children learn about the world is through interacting and internalizing the values and expectations that we have of them. Cognitive skills – thinking, conceptualizing, problem-solving – are assimilated through interaction with competent adults before they come under a child's control. The initiation of a child into the wider social world takes place through the guidance of adults. That is why the way that children think about themselves and the world is influenced by, and inseparable from, the adult imagination.

In recent decades the adult world has become more interested in the voice of children. It has become fashionable to advocate children's rights and to consult children on a variety of topics. Books are written to explore what children really think and what adults can learn from their messages. Ellen Galinsky's *Ask the Children: What America's Children Really Think about Working Parents* sought to find out what children thought of their parents and, in particular, what their reaction was to their parents working. This sensitive account – well received on both sides of the Atlantic – argued that from a child's perspective what mattered was not whether a mother worked or not, but how good she was at parenting. *Ask the Children* provides important insights into the dynamics of the parent–child relation. But it is important not to overlook the fact that what children 'really think' about their parents is inseparable from how adults define what constitutes appropriate forms of family life and child-rearing. Galinsky's findings can be interpreted as a portrait not merely of children's feelings but of contemporary adult expectations regarding maternal paid employment. Children's reaction to their mother's paid employment is to a considerable extent scripted through the stories that adults tell about it. If working mothers were more highly stigmatized by society, there is little doubt children's reactions would have been far more negative. And in that case this negative response would have been used as proof of the thesis that mothers who work outside the home are failing in their responsibilities.[1]

Many of the issues we associate with childhood are ones defined through adults interpreting children's lives through the medium of their own experience. Adults have always lived their lives through their children. From the moment of birth, when arguments break out about whether a baby resembles the mother or the father, adults never cease to discover themselves through their offspring. Some grown-ups conduct their lives through their children more than others. And too often, especially at times of uncertainty, parents find it difficult to avoid the temptation of seeing their children from the point of view of their own insecurity. The main point of this chapter is to outline how, in an important sense, parental paranoia represents the transmission of adult anxieties through the experience of children.

Parent identity

Child-rearing is not the same as parenting. In most human societies there is no distinct activity that today we associate with the term parenting. In agricultural societies, children are expected to participate in the work and routine of the community. Until recent times children were not regarded as requiring special parenting attention or care. They were perceived as little people, not yet fully formed. There was not very much concern or interest in their cognitive or physical development because it was assumed that these biologically immature people would eventually mature of their own accord. Compared to today, this relative absence of adult interest in children is striking. Mothers and fathers tended to leave the development of their offspring to fate. Allowing nature to take its course assigned a minor and passive role to adults in the process of child-rearing.

The belief that children require special care and attention evolved alongside the conviction that what adults did mattered to their development. These sentiments gained strength and began to influence public opinion in the nineteenth century. The view that certain forms of adult actions influenced the development of a child in a particular direction created widespread interest in the behaviour of parents. The work of mothering and fathering was now endowed with profound importance. It became defined as a distinct skill that could assure the development of character traits necessary for a successful life. Alternatively, the absence of this skill – poor nurturing – could deprive a child of a positive future. Mothers and fathers were seen to have a pivotal role in the determination of a child's future. Parenting, as a distinct skill and activity, emerged with the cultural assumption that more or less linked the fate of children to the behaviour of their mothers and fathers. This view of parenting is closely connected to the decline of large households and the rise of individualized nuclear family arrangements. Once children are seen as the responsibility of a mother and father rather than of a larger community, the modern view of parenting acquires salience.

The social recognition accorded to parenting ensured that this role began to influence the way that mothers and fathers viewed themselves. Throughout most of human history, parents have always claimed a special relationship with their children. But once children were perceived as the more or less direct product of parenting, the status enjoyed by mothers and fathers became more intimately linked with the development of their children. For parents, children provide proof of competence. With the growing influence of parent determinism, children also come to embody a moral statement about their mothers and fathers. A child's behaviour, skill, intelligence and character traits serve as a testimony of parenting virtues or faults. Not surprisingly, parenting has an important influence on the self-image of adults. Successful parenting enhances the identity of adults. It becomes an important constituent of the identity through which adults make sense of the world. Parenting is not merely about how adults react to children, but is also about how grown-ups make a statement about themselves through their children.

So parenting is not simply child-rearing. It is partly to do with child-rearing but it is also about how adults construct their lives through and in interaction with their children. Adults do not simply live their lives through children but, in part, develop their identity through them. When expectant fathers and mothers debate what name to give to a child, it is often obvious that they are using this event as an occasion to express themselves. A 'cool' name of a newborn invites the conclusion that the parents are also cool. An unusual name for a child provides a hint that the parents are exceptionally clever. Parents who play classical music to their baby may do so because it reflects their agenda rather than that of the child. Parents who pierce their infants' ears, dress them like little adults, insist that they become vegetarians, are in part making important statements about themselves. Through raising children parents are also raising themselves.

In most discussions the problem of parenting is perceived as the difficulty that adults have with the management of their children. The importance of this question to parents is self-evident. But there is also another side to the parenting problem – that of how adults ought to behave in order to carry out their functions as child-carers responsibly and effectively. That parenting is to a surprising degree about adult behaviour can be seen from even a cursory review of parenting literature during the past century. Such books offer lots of helpful hints about what fathers and mothers ought to do with their children in a wide variety of circumstances. But they also contain guidance about how mothers and fathers should behave, especially in front of the children. A recently published manual, *Change Your Child's Behavior by Changing Yours*, provides an explicit formulation of this approach.[2]

During the past two decades the focus of parenting advice has shifted even more towards targeting the behaviour of parents. This shift is not surprising since the continuous expansion of the parenting role demands that greater attention be paid to the conduct of child-carers. Hardyment's review of the history of baby-care advice confirms the significance of this shift of emphasis. She believes that the 'single most striking new emphasis' in recent parenting advice is a change 'from a concentration on the child to concern for its parents'.[3] Our own review of child advice manuals suggests that not only has there been a shift of focus towards the parent but also that *this literature can best be defined by its project of altering adult behaviour*. Advice, which is promoted as child-centred, is often aimed at the behaviour of the parent. The opportunistic targeting of insecure parental identities has become a central part of the repertoire of child professionals. Children become the vehicles through which parents are instructed about how they should act in general. That is why a chapter usually titled 'Your relationship' has become a regular fixture in recently published parenting manuals.

Parenting advice is often predicated on the assumption that, unless guided and educated, parental behaviour represents a risk to children. An article in *The Times*, titled 'Advice aims to stop parents behaving badly', sums up the approach. The article reported on the publication of an advice booklet that sought to reduce the stresses of new parenthood in order to minimize the harm done to children. Parent-training programmes also adopt the approach of altering adult behaviour.

Helping stressed-out parents to cope with life is another theme in the parenting literature. Chapters titled 'When it all gets too much' advise mothers and fathers to take a 'relaxing' bath or to find some other way of switching off. Special breathing techniques are promoted for parents who feel 'trapped and exhausted'. Child-rearing books now routinely deal with 'your needs'. The HEA's guidebook adopts an understanding tone towards the stressed-out parent: 'Keeping healthy, feeling all right about yourself and your life, being you as a person as well as a parent, are all very important.' The HEA's message is that emotionally sound parents make for happy children. 'If you care for yourself, you're more likely to enjoy being a parent, and more likely to keep on top of a very hard job', it notes.[4]

One important way that parenting literature tries to alter parents' conduct is by attempting to give meaning to adult life through parents' experience with children. The appeal to parent identity represents a powerful bid to their self-image. At the most basic level, parents are advised that the more you love your child the more he will love you in return. This instrumental call for love is carefully directed towards the parent's hunger for status and recognition. Penelope Leach's *Your Baby and Child* is paradigmatic in this respect. Leach informs mothers that 'babies fall in love with people who mother them emotionally'. Appealing to a mother's desire for affirmation, Leach promises that 'the baby flatters you with his special attentions, making you feel unique, beloved, irreplaceable'.[5] The pledge of a special and uniquely fulfilling relationship is offered to the parent prepared to adopt the behaviour prescribed.

Appeals to parent identity are often directed at the self-preoccupation of the adult carer. *Parents Who Think too Much*, Anne Cassidy's provocative critique of today's parenting culture, draws attention to the growing phenomenon of publications which are ostensibly about childcare but which are really about the emotional problems confronting adult identity.[6] Books like *Mothering the New Mother, The Shock of Motherhood, Coaching for Fatherhood, The Gift of Fatherhood: How Men's Lives are Transformed by Their Children, Growing up Again: Parenting Ourselves, Parenting Our Children*, aim to alter adult behaviour through engaging with tensions contained within parent identity. In Britain, books such as *How Love Works: How to Stay in Love as a Couple and be True to Yourself . . . Even with Kids*, by childcare guru Steve Biddulph, provide guidance to the emotionally confused parent. Parents are offered advice about how to survive and keep their marriage going after having children. In some cases, child-rearing is represented as a form of therapy through which an adult embarks on a voyage of self-discovery. 'Many older fathers speak of a "deepening" of their lives, or an "opening out", or "loosening up", conveying a sense of recognising something new in themselves', writes Jeremy Hamand with reassuring authority in *Father Over Forty*.[7] Psychiatrist Frank Pittman writes in *Man Enough* that 'fathering is not something perfect men do, but something that perfects the man'. In case the reader is confused by what fathering is about, Pittman remarks that the 'end product of child raising is not the child but the parent'.[8]

Anne Cassidy takes the view that the fact that 'child-rearing' is now called 'parenting' is not an accident. The term shifts the focus from children to parents. One reason for this shift, she believes, is that adulthood has become more self-absorbed and that it is now culturally acceptable to use 'our children's childhood' as the vehicle for adults' own psychic transformation.[9] Cassidy has a point, but as we shall see later in the chapter, there are other influences that shape contemporary adult identity. The shift in terminology does raise one particularly interesting paradox – which is that in the era where all aspects of family life are declared to be child-centred, many adults seem to have lost the ability to distinguish their own concerns from the issues that affect their children. Too often, child development is interpreted through the parenting agenda. This may mean that many of the concerns that society raises about parenting may have less to do with children than we are led to believe.

Emotional investment in children

Adult preoccupation with their identity as parents does not mean that mothers and fathers do not love their children. Children have never been so much loved by their mothers and fathers as today. In a world that is more and more dominated by instrumental calculation, the parent–child relationship stands out as a unique example of an interaction that is primarily guided by sentiment and altruism. The child has become a unique object of love and sometimes of veneration. This celebration of children has been characterized as the *sacralization* of childhood. This term refers to the important historical process through which contemporary childhood has come to be invested with sentimental or religious meaning.

The term 'sacralization' emerges out of an important study by the American sociologist Viviana Zelizer, titled *Pricing the Priceless Child*. Zelizer's text explores the profound alteration that took place in the economic and sentimental value of children between the 1870s and the 1930s. At the beginning of this period, children were still mainly valued because of the economic contribution they made to the upkeep of the family. However, important changes in the sphere of economic and social life ensured that child labour diminished in significance. With the passing of time children were less likely to be valued for their productive role and became more and more objects of sentiment. Zelizer argues that the expulsion of children from economic life at around the turn of the century was paralleled by the cultural process of 'sacralization' of children's lives. She believes that this process provides the platform on which the subsequent veneration of childhood has been constructed. She writes that the 'emergence of this economically "worthless" but emotionally "priceless" child has created an essential condition for contemporary childhood'. The normal pragmatic economic calculations that adults make about most aspects of life have little bearing on their decision to have children. Having a child in an industrialized society is primarily emotionally motivated.[10]

The sacred child of the modern era is an object of sentiment and veneration. This new conception of children as intrinsically precious and as an unequivocal source of love evolved alongside the new domestic role assumed by non-employed middle-class women. The American historian Carl Degler believes that the changing value of children served women's interest: 'Exalting the child went hand in hand with exalting the domestic role of women; each reinforced the other while together they raised domesticity within the family to a new and higher level of respectability.'[11] The exaltation of childhood and by implication the role of caring continues to influence parental ideology to this day. Through the care that adults provide to precious children, parenting acquired a new moral significance. Although the exaltation of childhood might have been an outlook that was initially restricted to a relatively small group of nineteenth-century middle-class professional mothers, it gradually spread to wider sections of society. Today it gives definition to the ideology of parenting. That is why parents who fail to provide the best care for their children are judged to be immoral.

Parental identity is also shaped by the expanding influence of parent determinism. The idea that the well-nurtured child was the product of the skills of his carers has proved attractive to many carers. However, the belief that parents bear so much responsibility for the development of their children also creates anxieties in case their offspring do not turn out so well. With so much at stake, parents have considerable moral incentive to implement the most up-to-date child-rearing practices as early as possible. As a result, the parent has become dependent on the information and advice offered by professional child specialists.

In recent decades, the exaltation of children has acquired far greater significance than at any time in the past. In most Western societies, children are less and less often brought into this world as an automatic duty. Increasingly the timing of a child's birth is carefully planned. In contrast to the pre-contraceptive-pill era, many women now have a real choice about when to have children, if at all. Consequently, greater control over fertility has led to a marked reduction in the size of families. From conception, children are far more likely to be 'wanted' and from the outset they are objects of a high level of emotional investment by their parents. In short, greater control over human reproduction makes every new child unique and priceless to parent and society alike. It also enhances the moral responsibility of the adult for guaranteeing the well-being of the precious child.

The immense emotional investment in children that society now expects of their carers is almost always readily accepted by parents. The status that is granted to the good child-raiser is a source of both moral authority and of parental identity. Many parents who positively embrace this status are also aware that every new stage in their child's development raises new questions about their skill and competence. With so much emotional investment at stake, parents are often seriously preoccupied with how their performance is judged in public. Parents are remarkably vulnerable to the many busybodies who continually instruct and advise them about their role. Since the identity of parents develops through public affirmation, mothers and fathers can never be indifferent to the way that others view them. Part of this identity is constituted through demonstrating competence in the skills of child-rearing. That is why advice that is oriented towards altering the behaviour of parents is so rarely contested by mature adults. A sense of performing for an audience is liable to weaken the confidence of even the most self-sufficient adult. Mothers and fathers who are never entirely confident about their performance as child-carers are therefore quite vulnerable to external pressure and influence. Consequently, parents listen and in many cases seek out advice from individuals who wear the mantle of expert authority.

Parents also anxiously watch one another and continually compare their performance. The pressure to keep up, or at least not to be seen to be falling down on one's duty, is one that very few can resist. Parenting identity is established not only through how mothers and fathers handle their job of child-raising but also in part through comparison with other child-carers. This aspect of today's parenting culture is rarely debated and yet it places an enormous burden on the lives of carers. Mothers and fathers who feel that they are under constant scrutiny cannot help but perform for others. Parents who are distracted by the need to perform can sometimes lose sight of what child-rearing should be about. Competitive parents often end up being pushy mothers and fathers. In recent years, there has been an outcry that many parents are going over the top and are in effect hothousing their youngsters. Well-to-do middle-class parents, who push their offspring hard to learn new skills at far too early an age, are often accused of placing their children's mental health at risk. The phenomenon of hyperparenting is prevalent in Britain as well as in the USA.

Hyperparenting is often one-sidedly blamed on insecure and ambitious parents. In his classic account of this form of parental pressure, David Elkind in *The Hurried Child* pointed the finger at self-obsessed carers who are insensitive to the feelings and needs of their children.[12] Such an accusation is not without foundation. The parent identity does little to discourage adults from living through their children and, as we note later in this chapter, this trend has become more noticeable in recent years. But there is more to hyperparenting than the archetypal pushy parent. Pushy parents have been around for a long time – hyperparenting has not. The roots of hyperparenting are not to be found in the pushy parent but in the culture of parent-scaring. Many of the trends previously outlined – perceptions of childhood vulnerability, infant determinism, the expanded definition of parenting – work as mutually reinforcing influences on the worldview of mothers and fathers. The constant exhortation, 'you can never do too much for your children' has had the unfortunate consequence of fostering a climate in which parents actually *do* do too much for their children. For many individual mothers and fathers this approach is not a matter of choice. 'Sophie was the only one amongst the girls her age that did not do ballet lessons', explained her mother Ruth. Ruth was made to feel that she was cheating her 4-and-a-half-year-old daughter by depriving her of this valuable activity, as well as of the company of her friends. 'Sophie felt excluded and I got fed up with her friends' mothers wanting to know why she didn't do ballet', said Ruth with a hint of resignation. 'And yes, after four weeks we gave in', she added. Even some parents who cannot financially afford to 'give in', still do.

Hyperparenting reveals just how far the insecurities contained in the identity of parenthood can contradict the real needs of children. The most obvious response to the pressure for parenting on demand is to *over-parent*. Unfortunately, such a response has little to do with improving the quality of the child–parent relationship. It simply implies a quantitative increase in the range of 'stimulating' activities and possessions made available to children. This is a classic example of how the expansion of parenting time has little to do with child-rearing as such. After-school activities take up a lot of parenting time. Their contribution to improving child-rearing is debatable. Hyperparenting is generally criticized for placing too much pressure on young children. But hyperparenting can also be seen as depriving children of precisely the kind of pressures they need. One of the most stimulating activities for young children is that of unsupervised play with others of their own age. Learning from and through other children encourages the acquisition of coping and communication skills and the habit of independence. But allowing children to be children is perceived as far too much of a risk by adults who have been trained to believe that they can never do too much for their children. Hyperparenting is merely a logical extension of parent determinism.

The emptying out of adult identity

The emotional investment that adults make in children is far greater today than in the early days of the sacralization of childhood. Our culture today is probably more child-obsessed than child-centred. The continuous rise in the demands imposed on parents is fuelled by the steady elevation of the moral significance attached to children. The reason for this development has little to do with any new insights into the world of children. Current concern with the position of children is sometimes interpreted as the consequence of a more enlightened and caring society. An examination of our culture's preoccupation with the child suggests that this development is inseparable from some of the problems that afflict the world of adults. It is the uncertainties which surround the meaning of adult identities that motivate many parents to put so much of their emotional capital into their children.

That today's world is one of uncertain identities is something of a truism. It is widely recognized that we live in a time of insecure attachments. Many of us have serious difficulties with offering more than a provisional answer to the question 'Who am I?' It is generally appreciated that the identities that served previous generations in the past fit rather uncomfortably with the demands of life today. The sense of belonging that we derive from being connected to others has in recent decades been undermined by important changes in the way we live and organize our lives. Take the role of work. Work has tradition-ally been an important source of collective experience that connected people to one another. It was and still remains an important part of an individual's identity. When people ask, 'Who is he?' they expect an answer bound up with work. 'He is a mechanic', 'She is a nurse' are not just statements about people's jobs, but also about their identity. An individual's personality and status is in some sense inextricably linked to his or her job. Today, however, work has a less permanent and identity-forming role than it had during most of the last century. In an era in which the idea of a job for life is dismissed as an illusion and in which people are expected to train to be flexible and responsive to the changing needs of the labour market, people's sense of who they are becomes more ambiguous. *Corrosion of Character*, written by Richard Sennett, a sociologist from the London School of Economics, provides a powerful account of the consequences that work insecurity has on the way that employees regard themselves. His study highlights the impact of this development on people's sense of themselves. The experience of insecurity makes it difficult for many workers to achieve a sense of moral identity. Work insecurity breeds detachment and a feeling of estrangement from others. Finding fulfilment through work becomes difficult for those who are unable to identify with their jobs. He claims that the question, 'Who needs me?' has become difficult to answer in modern capitalism. According to Sennett, a system that 'radiates indifference' generates personal confusion and confers on the individual a profound sense of personal isolation.[13]

The insecurities that many people experience in relation to work are also felt in other spheres of everyday life. The satisfaction that we derive from being connected to others is radically challenged by uncertainties about our communities. What does it mean to be British? At a time of devolution and of the powerful role that the European Union plays in everyday life, the answer to this question is not self-evident. Lack of clarity about national, ethnic and even community affiliations tests people's sense of belonging. Debates about national identity, Europe and the effects of globalization also reflect concerns about the human desire for recognition. When we fail to recognize ourselves through work or feel detached from others and have a weak feeling of community, then our very identity becomes unclear.

Weakening of durable relations

Nor is the question of who are we restricted to issues to do with work and community. The cumulative effect of social and cultural change has had a major impact on the way we conduct our affairs as men and women. Relations within the family and between people are generally experienced as unstable and transient.

Today, a growing proportion of adults are opting to cohabit either before, or instead of, marrying. According to the Office for National Statistics, over the last three decades there has been a dramatic increase in the proportion of women who have cohabited with a partner before their twenty-fifth birthday. In 1997, almost 40 per cent of women aged 25 to 29 had cohabited before the age of 25, whereas the proportion was just over 2 per cent for those aged 50 to 54. Not only are more people cohabiting, they are also living together for longer periods. This increase in the incidence and duration of cohabiting coincides with a decline in the number of people marrying.[14]

The number of first marriages in the United Kingdom has decreased by about 50 per cent since their highest number in 1970. Annual marriage rates are now at their lowest level since records began 160 years ago. In part, this decline in the number of first marriages is associated with the increase in the average age of men and women when they first marry. During the past three decades the average age at first marriage in Great Britain rose from 25 years to 28 years for men and from 23 years to 26 years for women. These trends have led some commentators to conclude that the traditional family is dead. A report published in 1998 by the Henley Centre, a well-known fore-casting company, claimed that marriage and the traditional family would be history within 25 years.

The decline of the so-called traditional family is so clear that it is no longer in dispute. But its impact on adults' and children's lives is not self-evident. The trend towards cohabitation and the decline in the rate of marriage are associated with a substantial increase in the rate of divorce. The number of divorces in the United Kingdom more than trebled between 1969 and 1994. At present, more than a third of marriages end within six years. The Office for National Statistics estimates that, according to the present trend, 40 per cent of marriages will ultimately end in divorce and just under half of married couples are likely to celebrate their silver wedding. If present divorce rates continue, it is estimated that 28 per cent of children will experience the divorce of their parents before they reach 16.[15]

The decline of marriage, and the rise of cohabitation and divorce have led to the emergence of important variations in family life. Since the 1970s, there has been a fourfold increase in the proportion of births outside marriage. By the late 1990s, more than a third of all births were outside marriage in England and Wales. Today, almost four in ten babies are born outside marriage. The growing instability of adult relations – married and non-married – means that a growing number of children are brought up in lone-parent families and in stepfamilies. Almost one child in three lives with a lone parent or in a stepfamily.

The instability that surrounds family relations in part reflects and in part consolidates the emptying out of adult identity. The emptying out of adult identity reflects a process whereby men and women find it increasingly difficult to derive a secure sense of affirmation through their relations with one another and with other adults. Other sources of adult affirmation – vocation, career, work and community – have also become less reliable means of conferring stable identities.

Uncertainty about adult identity is most intensely felt through our intimate private encounters. At a time of changing gender roles, certainty about the meaning of being a man or a woman sometimes proves to be elusive. Even relationships bound together through passion and love are experienced in a peculiarly short-termist and insecure manner. The emotion that adults invest in one another is tempered by expectations of impermanence. In everyday life, love between men and women is often treated in a calculating and pragmatic fashion. There is a heightened public awareness of marital breakdown and of the fluidity of intimate relationships.

For many, the emptying out of adult identity is experienced through a sense of estrangement from other people. In such circumstances, people's relating to one another is guided more by calculation and less by sentiment. Our very ability to make emotional investment in one another is restrained by a public mood that continually stresses the difficulties inherent in human relations. The British Government's recent proposal designed to encourage couples to make legally binding pre-nuptial agreements illustrates the temper of our times. The aim of a pre-nuptial agreement is to settle the division of property if and when a marriage breaks up. From the standpoint of legal and business calculation it makes perfect sense to enter into such an agreement. However, the adoption of such an agreement represents an assumption that the marriage is likely to break up and end in divorce. In August 1999, it was reported that the Government is to warn women about the risk of opening joint bank accounts with their spouses, in case the marriage breaks down and leaves them vulnerable. The assumption behind such policy initiatives is that marriages cannot be expected to work, and so provision should be made for individuals in the event of failure. For some this assumption represents a realistic appraisal of social trends. However, the expectation of failure necessarily changes our view of this institution when we no longer see it as an unquestioned commitment for life. At the very least, the expectation of impermanence is likely to limit the emotional investment that the two contracting parties make in one another.

It is not only governments that advocate a cold, calculating approach towards intimate relationships. A number of social scientists and commentators have taken it upon themselves to warn people about the 'illusion' of romantic love. University of Lancaster academic, Wendy Langford, has written a book entitled *Revolution of the Heart*, which warns women about the danger of investing romantic love with sacred and spiritual meaning. Ed Straw has published a pamphlet, *Relative Values*, for the think-tank Demos, which unequivocally insists that since romantic love is an insufficient basis for fostering long-term relationships, adults should be educated to adopt more realistic assumptions about parenting. The view that it is not possible to turn the clock back to the days when marriage was based on the illusion of romantic love provides the premise of a 1999 study by Jane Lewis for the Lord Chancellor's department. The message 'get real' is also promoted by numerous individuals claiming an expertise in the management of relationships.[16]

It is ironic that precisely at a time when personal relationships have been freed from many of their traditional constraints, they are often represented as more tortuous and problematic than ever before. Even intimate friendships are portrayed as belonging to a bygone era. Some academics claim that people today fear intimacy because they have become more individualistic, more self-protective and cynical. This was the thesis of Dr Robert Firestone's study, *The Fear of Intimacy*.[17] British researchers who argue that there is a trend for the middle classes to have fewer emotionally demanding friendships have echoed this US clinical psychologist's verdict.

Although most people still long for durable romantic attachments, contemporary culture appears to encourage a sceptical stance towards long-term emotional commitment. Such attitudes are also reinforced by popular culture that continually highlights problems associated with family life. The romantic notion that love can conquer all has been laid to rest, condemned as naïve idealism that never works in practice. Instead there is a growing wariness about love and romantic attachments, as a result of which individuals are encouraged to adopt a self-centred, calculating and short-term attitude to their emotional commitments, and not to invest too much in anybody other than themselves.

The elusive character of romantic love is not in doubt. However, this focus for adult passion and emotional attachment has not been replaced by any plausible alternative. Jane Lewis's study *Individualism and Commitment in Cohabitation and Marriage* claims that what has happened is an increase of individualism in relation to personal relations and that selfishness has 'undermined the commitment of men and women to each other and their children'. It is far from evident why individualism should lead to a fear of commitment. Nor is it self-evident that people have become more selfish. The problem of commitment is inextricably bound up with the emptying of adult identity. Today, many of us find it difficult to know what we can be committed to. The sense of confusion about who we are also makes it difficult to establish durable ties to one another. As a result, our expectations of relationships diminish and sometimes our ability to forge bonds of intimacy becomes weaker.

The problems associated with the self-perception of adults and the difficulties associated with long-term commitments have a decisive impact on relationships between adults and children. The tremendous moral significance which society invests in childhood is directly linked to changing adult identity. Above all it is the emptying out of adult identity that gives childhood its unprecedented importance. As adult identity becomes less distinct and more problematic the search for certainty finds an important focus in childhood.

The moral significance of the child today is directly linked to the emptying out of adult identity. At a time when the desire for recognition lacks an obvious outlet, the validation of the sense of self through one's child has acquired a new importance. When, in previous eras, adults lived through their children they did so as members of at least outwardly relatively stable families and communities. The child was used as a means of self-realization and sometimes as an instrument of family advance. Today, the child has been transformed into a far more formidable medium for the validation of the adult self. At a time when very few human relations can be taken for granted, the child appears as a unique emotional partner in a relationship. 'The trust that was previously anticipated from marriage, partnership, friendship, class solidarity and so on, is now invested more generally in the child', writes the sociologist Chris Jenks.[18] Unlike marriage or friendship, the bond that links a parent to a child cannot be broken. It is a bond that stands out as the exception to the rule that relationships cannot be expected to last for ever.

The general perception of transient relations between men and women stands in sharp contrast to the distinctly durable bonds that bind a parent to a child. The short-term perspective of marriage does not extend to the emotional commitment of a parent to a child. The difference in attitude to a partner and to a child was widely commented on in a series of articles on the attitude of female youth icons towards their partners and children. One commentator contrasted the pragmatic orientation of media personality Zoë Ball towards her marriage, with the sense of permanence she expressed towards a future child. She remarked that both she and her husband 'were quite realistic' about marriage. She added that 'things aren't always going to be for ever, but he really is a lovely man and he will be lovely to my kids, no matter what happens between us'.[19] Zoë Ball's realism and expectation that things don't last for ever suggest low expectations about relations of intimacy, and that it is not the commitment between two adults that is permanent, but of adults to their children. Marriage partners and lovers can come and go, but what must remain is commitment to the offspring of the relationship.

This reorientation from a commitment to a permanent adult relationship to commitment to the child is invariably accompanied by a rise in the emotional capital invested in the child. This development has been well expressed by the German sociologist Ulrich Beck:

Partners come and go, but the child stays. Everything one vainly hoped to find in the relationship with one's partner is sought in or directed to a child . . .

The child becomes the final alternative to loneliness, a bastion against the vanishing chances of loving and being loved.[20]

Of course most people have not abandoned the hope of finding fulfilling intimate relationships. But the desire for long-term commitments coexists with a heightened wariness of intimate relationships. Children offer a sense of permanence, which in the circumstances that confront them appears to elude adults attempting to forge secure attachments.

Present-day perceptions of childhood are primarily shaped by the changing world of adults. Parents, like non-parent adults, are subject to influences that weaken the sense of belonging and the ability to sustain long-term commitment. These wider concerns about the way that adults relate to one another help shape parental behaviour. In an uncertain adult universe there is a formidable incentive to expand emotional investment in children. Excessive affection and concern for children results from an outlook that regards them as one of the few permanent facts in people's lives. Mothers and fathers can lose their jobs and the status that is attached to them. Divorce and separation have become so common that many men and women are conscious of the prospect of future disappointment. Lovers, husbands and wives come and go. But whatever happens with adult relations, a person's daughter or son will always be their child. Children thus provide a sense of permanence in an otherwise fluid world. That is why mothers and fathers have such a formidable incentive to invest so much of their emotion in them.

Uncertain attachments

One of the consequences of the uncertainty of attachments in the place of work, in the community and the family is to elevate the role of parent identity. In many cases, emotional investment in children becomes so encompassing that parents' social and moral identities become inseparable from their parenting identities. Ideas about parenting and child development reflect the adult quest for secure attachment. Jerome Kagan has drawn attention to the way in which current concern with an infant's attachment to its parent is linked to anxieties about people's connectedness to their community. 'The sacredness of the mother–infant bond and therefore the psychological significance of the attachment of a baby to its mother are amongst the sturdiest of our dwindling set of unsullied ethical beliefs', writes Kagan.[21] In a world of transient encounters, the promise of permanent attachment through bonding endows the mother–infant relationship with deep meaning.

Parenting strategies that are based on an all-consuming emotional focus on one's child are paradoxically often indifferent to children in general. There is little that is altruistic about adults' emotional investment in children. Parental identity is focused on a particular child or children. Adults, who greatly value their own child and who lavish attention on them, can also feel little responsibility for other people's children. There is an important divergence between the private and public value of children. As Viviana Zelizer noted, the sentimentalization of childhood often stops at the family's doorstep.[22] The deep emotion that parents direct towards their own child in the privacy of their home stands in sharp contrast to the lack of responsibility that they, as mothers and fathers, feel towards other people's children. Other children make a noise in restaurants, howl and yell in supermarkets, compete for scarce places in the schools of our choice or bully our own sons and daughters.

The reluctance to take responsibility for children in general represents an important statement about the quality of parental altruism. Emotional investment is often inseparable from the motive of validating the self through one's own children. Cultural pressure to love on demand reaffirms this orientation and makes it difficult for adults to distinguish their own private preoccupation from the wider issues concerning children. It would be wrong to imply that parents have become peculiarly selfish or self-absorbed. The emptying out of adult identities, reinforced by current notions of parent determinism, has fostered a climate in which for many the search for the self has become bound up with their relation to children. With so much at stake in this relationship, adults are sometimes prepared to alter their conduct to fall in line with conventional norms regarding parenting identity.

I could not live with myself if . . .

Many parents know that their concern for their children borders on the obsessive. But they believe they need to be this way for their children's sake. Almost every parent that I talked to about their views on child-rearing referred to the external dangers facing their children. 'There never used to be so many drug dealers hassling young kids', said a 36-year-old father of two children aged 7 and 9. A mother of a 13-year-old, who does not allow her daughter to walk to school 700 yards down the road, complains that there have never been so many paedophiles on the streets of Britain as today. Larry lives in a peaceful leafy suburb – outwardly just the sort of place where parents ought to feel relaxed about letting children wander around. Yet neither his 11-year-old nor his 13-year-old son are allowed to go outside to play on their own. These reactions are regularly confirmed by surveys and opinion polls. A report by the Future Foundation noted that 'parents are increasingly reluctant to compromise their children's safety by leaving them unsupervised'.[23]

Although parental over-reaction to statistically insignificant risks is widely reported, its relationship to the way that adults perceive their roles as parents is seldom considered. And yet the inexorable rise of parental fears should be seen neither as simply an over-reaction nor as an irrational response to external developments. In conversations, most parents are prepared to concede the fact that the likelihood of their child being abducted is minimal. Most parents have a reasonably good grasp of the specific threats faced by their offspring and have no problem about discussing them in a rational and balanced manner. However, such good common sense does not prevent the very same parents from feeling burdened by a general sense of external danger, nor does it prevent parents from feeling extremely concerned when they hear a news report of a tragic incident involving a child. It is not so much the case that parents over-react all of the time but rather that they have a disposition to do so in a variety of circumstances.

Parental paranoia is in part symptomatic of the concerns that carers have of their own sense of self as parents. Parental perceptions of the risks facing their children are grounded in a tension that many mothers and fathers experience between their identity as parents and a lack of confidence in their ability to live up to that identity. Many parents who derive considerable affirmation from their role of nurturing and protecting their children also feel that they have insufficient moral and psychological resources to effectively discharge these responsibilities. Sometimes the external world is perceived to be a threat precisely because it is external to the parent–child relationship. It is difficult to reconcile the comfortable feeling of certainty promised by this unique relationship with the sense of uncertainty that prevails in the external world. For some parents, the question is the threat not simply to one's child but also to this unique, taken-for-granted relationship.

From talking to parents about their fears, I have drawn the conclusion that the concept of 'children at risk' serves as a metaphor for conveying the diffuse insecurity that many adults possess regarding their identity as parents. When parents talk about their fears for their children, one phrase keeps recurring. This frequently repeated statement, 'I could not live with myself if something happened to my child', provides an important insight about the meaning of parental anxieties today. The phrase refers to the vulnerability not so much of children but of adults. The sentence, 'I could not live with myself if something happened to my child', is a statement about the adult consciousness of insecurity. With so much emotional investment in a child, it is difficult to take risks. Their fear of losing the defining relationship of their identity encourages a heightened sensitivity to the troubles of childhood. Sadly, being able to live with oneself – a key issue confronting adult identity – has become a burden on children's lives.

Seven

Confusions about Facing up to Adulthood

Parents not only confuse their problems with those of their children. Sometimes they are also unsure about where to draw the line that separates adulthood from childhood. When adults begin to perceive their self-identity through children, the parent–child relationship becomes confused. In contemporary society this confusion has been reinforced by cultural trends that dispute adult authority. Since the 1960s and the institutionalization of youth culture, many parents have felt uncomfortable with their roles as 'responsible adults'. Today, it is common for adults to cling on to a youthful identity, insist that they still have a lot more growing to do and shamelessly copy the fashion of the younger generation. For some time now, parents, teachers and other adults involved with children have gone out of their way to cross the generational 'authority' divide to be the 'friends' rather than 'mentors' of young people. This changing conception of adulthood – an unconscious process of 'infantilization' – both reflects and reinforces weakening adult authority. The blurring of the line between adulthood and childhood plays an important part in parental anxieties.

Uncertainties about adulthood are invariably linked to changing ideas about childhood. Adults who sometimes behave like children are likely to treat children as adults. Maturity is actively discounted as being 'past it' and having no special claim to wisdom. The corollary of this infantilization of adulthood has been the promotion of the concepts of children's rights and autonomy. Confusion about the status of adulthood weakens the ability of parents to act authoritatively with their children.

The depreciation of adulthood

In a world in which a parent's word is not the law, a sense of power-lessness and the fear of losing control haunt most parents. Mothers and fathers often react by doing whatever they can to make home life as attractive as possible for children. Since the 1930s, parenting experts have been in the forefront of encouraging parents to adopt a more open and playful relationship with their children. Historians of family life have remarked that the caring professions played a crucial role in convincing parents to abandon their old-fashioned authoritarian ways for more fun-loving interactions with their children. Childcare professionals warned parents to change their ways or risk losing the affection of their children. Lisa Jacobson's study of this modernization of the American home points out that 'child experts urged parents to adapt [the] language of salesmanship, persuasion, and enticement and to forsake harsh discipline for understanding companionship'. These new authorities stated that the ideal father should be a friend and 'enjoyable companion' rather than a 'policeman'. A new conception of middle-class motherhood and fatherhood emerged based on the belief that parental authority was most effectively exercised through play and friendship rather than obedience and discipline. The ideal parent was someone who was 'with it', learned his children's slang and adapted to their world. By the 1950s, what Martha Wolfenstein characterized as 'fun morality' became a dominant influence on American parenting styles. A decade later, it also emerged as the norm in Britain and parts of Western Europe.[1]

Playing and having fun is an important part of any lively parent–child relationship. It helps establish a multi-dimensional relationship between parent and child. An easygoing atmosphere makes for greater openness and flexibility in family life. There is potential difficulty with fun morality, however. Parents often have difficult choices to make. They need to insist on forms of behaviour that a child will experience as anything but fun. Sometimes fathers and mothers have to adopt a policing role and demand unquestioning obedience of their child. For many parents the shift from the role of a friend to that of a disciplining authority is a difficult one to make. Fathers who have become too friendly with their children frequently find it difficult to gain and exercise authority when they have to act with firmness and decisiveness. The difficulty of reconciling these apparently conflicting roles often means that parents find it difficult to take hard decisions.

Parents complain that their authority is continually weakened by outside pressures. They assert that it is difficult to insist on a high level of discipline from their children when the rest of the world encourages lax behaviour. Children can effectively tap into this uncertainty and manipulate it. Children are good at finding contradictions between their parents' instructions and the standards of behaviour promoted by other adults. They point to the examples of their peers and complain that the rest of their friends are not subjected to such unreasonable demands as, for example, having to be home by suppertime. Of course, parents who are aware of their own difficulty in negotiating compliance from their children find it easy to blame others for their failure. But whatever the situation, it is the case that mothers and fathers receive virtually no public support or encouragement in the exercise of parental authority. And yet without a degree of cultural support it is difficult for parents to hold the line. Contemporary culture, instead of affirming that holding the line serves children's best interests, transmits the signal that parental authority ought to be viewed with suspicion. For example, the exercise of discipline is often presented as harsh, authoritarian, inflexible and sometimes as a form of abuse.

Everywhere we look, parents appear in an unattractive light. Popular culture and the media continually portray parents as out-of-touch deadbeats who are totally insensitive to their children's needs. In contrast, children are represented as essentially smart, streetwise, resourceful. In particular, parents who try to discipline their children are treated as objects of derision. This depreciation of adulthood and the elevation of the child are strikingly conveyed through a television advertisement for the Cheltenham and Gloucester Building Society. The ad sharply counterposes the lithe figure of a child diving for pearls with the lumbering adult uncomfortably confined in a cumbersome diving suit, representing the alleged inflexibility of adulthood. The child gets the pearl and the audience get the message about the superior skills and attitudes of the child. Young Ricky Fitts is the cleverest person in the Oscar-winning film, *American Beauty*. The middle-aged

Lester Burnham looks to him as an inspiration for his new life model. The highly acclaimed *Sixth Sense* is emblematic of the theme of dumb parent and resourceful child. The little kid, Cole Sear, is the smartest person in this film. His mother doesn't believe that he sees dead people, but he does. The boy also appears to understand the behaviour of grown-ups better than the adults. The film *Parent Trap* sees the clever twin sisters of separated parents conspire to get them back again. They succeed and show up the adults who are, in striking contrast, hopeless in managing their emotional affairs. The television series, *The Simpsons*, provides the definitive portrayal of adult dysfunctionality. Lisa is the smartest individual in the family. All the rest are dumb – really dumb. Repellent images of parents are also conveyed in blockbuster films such as *Home Alone*, *House Arrest* and *Honey, I Shrunk the Kids*. More 'thoughtful' films, such as the award-winning movie *Shine*, present parents as obsessed child abusers.

Parents are really bad news. At least, that is the verdict of the popular media. Sylvia Ann Hewlett and Cornell West have condemned what they characterize as 'a poisonous popular culture' in the United States for continually denigrating parental authority. During the summer of 1997 they monitored daytime talk shows to see how the shows treated parents. The conclusion they came to was that parents tended to be portrayed as either 'irresponsible fools or in-your-face monsters'. Hewlett and West contended that talk shows had no monopoly in the promotion of negative stereotypes of mums and dads.[2]

This negative stereotyping of parents flows from a culture that regards maturity with mixed emotions, as something to be avoided. The crisis of adult identity and the special moral status accorded to children, discussed in the previous chapter, have encouraged a cultural process that can best be described as a flight from adulthood. Popular television programmes such as *Men Behaving Badly* portray immature adult men as an indisputable fact of life. Many of the leading comedy series – *Frasier*, *Friends*, *Ellen*, *Absolutely Fabulous* – present grown-up men and women living a life of extended adolescence.

Not surprisingly, some parents do not want their children simply to like them, but also want to be like them. Everyone knows a forty-something father who feels that he has a 'lot more living' to do. These grown-up men make a virtue of identifying with their sons and daughters and want to be treated as their equals. Of course, they insist that their children's mates call them by their first names. They possess a curiously up-to-date knowledge of the music scene and, when you visit them, they ostentatiously flaunt the latest 'indie' CD in your face. The advertising industry even has a special name – kidult – to describe the growing number of Peter Pan adults.

Andrew Calcutt's book, *Arrested Development*, offers a compelling account of the erosion of adulthood in popular culture. Calcutt claims that what was once the exclusive preserve of youth – 'youth culture' – is now popular culture, which commands the allegiance of the majority of the population under 60. This culture promotes a forever-young, Peter-Pan-like aspiration to stay immature. Such influences make it difficult for many adults to accept the fact of life that they have grown up. There is little kudos attached to being grown-up. The world of advertising is sensitive to this development and understands that there is not much to be gained from appealing to the experience of grown-up middle-aged men and women. One executive of a leading advertising agency is cited by Calcutt as stating that, 'If all advertising seems to be directed at the young it's because we've found the most effective way to appeal to everyone is to make commercials which embody attitudes associated with youth.'[3]

The depreciation of adulthood and the current obsession with youth has important implications for the exercise of parental authority. Ambiguities about adulthood undermine the exercise of the moral bases for parental authority. At its most extreme, adults who behave like children are unlikely to enjoy the authority essential for the management of their parenting function. Curiously enough, the idea of infant determinism, which we encountered earlier, has provided the intellectual underpinning for a diminished sense of adulthood. The proposition that the experience of early childhood directly determines future character traits and behaviour transforms the adult experience into the mere playing out of a script written decades previously. Adults damaged during childhood simply can't help it. Such a vision of a helpless adult is by no means confined to the margins of our culture. Therapeutic professionals often claim that childhood experience does not merely shape, but unequivocally determines, adult identity.

The corollary of the importance attached to the childhood

experience is a diminished version of adulthood which suggests that grown-up men and women often lack the resources to exercise control over their lives. That is why in contemporary therapeutic literature the line that divides children from adults is difficult to discern. The concept of the *adult child* is emblematic of this infantilized version of the self. The notion that adults are merely acting out a script set in motion during their childhood has encouraged people to look continually for clues about their lives in the past. Accordingly, the key to understanding the adult self lies somewhere in childhood or beyond. 'Primal therapy' and 'past life therapy' are oriented towards the extraction of existential meaning through the process of moral archaeology. Unusual and profound insights are associated with the recovery of memory and the recovered memory movement never fails to discover acts of deep significance, which are said to account for the adult's predicament. According to one version of the therapeutic ethos, self-identity is based less and less on what people do and know about themselves than on what they can no longer remember. Hence the privileged role assigned to therapy for uncovering the lost identity of the self. The importance attached to the character-forming role of childhood and even pre-childhood experience is based on a highly deterministic perspective of the human condition. It suggests that people's adult existence is predetermined by their childhood experience. The many experiences we have as adults pale into insignificance compared to the trials of life we experience as children. As in a Greek tragedy, we are doomed throughout our lives to realize a predestined existence. People are encouraged to see themselves as victims of their childhood, rather than as self-determining agents. This renunciation of self-determination coincides with a dramatic reconceptualization of the adult self. It is a weak or diminished self, which is explicitly dissociated from many of the historically idealized characteristics linked to adulthood: moral autonomy, maturity and responsibility.

The depreciation of adulthood coincides with the idealization of childhood and of childishness. What is contained in this orientation towards the idealization of childhood is the implicit renunciation of adult values. The significance attached to childhood not only demeans adulthood but also posits it as morally inferior. In a secular variant of the religious theme of humanity's fall from grace, innocent children are said to be ruined by 'toxic parents' in a 'toxic society'. Campaigners promoting the idea of 'stranger-danger' contribute to a climate where the stranger – that is almost every adult on this planet – is not worthy of a child's trust.

The weakening of the association between moral maturity and adulthood is by no means a fully consolidated and irreversible process. It would be wrong to suggest that all adults behave like children. To be sure, there is strong cultural pressure on grown-up people to cherish immaturity. But most grown-ups continue to do their best to act as mature adults despite the cultural pressures that question their role.

The depreciation of adulthood can be best understood as a manifestation of the crisis of adult identity, discussed in the previous chapter. Often, what is described as the 'search for identity' turns into a journey back to childhood. Most of the time this psychological retreat from maturity represents a temporary episode in the larger project of making sense of who we are. But at a time when uncertainties are framed through the cultural interrogation of adulthood, it is easy to become confused about the line that divides grown-ups from children.

The future of every community depends on the successful socialization of its children. Every society needs to work out a solution to the problem of transforming children into adults. Parenting is the principal medium for realizing this goal. When parents try to act as their child's equal, it is far from evident what they are socializing their charges into. Are they socializing them into adults, or into adults who would like to go back to being children, or into adults uncertain of their roles? Confusion about how to face up to the responsibilities of adulthood places an extra burden on the shoulders of parents. It contributes to the weakening of adult solidarity. In particular, it intensifies the tensions contained within the exercise of parental authority.

Eight

The Problem of Holding the Line

How do we get our children to behave themselves? Parents know that children cannot be properly socialized unless they learn to draw lines, respect certain rules and gradually acquire the habit of self-control. Unfortunately there is no obvious guide as to how to gain the compliance of a child.

Testing boundaries is part of a child's development. Young children live for the moment; they want instantaneous attention and find it hard to accept that they should not watch more television, or that they must go to bed at the prescribed time. Some aspects of a child's defiance of parental authority can be creative expressions of their developing personality. Others, however, are positively dangerous. For a parent, knowing when to hold the line and when to overlook bad behaviour is a difficult problem to negotiate. Although we all try to be consistent, in practice it is impossible always to get things right. Mothers and fathers sometimes over-react and sometimes, for the sake of an easy life, tolerate behaviour that could store up problems for the future. It is not surprising that discipline is at the top of the list of issues raised with child professionals and providers of parenting advice. A look back at parenting publications shows that the discipline issue has been their readers' chief concern for most of the past century.

In recent times, the question of discipline has been complicated by the fact that family life is no longer governed by unquestioned rules enforced by the head – usually the patriarch – of the family. Modern families tend to rely on reason and negotiation to sort out their affairs – or at least they try to. The 'democratization' of family life has been driven by a more enlightened appreciation of human behaviour. The contemporary family accords individuals more freedom and choice, and gives children more status and respect. The decline of an authoritarian style of parenting means that mothers and fathers have to adopt a more open, sensitive and responsive set of tactics for managing their children's behaviour. This has been a positive and welcome development.

The question of discipline is further complicated by the ambiguities that many grown-ups feel about their own identity. The high level of emotional capital invested in parenting means that, for some mothers and fathers, their very identity is experienced through their children. This makes the issue of discipline fraught with tension. Taking disciplinary action invites rejection, or even the withdrawal of a child's love. One of the recurring themes in the drama of parenting is the fear that firm discipline might drive children away from their parents. Parents are particularly concerned about how to exercise control over what their children get up to in the outside world. Just saying 'no' may mean losing a child to the wrong crowd. Parents who fear that disciplinary measures could turn their children against them will resort to bribery, selective amnesia or just simply giving in.

The uncertainties that adults experience about knowing when and how to draw a line have helped to consolidate parental paranoia. Mothers and fathers have always felt unsure about what to do when their child said 'no'. Today, some of them are not only unclear about how to control their children, but are often uncertain whether they should even try to do so.

Drawing the line

Where do we drawn the line between adulthood and childhood? The lack of clarity on this issue poses big problems. Not only is parental authority being deprecated these days, but the moral standing of children is being elevated at the same time; while adulthood is degraded, the childhood state is celebrated. Children are often cast in the role of 'little adults', deemed capable of making informed choices – even presented as equal decision makers within the family. A particularly absurd expression of this in Britain is the on-going discussion about whether children should be endowed with the right formally to divorce their parents. The assumption that children are capable of bearing the responsibilities that attend having 'adult rights' reflects the uncertainties surrounding the status of adulthood. It is a prime example of a failure of nerve when it comes to drawing lines between a child and an adult. Such confusions can only undermine the ability of parents to guide and discipline their children.

Children these days are represented as victims of a split personality syndrome. On the one hand they are depicted as vulnerable creatures, in need of constant supervision, while on the other they are often represented as competent persons, capable of making informed and responsible choices about their lives. Today, adults are advised to consult and negotiate rather than to act, or make decisions, on their children's behalf. These widespread sentiments are codified in the principle of Children's Rights. The proponents of these rights claim that children should participate in making the decisions that impact on their lives.

In reality, even the most radical supporters of Children's Rights are far from consistent in their advocacy of their cause and have to concede that children cannot exercise such rights. One leading British advocate of this cause, Bob Franklin, states that 'Children have been excluded from participation in formal decision making for so long, that it seems unlikely that they could enter this arena without the initial support and advocacy of adults.' Priscilla Alderson gets around the objection that children lack the resources to speak the language of rights by arguing that children have their own way of demanding that their voices be heard.[1]

There is a lot to be said for adults being sensitive to children's voices. Children make sense of the world in their own way and develop illuminating insights about their experience. But to equate a child's voice with the deliberations of an experienced and reasoning adult is to confuse the potential for mature reflection with the actuality of it. Such confusions stem from the current crisis of adulthood, and the parallel elevation of childhood, which together make the line that divides the two appear arbitrary and unclear. Some have given up on trying to hold the line. Many parents operate on the assumption that their children are their equals – 'my best friends' as one put it to me – and so should be treated as adults. Superficially, this response appears as child-centred and child-friendly. However, treating children the same as adults can have profoundly disorienting consequences. Children have the potential to become the equals of adults. But for this potential to be realized it is vital not to treat them as if they were already 30-year-olds. The very act of nurturing depends on being able to distinguish the potential to grow up from maturity itself.

As our understanding of childhood has developed, we have come to appreciate that children have their own unique feelings, aspirations, dreams and fantasies, and that they see the world differently from adults. Acknowledging the special way that children feel and understand has been the key to gaining important insights into the process of child development. We now know that children do not simply know less, but that they also know in a way that is different from adults. Of course the worlds of children and of adults overlap, and children develop through the interaction between the two. The moral and intellectual universes of a child are not the same as those of an adult, but nor are they simply different. It is difficult to get the balance right. Sometimes adults imagine children as their polar opposites. At other times they lose sight of what distinguishes them from their offspring.

When mature adults talk to each other, they do not simply issue orders or directives. Because they regard one another as equals, they expect to arrive at a decision through reasoned negotiation. Intelligent parents are also likely to seek to explain, reason and negotiate with their children. This makes sense because one wants to teach children what to consider in making decisions. Unfortunately, today's parenting culture seeks to turn this teaching device into an absolute principle of the child–parent relationship. This approach was vociferously promoted in the 1970s in Thomas Gordon's million-plus bestseller, *Parent Effectiveness Training*, which advised parents to stop punishing their kids and to start treating them 'much as we treat a friend or a spouse'. Since the 1970s, this outlook has been restated time and again. Penelope Leach is critical of parents who think their child impudent for refusing to obey them; she complains that they believe that they 'have the right to tell him what to do' but 'they don't want to concede him the same'.

The view that children should be treated 'the same' within the family informs the argument that they should have a say in all decisions affecting them. In a recent Demos pamphlet, *The Family in Question*,

Professor Stein Ringen proposed that children could be given a veto to stop their parents divorcing, or to prevent their mother having an abortion. Such ideas might seem bizarre to some of us. But once the tactic of negotiation becomes a principle governing family life, giving children a veto over their parents' actions is not a peculiarly maverick idea. Nor is there any logical reason why, once conceded, a child's right of veto over its mother and father should be restricted to abortion or divorce. Why should children not have the right to prevent their mother from going back to work? How about moving house or moving to a different part of the country? Who makes the final decisions about holiday destinations?[2]

There is a big difference between a sensible attitude of give and take, and giving children the right to override parental decisions. Negotiation is a valuable way to educate children about making choices and dealing with the consequences. When used effectively, it can help children to participate in making informal rules and to gain an appreciation of the limits on their actions. But this interaction should not be confused with the negotiation between two equal parties. Rather, it is a child-rearing tool, which is based on the understanding that an adult and a child are not equals. If children are genuinely treated as equal negotiating partners, knowing where to draw the line becomes a permanent source of anxiety.

The belief that parents should adopt the same standard of behaviour towards children as they do towards adults is also behind the controversy about smacking. Opponents of smacking argue that behaviour that is unacceptable among adults should not be used against children. They decry the fact that if a man hits another adult it is called assault but if he smacks his child it is called discipline. They believe that the defence of 'reasonable chastisement' legitimizes behaviour which would be 'illegal when directed at an adult'. These propositions have profound implications for the whole process of child-rearing. Their ultimate logic leads to the renunciation of any attempt to impose parental will on children.

But parents must do things to their children that they would not to do to another adult. From the moment of birth, mothers and fathers continually impose their will on their babies. Parents who would never dream of telling another adult it was time to go to bed have no problem demanding that their child should go to sleep on the dot at 7 p.m. Parents who check that their child's bottom is clean are unlikely to do the same to people their own age. Whenever they wash them, feed them or read to them in bed, mothers and fathers unthinkingly treat their children as children and not as adults. We may wish to negotiate over how these things are done, but only towards a non-negotiable end such as making sure that the child is clean.

In reality, the notion that parents should treat children like adults is wholly impracticable. This point is implicitly recognized even by the advocates of children's rights, who use the argument inconsistently. For instance, the fashionable idea of parental determinism, with its one-sided stress on the power of nurturing, is based on the premise of treating children very differently from adults. The two conflicting assumptions of parental determinism and the treatment of children as adults are rarely reflected on by professionals who uphold both arguments simultaneously. Some demand that parents should treat children as adults in one breath, while insisting in the next that they are vulnerable creatures who are permanently at risk. This confusion about negotiation expresses a deeper unease about the exercise of parental authority.

Some insist on the principle of negotiation because they want to limit parental authority, seeing the power that parents possess as potentially damaging to children. This sentiment informs the thinking of children's rights advocates. Bob Franklin writes that 'being a child continues to express more about power relationships than chronology'. While there is little doubt that parents have considerable power over their children, it is far from evident why this should be perceived as a problem. It only becomes a problem in practice if there is a fundamental conflict of interest between them. Unfortunately, that is increasingly the way that the relationship between parent and child is represented. Stein Ringen's proposal to grant children the right of veto over their parents' right to divorce is based on the premise that such a conflict of interest exists. He also believes that children's interests cannot be represented adequately by their parents in elections, and that therefore the voting age should be reduced to 16, while those who are younger than 16 should also have a vote administered by their mothers, presumably at the child's diktat.[3]

Most advocates of restraining parental authority through negotiation do not go as far as Ringen. However, they all embody an approach that believes that children have distinct interests, separate from and often contradictory to those of their parents. Parenting manuals continually contrast 'your needs' with 'your child's needs'. Parenting professionals often adopt the posture of umpire or mediator. They talk about getting 'both sides' to 'understand each other's needs'. The tone of parenting education literature resembles the language of marriage counselling, conveying the impression that the conflict of needs is of the same order as that between husband and wife. This conflictual model of the parent–child relationship can have damaging consequences for everyone concerned. Counterposing the interests of the adult to those of the child can weaken the very relationship through which nurturing thrives. If a relationship based on affection and sentiment becomes subject to narrow calculations of self-interest, it will have unpredictable consequences for parent and child alike.

The caring professions thrive on alleged conflicts of interests between members of a family. Such conflicts justify their existence and provide them with plenty of work. The conflict-oriented model of family life makes professionals indispensable to the resolution of parenting problems.

Assumptions about the conflict model of family life are rarely spelled out forcefully. In the end society requires adults to nurture and socialize the young. Too strong a representation of parents as self-serving selfish individuals would contradict the demand for mothers and fathers to behave as altruistic nurturers. That is why parenting is still so highly esteemed. But while responsible parenting is acclaimed by politician and childcare professional alike, support for parental authority is conspicuously absent. It appears that our culture wants devoted adults to parent on demand, but also to refrain from exercising their authority. One of the ironies of the present era is that, while politicians complain that parents don't control their children, powerful voices also decry the exercise of strong parental authority. We tend to believe that strict parental discipline is repressive and makes for a dysfunctional childhood. Even the term 'discipline' now carries connotations of an abuse of power. Predictably, most parents have internalized the confusion that surrounds the exercise of authority, and it is hardly surprising that they feel insecure about their ability to control their children. Sometimes they are uncertain whether it is even right to try to impose their will, and worry about the consequences of whatever course of action they adopt.

Discipline

Many parents report that the attempt to gain their child's compliance is a 24-hour-a-day struggle. Most of us find it difficult to simply say no. Parents spend an inordinate amount of time weighing up different options. 'Should I make an issue out of this now, or wait until we are alone?' 'Should I pretend not to notice that she has ignored me yet again – or come down on her firmly?' Child-carers agonize over every reprimand they issue and often go on to relive the experience. 'Should I have used different words?' 'Should I have waited until I was less angry?' Routine anxieties about everyday disciplinary issues are reinforced by more intense apprehensions about losing control altogether. A survey published in January 2000 by the *Times Educational Supplement* provided a fascinating insight into parental concerns about discipline. This poll of 1,000 parents in England and Wales indicated that parents were so preoccupied by the issue that a majority were even prepared to support the reintroduction of corporal punishment in schools. Two-thirds of the parents stated that discipline in schools had deteriorated over the past decade and 51 per cent thought that the reintroduction of corporal punishment was the answer to this problem.[4]

Anyone who mixes with other parents would not be surprised by the findings of the *TES* survey. Parents worry constantly about what happens to youngsters in school and in the outside world. Teachers are often criticized for being too weak or 'permissive'. On closer scrutiny, it often appears that worries about poor discipline in school are closely linked to a wider sense of a loss of parental authority. Sometimes parents end up blaming schools and teachers for the problems of discipline that they have failed to resolve at home.

Of course schools are not exempt from the effects of the erosion of adult authority. Indeed its most dramatic symptom is probably the problem of discipline in schools. Numerous surveys acknowledge that teachers find it difficult to control some of their students. A recent report indicated that four out of ten secondary school teachers had suffered physical or verbal abuse, nearly two-thirds of them at least once a year.[5]

It would be wrong to suggest that discipline is a unique problem of our times. Parents have always faced the challenge of dealing with their infant's defiance and with adolescent rebellion. This is an age-old issue that is inextricably bound up with the parent–child relationship. Today, however, this problem has become even more complicated and far more difficult to tackle because of changing cultural attitudes to adulthood, parental authority and the exercise of discipline. It seems to this author that the widely held expectation of treating children the same as adults makes the task of maintaining discipline a very difficult if not impossible task.

For all its hundreds of manuals and periodicals, the parenting industry avoids confronting this huge problem. Parenting manuals often provide a bag of tricks for anxious parents and hint that the compliance of a child can be gained through clever psychological manoeuvres. Some of the advice is sensible and may help a father who has tried everything and has still not managed to get his son to put his toys away. Unfortunately, there are no foolproof techniques for gaining compliance. Managing a child's behaviour requires drawing a line, insisting that children respect rules, and also enforcing them.

Parenting manuals counsel us to be firm, consistent and to draw boundaries for our child. Unfortunately, such good advice is linked to disciplinary techniques that deliberately evade the question of punishing negative behaviour. Disciplinary techniques based on reasoning, positive reinforcements and negotiation can play a useful role in managing a child's behaviour. But such techniques are unlikely to be effective in all circumstances, and other more power-assertive methods are sometimes required to discourage a child from negative behaviour.

In an ideal world parental authority could be discharged through the power of reason. In the real world matters are quite different. Any mother or father who is prepared to renounce entirely the use of all forms of punishment, also risks having to abandon the claim to parental authority. Parents recognize that they need a wide range of sanctions to carry out their role, which is why we continue – albeit reluctantly – to punish disobedient children. This intuitive response to circumstances now faces a challenge from anti-smacking campaigners.

The new wisdom that dominates the parenting industry is that discipline is actually a teaching tool through which children learn how to negotiate the world they face. Jan Parker and Jan Stimpson describe discipline as an 'investment'. From this standpoint discipline is about teaching children what they have done wrong, the consequences of their behaviour and how they can go about modifying it. Discipline as an enlightened teaching tool is favourably contrasted with punishment, which the authors portray as an inferior tactic that aims to 'shame, frighten or otherwise force children into compliance without them understanding why'. This redefinition of discipline contains the clear assumption that punishment is an inappropriate act for the enlightened parent. Some psychologists oppose all forms of punishment. The American psychologist Joan McCord takes this attitude, on the grounds that it means 'giving physical or mental to pain to others'. Opposition to punishment is predicated on the belief that it must damage children. The leading American child psychologist T. Berry Brazelton thinks that punishment can promote aggression and discourage children from co-operating with others.[6]

There are considerable problems with the redefinition of discipline to mean an act of enlightened teaching. It could be argued that everything that carers do with children contains an important element of teaching. But there is teaching and teaching. Teaching children about different shapes or colours or how to cross the street is not the same as disciplining them. Whether we like it or not, on occasions we as parents need to demand unqualified obedience, we have to assert control over a child's behaviour and punish the transgression of an important rule. We have to do this, not because discipline has an intrinsic educative value, but because the child needs to be stopped from doing what could harm herself and others.

As it happens, discipline can have an important educative value. A child learns that his actions have important consequences, and that certain forms of behaviour are so unacceptable that they invite serious sanctions. Diana Baumrind, one of the foremost American authorities on parenting, argues that the 'judicious and limited use of power-assertive methods, including punishment' helps children to internalize their parents' values.[7] Although the primary aim of punishment is not 'teaching' it can constitute an important learning experience for children. A disciplining strategy that is based entirely on reasoning is likely to be neither effective nor a particularly valuable teaching tool. A discussion over a troublesome episode may teach a child very little unless the small boy or girl understands that it has important consequences. When discipline is equated to teaching it becomes neither a teaching nor a disciplining experience for a child.

Effective parenting requires a judicious mix of disciplinary tactics that encourage positive behaviour, and power-assertive sanctions that punish negative ones. Effective discipline depends on parents praising good behaviour and punishing that which they deem unacceptable. Both of these tactics play an important role in encouraging good behaviour. But they are unlikely to be enough. Parents also need to explain the point of discipline, so that a child learns why he has been praised or punished. It is at this point that reasoning becomes particularly significant. The explanation of parental action helps to generalize from a specific act what is expected from the child in other similar circumstances. Effective discipline is part of a unitary system that links together reasoning, punishing, praising and communication. Punishing unwelcome behaviour is part of this system, not its polar opposite.

Child professionals who stigmatize punishment work on the assumption that parental discipline constitutes a danger to the child. Parenting guides continually warn mothers and fathers to reflect on why they want to punish their child. 'Ask the members of the group to think about what makes them snap', advises an NSPCC manual written for tutors of parenting classes. Tutors are advised to guide parents to think about their feelings so that they can learn to defuse their anger. Throughout the manual there is a clear sub-text that implies that the real issue is the behaviour of parents rather than children. The Health Education Authority's *Birth to Five* quite explicitly assumes that the real problem is how parents react to their child's difficulties, not the child's behaviour. After lecturing mums and dads about their behaviour, it offers an olive branch with the soothing words, 'If the problem is more yours than your child's don't blame yourself for that.' The HEA also warns that sometimes the response of the parent to a child's behaviour 'changes it from something that's irritating for you into a real problem for your child'.

It seems that every form of disciplinary tactic used by parents can be interpreted as a positive danger to children. One objective outlined in the NSPCC manual *Positive Ways of Managing Children's Behaviour* is 'to enable parents to establish authority without resorting to physical coercion, shaming or blaming'. So what can a parent do to establish authority? According to current wisdom not very much. What is offered is a pretence of authority, kept up through avoiding the question of punishment. The HEA approach sums up this evasive stance: 'Is it a problem that you feel you *must* do something about; or might it be better to just live with it for a while?'[8]

Those who want to sidestep the issue of punishment tend to play down the significance of a child's bad behaviour. Parents are consistently advised to analyse their child's behaviour and to understand what has caused it. Once these causes are understood, children's bad behaviour can be reinterpreted as 'difficult' or even as a 'normal' response to a particular experience. 'It's just a stage' is the stock answer offered by editorials in parenting publications. Such publications regularly rehearse the argument that children's defiance of parental authority is quite normal. They rightly claim that youngsters need to explore, to test the boundaries of what is acceptable and what is not acceptable and that they need to assert their independence. But instead of encouraging parents to work out an appropriate response to acts of defiance and to maintain the boundary of acceptable behaviour, parents are advised not to over-react. 'Children can be astonishingly unresponsive to requests from their parents, especially when deeply absorbed in pretend play', reports Professor Thomas G. Power of the University of Houston. Power's assurance that a child's naughty behaviour is quite normal encourages parents to evade the issue of how to curb normal but anti-social behaviour. When he states that defiance is often 'really nothing more than the difficulty a child experiences making the mental switch from one activity to another', Power offers an argument for avoiding the issue of discipline. The proposition that 'it is just a stage in a child's development' rather than an expression of negative behaviour is a call to inaction.[9]

Children's disobedient behaviour is not only rendered acceptable through the 'it's just a stage' argument but also by the tendency to treat misbehaviour as a medical condition. In recent years we have witnessed the discovery of a variety of 'hidden syndromes' which are reported to afflict children. Attention deficit hyperactivity disorder (ADHD) is only the most recent childhood syndrome to be highlighted in the media. ADHD is characterized by many of the traits that would, in the absence of a medical definition, be frowned upon as bad behaviour: inability to concentrate, lack of application, unruliness. For some parents, it seems, the discovery of new childhood disorders provides a welcome explanation for their children's bad behaviour or poor performance in school: 'She isn't naughty, she's ill.' There has been a phenomenal upsurge in the number of parents who demand that their children be labelled as suffering from ADHD or some other disorder. In some parts of the United States, 50–75 per cent of children newly referred to child neurologists and behavioural paediatricians are diagnosed as ADHD. It is claimed that 10–20 per cent of children of school age in the USA are affected by this disorder. In the UK, ADHD is estimated to affect 1.7 per cent of boys of primary school age. But given current trends in Britain, it is only a matter of time before this gap is substantially narrowed. It is evident that in the United States large numbers of parents and their children are using ADHD as an excuse for poor school performance. Failure to finish homework, inability to focus on class discussion, and boredom in school are regularly blamed on the ADHD affliction.

The readiness with which parents accept medical labels for their children's bad habits and behaviour suggests that few mothers and fathers need to be lectured about the pitfalls of harsh discipline. Most parents have for some time assimilated the 'fun morality' advocated by care workers in the middle of the last century. To a surprising degree, parents have also internalized the stricture to negotiate and to use reason instead of punishment. We all want to rear our children in an atmosphere that is free of intimidation. But parents are far from certain about what to do when the child refuses to obey reasonable demands. 'Hold the line' is the sensible answer offered by most child-care manuals. Unfortunately, it is difficult to hold the line without the assertion of parental authority. And parents are rarely encouraged to be tough. Parents are told to control their children but are warned not to rely on punishment. No wonder many parents feel not in, but out of control.

The smacking debate – evading the issue

The rights and wrongs of the physical punishment of children is the most controversial subject in the field of parenting. The debate about smacking excites formidable passions on both sides of the Atlantic. Its opponents portray it as a form of child abuse that is likely to stimulate long-term violent behaviour. Among child professionals, the campaign against smacking has assumed the character of a moral crusade. They have organized lobby groups to push for a ban on parents smacking a child. This campaign has proved remarkably effective in influencing the opinion makers and politicians. In general, the media reflects the sentiments of the anti-smacking crusade and frames its stories according to a script that defines a smack as a form of outdated and brutal behaviour.

There are very few robust defenders of smacking. Most of its proponents strike a defensive chord and fear being castigated as brutal apologists for child abuse. The only obstacle that stands in the way of the anti-smacking crusade is the behaviour of the great majority of parents. Surveys carried out on both sides of the Atlantic indicate that a significant majority of parents continue to use physical punishment to regulate their children's behaviour. Campaigners against smacking recognize that their main job is to alter the behaviour of parents. An editorial in the *British Medical Journal* has called for a 'public education campaign' to teach parents not to smack.[10] Campaigning groups like the NSPCC also use parenting education programmes as a vehicle for changing attitudes on smacking.

On closer examination it becomes clear that the campaign against the physical punishment of children is not simply about the appropriateness of smacking. Some leading opponents of smacking are actually against all forms of punishment. They believe that parents who rely on the withdrawal of affection as an alternative to smacking may cause even more damage to a child. They claim that punishments which are designed to make children feel stupid or undignified are just as ineffective and emotionally dangerous as the physical kind. 'Withdrawal of affection is often used as an alternative to smacking, but in the opinion of many psychologists, this can be more damaging than corporal punishment', comments Frances Hamcock in *Nursery World*.[11] Such concern about emotional punishment suggests that all power-assertive methods are liable to be criticized for the damage they inflict on children. However, since it is not realistic to campaign against the rights of parents to punish as such, smacking provides the crusaders with an emotive target. Anti-smacking campaigners are often motivated by a deep-seated animosity to all forms of tough parenting. Their opposition to the physical punishment of children is linked to a wider hostility to what they perceive as authoritarian parenting styles.

The implicit objective of the campaign against smacking is to restrain the exercise of parental authority. As noted previously, this project is inspired by the conviction that parent and child have contradictory interests. Penelope Leach eloquently represents this standpoint when she advises her readers to stop thinking about a child's behaviour in terms of 'obedience' and 'disobedience'. Leach thinks that what parents interpret as an act of disobedience is actually a manifestation of a child's separate and distinct interest. If a child refuses to go to bed, 'it is not his disobedience that is causing trouble, it is a simple conflict of interest'.[12] From this perspective, the way forward is always to negotiate a compromise and never to punish.

The debate on smacking is actually a product of our confusion about what it means to be an adult and a parent. It raises questions about the boundary that separates childhood from adulthood and the legitimacy of parental authority. Unfortunately, the debate evades these wider questions and unhelpfully places the spotlight on a single disciplinary technique. This has led to a simplistic debate that has polarized opinion between those who condemn and those who support smacking. In such a debate, there is always a temptation to adopt one-sided and misleading arguments on both sides. In America, Gary and Anne Marie Ezzo have published several books which recommend spanking for toddlers as young as 18 months for being naughty. They believe that physical punishment has inherent virtues for raising children. Opponents of smacking, who represent the mainstream of the parenting profession, take a diametrically opposite stance and condemn this practice as a form of abuse that is likely to have long-term damaging consequences for the child.[13] Such sharply polarized opinions have helped create an atmosphere in which hysteria and moral outrage make it difficult for parents to work out their own rules for disciplining their children.

So what do we actually know about the consequences of smacking children? Opponents of smacking claim that scientific research conclusively demonstrates that smacking has long-term negative effects on the behaviour of children. They continually appeal to the authority of research to justify their indictment of what they characterize as 'violence to children'. One of the most robust claims is to be found in a recent publication by Penelope Leach, *The Physical Punishment of Children: Some Input from Recent Research*. Leach writes that 'respected research tells us that the more children are hit, the more aggressive, disruptive and anti-social they are'. She claims that research provides evidence that smacking can even lead to criminal behaviour in adolescence and adulthood. To support her argument, Leach repeatedly refers to research carried out by Murray Strauss, a veteran American campaigner against corporal punishment. Yet Strauss's own work is far less robust than the claims made by Leach on its behalf. Strauss concedes that the case against smacking is 'not truly conclusive' and raises the question of 'whether advising parents to spank is ethical and responsible'. Strauss believes that it is not – not on the grounds of scientific research but on moral ones.[14]

There are good arguments for opposing the smacking of children but they are not to be found in the realm of scientific research. Despite dozens of studies on this subject, nobody has established a causal relationship between smacking and negative behaviour. A recent anti-smacking editorial in the *British Medical Journal* concedes that there is a lack of evidence supporting its position. Nevertheless, the *BMJ* insists it is possible to 'apply good judgement' to this issue. Once again, the rejection of smacking is based on a moral judgement rather than scientific fact.

American opponents of smacking are often disarmingly open about the need to mount research that will prove their point and convince parents to abandon this practice. At a 1996 meeting of the American

Academy of Pediatrics, Irwin Hyman proposed a campaign of what he called advocacy research, using bits of research as propaganda to change public policy. His colleague, Leonard Eron, urged the audience to have the courage of their conviction regardless of the state of current research. 'How much evidence must we have and how incontrovertible must this evidence be before we can act?' he pleaded. Other doctors attending this conference managed to retain a measure of objectivity. After hearing the evidence or the lack of it, this meeting of doctors and psychologists refused to condemn smacking.[15]

No study has managed to prove the thesis that smacking leads to child abuse or long-term violent behaviour. The experience of Sweden, often used as a test case by anti-smacking campaigners, has not provided them with any new ammunition. After Sweden outlawed smacking by parents in 1979, reports of serious child abuse actually increased by 400 per cent over ten years. The Swedish experience does not prove that banning smacking leads to an increase of abuse, but it clearly suggests that it does not have the effect of lowering the rate.[16]

There is also some evidence that suggests that in certain situations smacking can be an effective disciplinary tool. In 1996, the psychologist Robert Larzelere published a major review of the existing state of research on the subject. Focusing on the 35 most rigorous empirical studies, he concluded that there was no convincing evidence that non-abusive smacking, typically used by parents, damaged children. Larzelere's review also came to the conclusion that no other disciplinary technique – including time-out and withdrawal of privileges – was more effective than smacking for gaining the compliance of children under 13. Larzelere's review is confirmed by the work of the psychologist Diana Baumrind of the University of California at Berkeley. Baumrind, the innovator of the concept of authoritative parenting, believes that the smacking debate wrongly polarizes punishment and reasoning. She claims that authoritative parents are warm, firm and responsive, and that in this context the occasional smack will have no long-term damaging effect.[17]

Baumrind's approach offers a useful antidote to the narrow clash of opinions on smacking. The main merit of her work is that she continually underlines the *context* within which disciplining takes place. Her argument is that disciplinary methods are mediated by children's perception of their legitimacy. In the context of a warm and responsive relationship, children can understand the imposition of authority, even the odd smack. Any form of punishment can have unexpected negative consequences. But such an outcome has less to do with the form of punishment than with the nature of the particular parent–child relationship. The outcome of an act of discipline is closely bound up with how a child experiences that relationship. That is why the mother or father is in the best position to work out what form of punishment is appropriate for their child.

Unfortunately, in the zealous climate that surrounds this issue, the sensible approach outlined by Baumrind tends to get overlooked. The terms in which the debate is framed militate against the possibility of a reasoned exchange of views. Campaigners define smacking as violence against children. They then contend that violence can only lead to more violence and that therefore it should be stopped. The argument that violence breeds more violence is a powerful one. After all, who can stand up and extol the virtues of violence? However, the equation of smacking with violence is a verbal trick designed to associate this form of punishment with the act of abuse. Parents who occasionally smack their children are not behaving violently. Violence represents the projection of physical force designed to injure or abuse. Caring parents who administer a smack in response to a child's act of wilful defiance, with the objective of discouraging unacceptable behaviour, are not behaving violently.

The inability to distinguish violence from the caring discipline exercised by loving parents says more about the outlook of anti-smacking campaigners than about real-life mothers and fathers. It is an outlook that assumes that parental abuse is the norm rather than a rare exception. Such a harsh view of parental behaviour also extends to a suspicion of other forms of punishment. But it makes better PR to confine hostility to punishment to the easy and highly charged target of smacking. Smacking serves as a symbol for a campaign that believes that the exercise of parental authority is potentially damaging to children.

An invitation to over-react

Whatever the outcome of the debate on smacking, its impact on the parent–child relationship will be unhelpful. At a time when parents are already apprehensive about exercising discipline, the debate is likely to undermine their confidence further by strengthening the association between punishment and abuse. It will enhance the pressure on the exercise of parental authority.

With all the publicity that surrounds the smacking debate, it is easy to overlook the real issues facing the vast majority of parents. For most parents the real question is not smacking, but one of discipline. Many parents are uncertain as to how to regulate their children's lives. They understand that their role is to guide their children's development but are far from clear about how to realize this objective. Parents are continually told what is wrong with different disciplinary methods, but they are at a loss to know what is right. We are urged to adopt techniques of positive parenting. But these turn out to be banal exhortations to be consistent and sensitive. The techniques promoted by advocates of positive parenting are based on the assumption that the effective alternative to punishing children is to reward children who do right. In theory this advice seems sensible. Praising children for their good behaviour is an important part of sensitive parenting, but it provides no help to parents who want to know what to do when their child behaves badly. Real children behave in a variety of different ways. Sometimes the model well-behaved child turns into a destructive little monster who needs to be contained for her own good. There is a time for rewarding and a time for punishing. The one-dimensional approach of the disciplinary strategy based on positive reinforcements leaves parents with no resources for coping with bad behaviour.

'Pick your battles.' 'It is only a stage.' 'It is your problem not your child's.' 'Your child's defiance is only a call for attention.' 'It is better to ignore bad behaviour than to reward it with attention.' 'Compromise.' 'Communicate your feelings.' Most advice these days provides a ready-made excuse for not holding the line and for avoiding the exercise of parental authority. Mothers and fathers, who in any case are worried about losing the affection of their children, are often happy to postpone taking hard decisions. There is very little public support for any other option.

Parents often lead a schizophrenic existence. They are worried about the effects of disciplining their children and also feel uneasy about losing control if they don't punish them. Lack of confidence about knowing when to hold the line encourages an unhelpful style of over-parenting. Parents who are reluctant to say 'no' have sought other means to control their children's lives that avoid conflicts. Many of the characteristic features of paranoid parenting – using surveillance technology to keep an eye on children, preventing kids from participating in outdoor unstructured activities, a reliance on constant adult supervision – represent a form of control that serves as an alternative to parental discipline. In this way the issue of discipline is displaced and re-posed as a question of safety. Parents who feel uncomfortable about refusing to give yet another piece of chocolate feel much more relaxed about imposing their will by preventing their son from playing in the park with his friends. Regulating children's lives on the grounds of safety is accepted without question as an act of good parenting. Over-reacting to the risks faced by children allows parents to maintain a semblance of control without exercising too much authority. Keeping children under constant adult-supervision creates the illusion of retaining control without having to confront the issue of discipline. These excessive restraints on the experience of childhood are the price that children pay for the problems that grown-ups have in coming to terms with their role as parents.

Nine

Unclear Rules – Prejudice Masquerading as Research

Practical ideas about child-rearing are inseparable from one's moral outlook. Today, the lack of consensus on the 'right' approach to parenting is reflected in the continual debates about the pros and cons of 'family values', marriage, cohabitation and single parenthood. Customs and traditions that could once be taken for granted seem to have lost their relevance in a world haunted by uncertainty and self-doubt. Many mothers and fathers think that what their own parents did has few lessons for child-rearing today. Changes in the status of women and gender relations have also broken some of the old habits associated with family life. The changing contours of family life create new complications for everyone concerned, adding to the already considerable burden borne by parents.

Everything about parenting seems open to question; nothing is certain, nothing can be taken for granted. As a result, almost any issue can turn into a controversy. Yet controversy is the last thing that we need when struggling with the day-to-day pressures of family life. Worse, precisely at a time when many parents lack confidence in themselves, they feel that they are under constant scrutiny. With so much public attention focused on 'parenting issues', parents feel forced to account for and justify their every action to teachers, health visitors, doctors and other professionals. Not surprisingly, parents who feel so exposed often find decision making onerous and feel less than confident about their ability to do what is right.

One way that parents try to resolve these ambiguities is by conforming to the demands of professional authorities. Unfortunately, the professional does not always know best, and often they turn out to be just as confused as parents. Their 'off-the-peg' advice does little to arm parents with the guidance they yearn for.

Starting from scratch

For the past two centuries ideas about child-rearing have been in a continual state of flux. New beliefs about nutrition, infant health and education, along with changing moral values about the family and the status of its members, have led to a rolling revolution in the way we think about parenting. Geographical and social mobility have also generated novel approaches to child-rearing. A significant number of new mothers and fathers live far away from their own family. Unlike the previous generation of parents, they are not subject to the unrelenting advice freely offered by relatives. Consequently, they are less likely to copy their own parents' approach to child-rearing. Some young parents welcome the absence of nosy relatives. But many others wish that they had access to a reliable source of sensible advice. In any case, mothers and fathers living away from their families are compelled to work out their own rules.

According to historians of the family, the expansion of the education and higher education systems has had an important influence on the way that young men and, in particular, young women, regard their future roles as parents. Young educated adults frequently believe that they know more about the world than do their own fathers and mothers. They often draw the conclusion that the old folks have 'old-fashioned' ideas, whereas they themselves understand the ways of the modern world. At a time of change, when many fields of knowledge are developing at a rapid rate, an intellectual and emotional distance opens up between the generations. This reaction to the old ways of doing things is inevitable and, as long as people are prepared to learn from the experience of the past, change will usually be for the better.

Reacting against the old ways of doing things does not have to mean dismissing 'family advice' about child-rearing. The notion that family advice was inherently flawed was the invention of a new group of experts that emerged at the start of the twentieth century. They claimed that parenting was a science that was too important to be left to ignorant mothers and fathers. Although parents had managed to bring up children for thousands of years without the help of scientific authorities, these professionals claimed that their science would provide a far more enlightened and effective approach to childcare. Writing in 1929, Susan Isaacs was delighted that 'mothers and nurses' had 'begun to turn away from mere custom and blind tradition to science'. She insisted that 'many practices that had been taken for granted for centuries have been found to be false guides when carefully tested'. Baby-rearing was now to be based on proven 'scientific knowledge about food and sleep and clothing, the effects of light and air, and ways of preventing disease'.[1]

By the 1950s, the practice of parenting advice was well established. The formidable influence of the childcare guru reflected an important shift in family culture. Since it was assumed that parenting practices would change alongside new discoveries about child-rearing, the advisory role of older family members diminished. 'American parents, for instance, do not expect to bring up their children in the way they were brought up, anymore than they would want to live in the house in which they were raised or to drive around in the family car of their childhood', observed Wolfenstein in the 1950s.[2] Similar attitudes were also evident in Britain.

However, the rejection of parental tradition 50 years ago was of a different quality from what we see today. In the 1950s, the reaction of young adults to the customs and child-rearing practices of their parents rarely touched on fundamental issues of values and moral principles. By and large they accepted the moral universe of their fathers and mothers but sought to do a better job of parenting than the previous generation. 'They hope to bring up their children better than they were brought up themselves', was how Martha Wolfenstein described the attitudes of young adults in the 1950s.[3] During this period of relative economic prosperity, there was also a sense of optimism about the future. The world had changed. New economic and educational opportunities meant that their lives would be very different from that of their parents, and that they in turn could do much more for their own children.

Today, attitudes are quite different. Martha Wolfenstein's generation of young adults wanted to bring up their children *better* than they were brought up themselves. Today, young adults are not so much encouraged to do it better than to do it *differently*. Traditional values have less of a significance today. Important changes to the structure of the family, to the position of women and to the institution of marriage indicate that such values have lost much of their authority.

Films, fiction, television documentaries and the rest of popular culture dwell on the so-called dark side of the family. Previous generations of parents are often depicted as emotionally illiterate people who either consciously or inadvertently damaged their children. It is increasingly rare to encounter public tributes to the wise parent. And there is a whole genre of confessional writing devoted to exposing the destructive practices of brutal parents. Negative stereotypes of traditional child-rearing practices are widespread in parenting magazines and influence the practice and thinking of professional experts. The advice is not so much to 'do it better' than your parents – in the sense of succeeding where they failed – but to 'do it differently' – in the sense of aspiring to different results.

Whenever any problem with child-rearing is under scrutiny, it is invariably treated as a hangover from the bad habits of previous generations. One of the standard arguments used by opponents of smacking is that parents hit their children because their parents hit them. 'Why do we smack at all?' asks a feature in *Parenting*. 'It makes sense to smack because we'd seen the generation before us do so, when smacking was considered acceptable.'[4] Child abuse is also routinely attributed to the copying of one's own parents. The argument is rarely extended to positive forms of behaviour. We don't ask 'Why do we love our children?' and invite the answer 'Because we have seen our parents smother us with love.' Positive acts of parenting are attributed to the effects of our enlightened society, while negative ones are blamed on our parents.

The premise that parenting practices from the past should be avoided like the plague permeates professional thinking. Parenting education programmes and publications encourage their target audience to turn away from the model provided by their incompetent mothers and fathers. A magazine titled *Get Ready*, part of the Birth Pack distributed by *Bounty* to pregnant women, never loses an opportunity to put a distance between the pregnant reader and her family or friends.

'Trusted friends and family are probably your first port of call when help and advice are needed, but times change and it's useful to work out your own ideas about being a parent and to have a fresh approach to raising each new generation', it notes. This exhortation for adopting a fresh approach – parenting from scratch – actually represents a call for ignoring the counsel of your friends in order to absorb the arguments contained in *Get Ready*.[5]

The appeal to 'work out your own ideas' is really a call to adopt a different approach from that of your parents. 'If you feel your own mum or dad didn't do such a great job bringing you up', warns *Get Ready*, 'you might feel worried about making the same mistakes.' This euphemistic reminder of parental incompetence is a prelude to more ominous hints. 'Having a baby can bring back strong memories of childhood', warns *Get Ready*, with the implication that such memories are likely to be negative ones. It concedes that for most people childhood memories are happy ones, before getting to the point: 'If they are not happy it's essential to get support and find a trusted, sympathetic listening ear.' In case you missed the point, you are advised to 'think about whether you now agree with everything in the way you were brought up'. Such advice inevitably leads to only one conclusion – 'No!' – since no one can possibly agree with everything that their parents did to them. After doing its best to distance the pregnant reader from her parents, *Get Ready* is happy to concede that they did not act entirely out of malevolent motives. 'Remember parenting styles have changed, and your parents probably did the best they could', it patronizingly notes before suggesting, 'If possible talk to them to see if any of this can be worked out.'

The crude approach adopted by *Get Ready* is rooted in the assumption that negative experiences with one's parents in the past account for one's own problems with rearing children in the present. Parenting education programmes push their clients to think critically about their parents' behaviour and to avoid the bad habits learned from their parents. This approach now also informs child-rearing manuals. 'Think back to the way you communicated with your own parents', counsels *Raising Happy Children*. Its authors ask: 'Did you feel that they listened to you and that you were able to express anything that worried, concerned or even interested you?'[6] These questions are followed up by seven similar questions that are rhetorically framed so as to invite a negative response. Emotionally distancing the reader from her parents appears to be the aim of a lot of child-rearing literature.

The indictment of yesteryear's parent is a powerful theme in current culture, and influences public discussion on child-rearing. Its practical consequences remain unclear. Most mothers and fathers continue to borrow and adapt insights and practices from their parents. But, more than ever before, they feel that the past is an unreliable guide to carrying out their responsibilities. It is almost as if they have to start from scratch. They have lots of questions and very few (and dubious) answers. Of course we talk to friends and peers and share views and experiences. Many also consult professionals and read a lot about child-rearing. Some of this information is useful and helps parents to make informed decisions. But professional opinion and advice is no substitute for the sort of guidance that is based on commonly accepted rules and values. As we argue below, instead of providing certainty, in the absence of consensus such advice may well become the source of further doubt and confusion.

Unclear rules – conflicting advice

Parenting and childcare advice is shaped by the moral and cultural values of the time. Parenting experts, agony aunts and others who inform the public often draw on the prevailing moral climate to work out practice advice. Anyone who cares to read the numerous editions of Dr Spock's *Baby and Child Care* will be struck by just how closely this authority reflected the shifting moral mood of the times. In the 1960s, Spock wrote in disapproving terms about mothers who went out to work. By the 1970s, when there was greater acceptance of maternal employment, Spock adopted a more positive attitude towards it. In 1991 Spock became a vegan. His next edition of his manual reflected this shift. 'We now know that there are harmful effects of a meaty diet', he observed, and stated that 'I no longer recommend dairy products after the age of two years.'[7]

Lack of consensus about rules and values governing family life means that advice offered to parents can be highly unstable. When my wife gave birth in 1995, I faced considerable pressure to be present during her labour. I was told that this was an essential experience that would bring me closer to my baby and to my partner. A few years later one of the world's leading childbirth gurus, Michel Odent, stated that men should be kept out of the delivery room since they impede women from getting on with the business of giving birth. The National Child-birth Trust, which had previously actively encouraged men to attend the birth of their children, indicated that 'there may be something' in what Odent argued.[8]

Childcare advice has always changed with the times. But today it changes faster than ever before. Sometimes, advice offered with the authority of science is called into question within a matter of months. For example, in May 1999 parents were informed that young children who sleep with the light on are much more likely to be shortsighted when they grow up. Parents were advised to get rid of night-lights in the nursery. This new source of worry for mothers and fathers was refuted by research published in March 2000, which claimed that it was perfectly all right to leave a nursery light on since it did not harm an infant's sight.[9] In October 1999, the British press publicized research which claimed that children were less likely to develop allergies, asthma and eczema if they were exposed to farmyard animals and plenty of muck. A few months later, after it was revealed that a child contracted the E. coli virus during a school trip to a farm, some safety advisers took it upon themselves to warn parents about the risks of contamin-ation facing children visiting farmyards.[10]

Advice that is offered at one time with great authority, a few years later is seen to be not only redundant but positively dangerous. Burning old parenting manuals is now one of the tasks of a responsible librarian. 'Parenting titles that do not discuss or even acknowledge contemporary conditions, current scientific information, and up-to-date additional readings have lost much of their value and should be weeded from working collections', warns an article in *Library Journal*. Kathryn Carpenter, the author of this article, stated that some advice in older texts – such as giving honey to infants or allowing babies to cry it out rather than attending immediately to their needs – might be 'harmful to life and well-being'.[11]

Lack of consensus about rules and values is reflected in the absence of a recognized authoritative voice on parenting. Today, there is no single dominant authority that has the stature and the influence of a Dr Spock. The influence of childcare gurus such as the American T. Berry Brazelton or Penelope Leach, is not comparable to that of Spock, a man whose name defined a generation. Parents today are much more likely to turn for advice to someone who reflects their particular values and lifestyles. Dr Hugh Jolly's *Book of Child Care* often suits middle-of-the-road traditional parents. Feminist mothers reacting to a male authority figure may find Dr Miriam Stoppard more to their liking. Everyone – the ambitious hothousing parent, the lone mother, the single father and the green parent – is able to find manuals that reflect their outlook.

Leading authorities continually change their minds, alter their advice and sometimes clash publicly. When Spock advised parents not to let their youngsters eat meat, and to avoid dairy products, T. Berry Brazelton told the *New York Times* that this was 'absolutely insane' since children needed the protein and calcium of milk and meat. Penelope Leach has called Gary and Anne-Marie Ezzo 'very dangerous people', whose harsh child-rearing techniques constitute a form of child abuse. The Ezzos in turn have blamed Leach for her 'immoral' influence on family life. Public arguments about toilet-training, childcare arrangements, early learning and quality time indicate that child-rearing advice is itself a source of controversy. Clashes between different childcare specialists sometimes involve little more than competition for status and authority. But often their contrasting opinions mirror competing moral standpoints on the issue of child-rearing.

Consider advice on the rights and wrongs of maternal employment. During the past century, opposition to working mothers has been fuelled by fears about its impact on family life. Some traditionalists regard maternal employment as the cause of family breakdown. From their standpoint, mothers who work undermine relations between husband and wife, and fail in their duty as mothers. This belief is based on the moral outlook that assumes that a woman's place is in the home, in her primary role as nurturer and housewife. Everyone is entitled to their opinions and to their moral vision of the world. Unfortunately, instead of openly acknowledging this moral outlook, opponents of maternal employment hide behind research and advice that claims it is wrong for mothers to go out to work.

Throughout most of the 1950s and 1960s, child-rearing professionals promoted the idea that children under 3 need the continuous presence of their mothers. Dr Spock led the way in declaring that maternal employment before the child had reached this age was likely to be harmful to his or her development. Fears were expressed that children exposed to nursery care would be emotionally deprived, and dangerously deprived of stimulation. Mothers were also warned that leaving others to care for their baby would weaken the parent–child relationship for ever. This approach, which Scarr and Dunn have dubbed 'psychology to keep mothers at home', dominated the parenting literature until the late 1970s, by which time the growth of female paid employment made it difficult to sustain such a one-sided condemnation of working mothers. As public opinion shifted in the 1970s, more liberal and feminist child-rearing experts began to offer their own advice, asserting that maternal employment had considerable benefits for family life. And even writers who had previously condemned the practice modified their criticisms. Spock acknowledged his earlier prejudices and wrote that 'both parents have an equal right to a career if they want one'. Kathryn Young's review of the received wisdom, published in the American *Parent* magazine, confirms this reorientation from hostility to acquiescence. By the late 1970s, its feature articles were advising readers that the quality of the mother–infant interaction plays an important but not exclusive role in the subsequent emotional health of the child.[12]

The pragmatic acceptance of maternal employment meant that traditional family morality could no longer be advocated in an undiluted form. Instead, opponents levelled a variety of fresh charges against maternal employment, appealing to the authority of research and science. They suggested that children who are cared for in nurseries end up with a lower IQ, or perform worse at school. They continue to insist that daycare is damaging to children. 'If your concern is the development of babies and toddlers into healthy, capable, well adjusted, and productive adults, substitute child-care is not only inferior, but damaging to human potential' is the claim made by Allan Carlson, an American critic of what he calls the 'Trojan horse of day care'. Carlson believes that the culture of putting children into daycare can lead to the destruction of family life. But instead of boldly upholding his ideological standpoint, he hides behind child-rearing advice and research.[13]

Unfortunately supporters of maternal employment tend to imitate their opponents. Instead of arguing the case for women's right to pursue a career on equal terms with men, they often seek to justify their cause through the medium of child-rearing advice. They argue that quality childcare will benefit children. They cite studies which claim that in the USA nursery children are five times less likely than non-nursery children to become delinquent. Some feminists attempt to divert attention from the absent mother by pointing the finger at the absent father. Many writers now insist that the quality of a father's parenting skills has a significant impact on a child's intellectual and emotional development. 'What and how often boys read is influenced by what their fathers read at home', claims one writer in *Parents*. The NSPCC publication *Baby's First Year* makes the startling assertion that, if their fathers are involved, babies smile more quickly and smile more, and, 'as they grow into children, they have fewer problems'. Advice promoting the father's involvement in childcare today is a mirror image of the approach that demanded continuous maternal attention 30 years ago. Parent-blaming has shifted its focus from maternal to paternal deprivation. Delegates attending a Home Office seminar in November 1999 heard how boys who had no contact with their fathers were more likely to become violent, get hurt and do less well in school. Proponents of the dad-bonding thesis could not identify a causal link between absent fathers and damaged children. But lack of evidence did not prevent them from confidently asserting this thesis.[14] Mothers are still expected to be the prime carers, but fathers have also been pulled into the frame.

There is nothing wrong with open and intelligent debate about the moral issues pertaining to family life or the role of fathers and mothers. But when moral statements are recycled through the medium of child-care advice they are likely to confuse matters. Worse still, the promotion of an unacknowledged ideological agenda complicates matters, transforming a practical parenting issue into a source of anxiety. Take the current discussion on breast-feeding. Breast-feeding involves a lot of practical issues, especially for working mothers. But the transformation of breast-feeding into a moral crusade makes it almost impossible to make an informed choice about whether to breast- or bottle-feed.

Throughout most of the twentieth century, breast-feeding was promoted on the ground that it was essential for maternal bonding and for the emotional well-being of the child. The growth of maternal employment led to the modification of this position. By the 1970s, a new consensus was forged which conceded that either method of feeding would work; however, expert preference was still for the breast because of its alleged emotional benefits for the child. Since the 1970s many mothers have opted for bottle-feeding, though sometimes feeling guilty that they may be acting 'unnaturally'.[15]

In recent times cultural concern about the environment, food safety and anything that appears unnatural has boosted the appeal of breast-feeding. Parenting experts also regard breast-feeding as an important experience for bringing mothers closer to their children. There are good health arguments for opting for breast-feeding, at least during the first three months of a child's life. Unfortunately, the health benefits associated with breast-feeding have become so politicized, that it has become difficult to discuss as merely a practical feeding issue.

Whatever the merits of the arguments, the crusade promoting breast-feeding sometimes acquires an authoritarian tone. Childcare publications continually promote the same message. The article might be titled 'Breast or bottle?' – but instead of helping women to make an informed choice, the message is that bottle-feeding is an inferior option chosen by irresponsible mothers. 'Only you can decide how you want to feed your baby' states a journalist in *Baby Magazine* before pointing out that the 'benefits of breast milk are obvious'. The moral message conveyed is that opting for the bottle is an error with potentially damaging consequences for mother and child alike. Another 'Breast or bottle?' feature in *Mother and Baby* published in May 2000 turned into a celebration of the fact that most of the women it surveyed breast-fed their babies. It boasted that 'the great news is that 72 per cent of you breast feed'. Turning to the other 28 per cent, who bottle-feed, the article notes that not all is lost since most of these women 'did try to get to grips with breast feeding first'. Like smokers who tried to give up but failed, these unsuccessful breast-feeders are offered a measure of recognition.[16]

Women who have chosen to bottle-feed their babies face a barrage of propaganda. 'What's stopping you breastfeeding?' asks *Prima Baby* in disbelief. It complains that 'it's perfectly natural and will help protect your baby from many illnesses from asthma to diabetes, but despite that, most mums still don't breast feed'. *Prima Baby* also has a clear message for any woman tempted to abandon breast-feeding: 'keep going if you can – persevere and both you and your baby will benefit'. Advocates of breast-feeding continually discover new reasons to support their cause. They have seized upon a New Zealand study published in 1998 that suggests that children who have been breast-fed are more intelligent. Throughout the summer of 1999, *Prima Baby* linked having a 'brainy baby' to breast-feeding. 'Breast-feeding will help add even more points to your baby's IQ because breast milk contains more long chain fatty acids than standard formula milk', it revealed. And *Parents* stated that breast-feeding 'may help reduce the risk of childhood deafness in the first two years of life'. It has also been argued that breast-fed babies are less likely to be cot death victims, and that breast-feeding is the best remedy for teething as it provides maximum comfort for the baby. The positive advocacy of breast-feeding has been complemented by scare stories about formula milk. *Practical Parenting* and *Mother and Baby* have both warned mothers about the risks of scalding babies by using hot water. These stories typically exaggerate the risks involved in heating bottles. They suggest that this is a common occurrence even though the figure they cite is 23 burn cases over a three-year period – that is, fewer than eight cases per year.[17]

There are lots of health benefits for a baby who is breast-fed. But when a sensible practical matter like breast-feeding is transformed into a crusade, advice turns into a form of moral blackmail. In 1996, zealous advocates of this cause in Dundee used their influence to ban health visitors from teaching mothers how to make up bottle feeds in ante-natal classes, unless specifically requested to do so. An editorial in *Nursing Standard* argued that the clinical judgement of frontline professionals was being compromised by top-down edicts, and that women who had chosen to bottle-feed were being ostracized or made to feel ashamed of their choice. The editorial singled out the activities of the Baby-Friendly Initiative, an advocacy group campaigning to promote breast-feeding, for its insensitivity. Many health professionals justify their stance on the ground that teaching how to make up formula feeds in ante-natal classes 'sends out the wrong message'. It seems that professional campaigners, who think they know what's best, have taken it upon themselves to prevent mothers from making an informed choice about feeding their babies. In recent years this campaign has gradually turned into an informal policy pushed with vigour throughout the country. In April 2000, the campaign won official recognition when the Government announced plans to award new mothers an extra £10 a week if they breast-fed.[18]

The heavy-handed campaigning by the breast-feeding lobby is not only intrusive and intimidating, but is also a source of unnecessary worry for many women. Numerous mothers have complained that they find it difficult to gain access to quality information about bottle-feeding. Their attempt to find information on this subject is often met with a look of incomprehension, as if to suggest that surely a responsible mother like you would not be so selfish as to put her baby at risk by using formula milk. Many new mothers are placed in an impossible situation. Matters are made even worse for those mums who for one reason or another simply cannot breast-feed. For some women, breast-feeding is not an option and the frenzied climate of hostility against the bottle can only serve to make them feel guilty about not doing what's right for their new baby.

The transformation of a practical feeding matter into a huge public issue helps to make parents more anxious about nurturing babies. Since advice is predicated on the latest bit of research, it is by definition provisional and highly unstable. In a world where every experience seems to give rise to a risk, every health benefit can be potentially linked to some unexpected side-effect. Consequently, even mothers who breast-feed are periodically confronted with information that causes them serious worry. How is a mother to react when she hears claims that she may be inadvertently giving her baby toxic pollutants through her milk? Sir Kenneth Calman, then the Government's Chief Medical Officer, classified such risks as negligible in 1997. However, three years later a Dutch study reported that the breast milk of many European women contained levels of polychlorinated biphenyl high enough to damage a child's immune system. The authors of this study stated that the babies of these women were several times more likely to contract chicken-pox, ear infections and other illnesses. Supporters of breast-feeding immediately contested their findings; but in a climate where insignificant feeding risks are elevated into a major public health issue, a new focus for parental anxiety had been constructed.[19]

The instability of child-rearing advice encourages public conflicts of professional opinion. Such conflicts continually confront parents with new dilemmas. Take the issue of co-sleeping. Supporters of breast-feeding have traditionally supported the practice of parents sharing their bed with their baby since this form of feeding encourages co-sleeping. However, in recent years a group of researchers have claimed that there might be a link between bed-sharing and sudden infant death syndrome (SIDS). Parents are yet again forced to make a difficult choice. Matters are not helped by the tendency to confuse practical childcare problems with the moral concerns of different groups of advice givers. It is difficult to avoid the conclusion that such advice is often driven more by the agenda of the advice provider than the desire to tackle practical problems. The alleged link between sudden infant death syndrome and bed-sharing brings to the surface a potential tension between the objectives of three distinct groups of campaigners. Supporters of bed-sharing and of breast-feeding, and campaigners against cot death find themselves in potential conflict.

Whether a baby sleeps with the parent should be treated as a minor issue best left to the inclinations of those concerned. Sharing a bed or breast-feeding works for some but not for others. But instead of leaving it at that, bed-sharing threatens to turn into a highly charged discussion with the moral overtones that characterize the smacking controversy. Advocates of co-sleeping tend to preach rather than inform. Deborah Jackson's *Three in a Bed: The Benefits of Sleeping with Your Baby* makes many useful points regarding this subject. But instead of just sticking to the 'benefits', she often portrays parents who do not sleep with their children as morally inferior. She describes the practice of leaving a child alone and crying rather than picking her up and bringing her into the parents' room as a form of abuse. The practice of leaving a baby in his cradle in a separate room is represented as an 'obvious explanation for infant misery'. Jackson warns working parents that 'there could be a crisis looming' if they don't sleep with their children, since such separated infants could grow up 'more closely bonded to their minders than to their parents'.[20]

Childcare professionals who believe that allowing infants to sleep in a separate room is unnatural have argued that bed-sharing is essential for parent–child bonding. They have also supplemented this unproven claim with the argument that bed-sharing *prevents* cot death. In the early 1990s, the American anthropologist James McKenna carried out research which suggested that the practice of sleeping with babies could help prevent cot death. This argument convinced many childcare professionals to advocate bed-sharing. Mary Newburn, head of policy research at the National Childbirth Trust, states that the closer a baby is to adults, the safer he is because hearing the heartbeat and breathing of his parents will stimulate his own system. According to Newburn, this helps to avoid cot death in those cases where the child has simply forgotten to breathe. But in 1999, this case for bed-sharing was called into question by research carried out in Britain and the United States which alleged that this practice actually increased the risk of cot death. As a result the Federal Consumer Product Safety Commission warned that sleeping together posed a significant risk of accidental smothering or strangling to the infant. In Britain, the Foundation for the Study of Infant Deaths advises that a baby should always be returned to her cot if the parents have been drinking, taking drugs or if they are particularly tired or obese. Advice is now divided on this subject, and parents have been left to pick up the pieces.[21]

Since the debate on co-sleeping has been subjected to conflicting moral agendas, it is easy to overlook the fact that we simply do not know what, if any, risks are associated with either bed-sharing or sleeping separately. The alleged risks based on the authority of research are statistically insignificant, and in any case no one has been able to show any causal link between how a family sleeps and the incidence of cot death. As in the case of breast-feeding, the controversy is fuelled by ideology rather than practical considerations. Advice is often directly linked to what a childcare authority thinks about the wider moral issues to do with family life. Many opponents of bed-sharing, such as Spock and Brazelton, are concerned about the effect of parental nudity and of the possibility of the child witnessing its parents having sex. Others worry about the exacerbation of oedipal conflicts. Supporters of bed-sharing share a different moral outlook. They take the view that this practice is natural and essential for the emotional development of children.

Too often opinion, speculation and prejudice are presented as authoritative advice. Virtually every childcare issue – feeding, quality time, watching television, early education, discipline, etc. – is subject to conflicting advice. Professionals frequently change their minds. New fashions and fads come and go with ever-increasing frequency. Parents, who may not be aware of this whole process, are left in the difficult position of trying to decide how to interpret the latest claim about some newly discovered risk to their child's health. Advice is always presented to them as a matter of choice. Parenting manuals insist that it is up to parents to decide what is best for them, and that they are not in the business of providing recipes. The first words of Spock's book were 'Trust yourself'. Unfortunately, despite the non-prescriptive rhetoric, parents are not offered real choices. Parenting advice is highly prescriptive and with rare exceptions contains the implication that you had better do what has been suggested – or else.

With so much conflicting advice, parents are placed in a position where they are made to feel vulnerable and ignorant. Most of us are not aware that the moral uncertainties of our society, and the agendas of competing groups of professionals and campaigners fuel much of this supposedly unbiased information. So what are we to make of it all? It is worth asking the question, 'What do childcare gurus really know?' What do we actually know about the impact of parenting on children? For parents who are interested in the answer to this question there is both bad news and good news. The bad news, which will be outlined in the next section, is that most advice is based on speculation and common sense and not on science. In a nutshell: we actually know very little about the impact of parenting on children. The good news, the *really* good news, is that parents are likely to know as much about their children as anyone else. And since childcare advisers know so little about so many of their claims, we might as well ignore them and act on our instincts. Parents usually know better than anyone else what is the best way of bringing up their children.

Prejudice masquerading as research

Parenting advice is usually presented as resulting from the latest scientific studies. Backed by the authority of science, experts such as Dr Spock or Dr Penelope Leach exercise a formidable influence over the way parents behave with their children. Their views are not only treated as words of wisdom but as incontrovertible facts based on rigorous science. Many such writers try to formulate their advice conscientiously and do their best to communicate sound information after sifting carefully through the available knowledge. However, it is difficult to turn scientific knowledge into effective parenting advice. The problem is not just that our scientific knowledge is incomplete. Parenting is simply not reducible to a scientific endeavour. It involves a unique relationship that does not always readily fit into a general formula.

Child-rearing research and advice is also affected by prevailing moral and cultural attitudes. The expert is influenced by these attitudes and invariably selects and presents information in a manner that reflects them. Individual authorities are also the products of their own experience as children, adolescents, family members and fathers and mothers. These personal details invariably shape their outlook and often influence the quality and orientation of their advice. Most of the time parenting information is based on a combination of common sense, prejudice, and insights provided by research and interpreted through the prism of current moral values. Although many authorities are unaware of these influences on their pronouncements, their advice is frequently little more than prejudice masquerading as research.

Whereas today's childcare professional can be highly critical of the prejudiced nature of parenting advice in the past, they flatter themselves that their advice is sound and objective and beyond reproach. They do so even though such advice is continually contradicted by 'new discoveries'. The field of psychology is littered with parent pathologies announced as a major discovery, only to be discarded as nonsense a few years later. In the 1950s the schizophrenogenic and the refrigerator mother were blamed for producing autistic children. The 1960s was the decade of maternal deprivation, when working mothers were held responsible for causing irreparable emotional damage to their children. Today, these pathologies stand discredited – instead psychologists have invented new ones such as attachment disorder.

A close inspection of child-rearing literature shows that the advocates of particular parenting practices are continually shifting their argument from science to what they consider to be common sense. Take the discussion about the insights on child development gained from brain research. A leading feature in *Newsweek* enthused that this research confirmed what parents already knew. 'Cutting-edge science is confirming what wise parents have always known instinctively: young children need lots of time and attention from the significant adults in their lives.'[22] For the author of this report, the line between intuition and science is an arbitrary one. But if science simply tells us what we already intuit through common sense, what's the point of appealing to its authority other than to boost an argument? The experience of the past tells us that when science is used to provide legitimacy to speculation, there is always a possibility that we will find what we are looking for. Researchers sometimes admit that they are looking for research-based evidence to justify a cause. To return to the issue of co-sleeping. According to newspaper reports, a team at Durham University, led by anthropologist Dr Helen Ball, is embarking on a study to back up with scientific proof some of the positive claims made about co-sleeping. The team is hoping to discover the benefits of co-sleeping. It is highly likely that this team will stumble across the evidence they seek. When researchers set out to prove a case they already believe in, they usually succeed. But in such instances, the role of science is to provide a fig leaf to cover opinion.

Advocates of particular child-rearing techniques often display a disturbingly instrumental approach towards research and science. Many supporters of infant determinism welcomed research that claimed that listening to classical music had a powerful effect on the intellectual development of young children. 'We've always known that music is great for kids but now research shows that music should be an essential part of childhood', enthused Elizabeth Stilwell, the director of the Early Childhood Center at Cornell University. Music teachers were even more delighted by news of this discovery. An article in *Teaching Music* recognized the impact that the authority of scientific research was likely to have on parents; it noted that the 'long term effect on public opinion about music and education has been favourably altered to benefit all of us'. 'All of us' meaning music teachers. When the scientific claims made about the Mozart Effect were questioned by further research, its advocates changed their tune. According to them the benefits of listening to music were so obvious it did not matter that their claim was not supported by science. One wrote in *Time* magazine that maybe the case was not 'based on rigorous neuroscientific research' but it was 'pretty good advice nonetheless'. When it serves the cause, science is upheld as the last word on the subject – when it doesn't, then science is deemed an irrelevant distraction.[23]

Since science confers legitimacy on the views of professionals, advice continually appeals to its authority. It has become commonplace to use the formulation that 'research shows that . . .' The proposition that love boosts brainpower or that babies develop more quickly if they are systematically stimulated during their early years is often backed up by claims of evidence drawn from brain research. In actual fact, there is no evidence for these claims. Invariably, the advice offered on the basis of brain research is the same as that offered by proponents of infant determinism 20 or 30 years ago. The celebration of attachment and bonding is simply framed in scientific jargon about brain development.

Charlatans who know that they can cash in on science sometimes manipulate the hunger of parents for hard facts. But most often it is not dishonesty that drives professionals to misuse the authority of science. Rather it is a case of people failing to distinguish their opinion from what research actually shows. Surveys of parenting literature confirm that the information presented has little to do with the findings of serious research. Such studies have noted that there is often a lack of correspondence between scientific knowledge and the information that is conveyed to parents.[24] Cultural change and moral values influence the selection and communication of parenting advice. Research itself is often subject to similar influences. It is important for us to understand that media reports of research findings should not be seen as synonymous with scientific knowledge. Often parenting research is itself driven by an explicit agenda. And even when this process is not explicit, research has a habit of validating prevailing cultural practices.

There are good reasons why parenting and family research is so unreliable. Thirty years ago, Michael Anderson, editor of the widely cited textbook *Sociology of the Family*, said every sociologist 'knows at the outset too much about what he is supposed to be studying'.[25] In this respect experts are no different from ordinary mortals. Since most of us have had some experience of family life, we all have opinions on the subject. The difficulty of maintaining a degree of distance from our inquiry has plagued family research. Matters are made more complicated by the fact that prevailing cultural values influence what researchers define as the problem and the kinds of questions they ask. Take the effect of maternal employment on children. Research on this topic was initiated at a time when there was widespread moral disapproval of working mothers. There was a clear expectation that children would receive an inferior standard of parenting if they grew up in a family where mothers went out to work. Is it any surprise that many researchers who went out to explore this topic looked for nothing but problems? Their questions were framed in such a way so as to solicit information about symptoms of anxiety, dysfunctional behaviour and disruption to family life. The possibility that maternal employment might bring some benefits to family life was simply not entertained.

These days, when maternal employment has become a reality, research questions about its impact are no longer posed so one-sidedly. There are many researchers who believe that it may have some positive outcomes for family life, and frame their questions accordingly. However, they often fall into the same trap as the other side, and allow their value judgements to shape their research. In an important study, two New Zealand academics, John Horwood and David Fergusson, conclude that the question, 'Is maternal labour force participation harmful or beneficial?' may be a misleading question to pose. They believe that what is required is research into 'patterns of family life, child supervision and support that may lead maternal labour force participation to have harmful or beneficial effects'.[26]

All research is subject to judgements of value, but parenting research is an extreme case. Often this research rests on the unproven assumption that what parents do explains the development of the child. It is only recently that psychologists have begun to popularize the notion that children are quite capable of exerting an important influence on their own development. During the past 20 years, sociologists have also begun to question the idea that parents are the most powerful influence on their children. The lack of evidence of any significant direct connection between parenting and children's behaviour has led sociologists to look at other influences, in particular those of other children.[27] Sadly, parenting research has not seriously engaged with this insight and continues to be driven by the ideology of parent determinism.

Even with the best will, parenting research is fraught with considerable difficulty. How children develop is only in part determined by the behaviour of their parents. Children's lives are rooted in a complex network of social, cultural, environmental, economic and family relationships. Research findings are specific to particular communities, cultures and social arrangements. Conclusions drawn from work carried out in Slovenia are not necessarily valid or relevant to the experience of children in Wales. Even work carried out within one society may often provide little insight into the problem. It is, for example, difficult to ascertain the virtues of breast-feeding over the bottle since the children studied may not be directly comparable. Breast-feeding is more widely practised by middle-class than by working-class mothers and claims made about the benefits may well also be due to differences in socio-economic factors and other variables. With so many influences and variables to consider, it is impossible to isolate the parenting effect on development. As children grow older, the variety of influences that bear on them increases and becomes more complex. Friendship circles, the quality of education, the amenities provided by the community and, most important of all, a child's own role in making her life take on an increased significance.

Serious researchers are characteristically tentative about drawing hard and fast conclusions. Objective research requires that others replicate its findings.[28] The history of research into parenting is one of non-replicated results. Sometimes this is because of different approaches to data-gathering. But most often it is because parenting behaviour involves so many unpredictable and unexplainable influences that it can never be a subject of an exact science. That is why reputable researchers rarely draw a relation of causality between parenting and child behaviour. However, parenting experts and professionals seldom appear able to exercise such restraint, and give the impression that we know far more about the influence of mothering and fathering than is warranted by the information provided by research.

Most of what goes by the name of parenting research is best described as *advocacy research*. Advocacy research does not set out to discover what's not known; it seeks to convince and influence public opinion. Its starting point is a belief that something is 'a good thing' and its aim is to marshal arguments that illustrate this in order to persuade a doubting public. Campaigners against corporal punishment promote this type of research in order to encourage parents and politicians to outlaw smacking. Child protection charities publish surveys and reports in order to raise awareness about their concerns. When the NSPCC publishes a report that claims that a million children might be abused, it is using advocacy research to influence the public and to promote its profile. There is nothing inherently objectionable about advocacy. It has a long and honourable tradition of highlighting important social issues. However, it is important to remember that such a cause-driven enterprise is in the business of propaganda and not of communicating scientific truths. Parents need to know that most of the surveys that they read about the problems facing children are the products of people's opinions and not of science.

Moral confusion

As outlined above, parenting advice and research bears the stamp of moral and cultural values and concerns. These days matters are further complicated by the lack of consensus about moral norms and values. We live in an era of moral confusion – where the absence of consensus encourages competition between moral values. Debates about 'family values', lone parenting, the role of women and men, homosexuality and parental responsibility are embedded in competing moralities. In this situation, parenting advice becomes subject to the competition between different values and attitudes to personal life. In such a time of moral uncertainty, it is difficult to resist the temptation to opt for simplistic solutions. 'Improved parenting' seems such a simple answer to our lack of clarity about how to conduct our everyday affairs. Confusions about how to rear children are superficially resolved by the demand for more and better parenting. We may not be clear about how to rear our children and what rules and values we want to impart to them, but we can give them more attention. We may feel unsure about giving children an inspiring vision of a good world, but we can spend a lot of time supervising their activities so that they don't get into any trouble. Mothers and fathers, who live this life of confusion but who want to do what's best for their children, are prey to the pressure to devote more time and energy to child-rearing. Children do need a lot from their parents, but in most British homes the one thing they can do without is more supervision.

Paranoid parents are ordinary people who are forced to pay the price for society's failure to provide them with a relevant moral outlook to guide their lives. In the absence of such guidance, mothers and fathers seek to find some measure of control over their predicament by over-parenting. As the next chapter suggests, this approach empowers not mothers and fathers, but the parenting professional.

Ten

Professional Power and the Erosion of Parental Authority

From the Government downwards, everybody involved in the parenting debate reiterates the need to support parents and families. Parents do need support, but not the kind that is generally on offer. Parents need access to quality childcare, and we need child-friendly communities. Most important of all, as parents we need to know that the decisions we take about the future of our children will be supported and not undermined by the rest of society. Sadly, the term 'support' is often used as a euphemism for offering advice and training about how parents should behave. Parenting education is primarily oriented towards altering adult behaviour, and providing mothers and fathers with skills that they allegedly lack. The pity is, however, that projects that aim to transform incompetent adults into skilled parents have the unintended consequence of disempowering mothers and fathers and empowering the professionals.

The intervention of professionals in family life has done a lot to consolidate paranoid parenting. Although child professionals mean well, they continually put into question parental authority. Their very existence serves as a sharp reminder of the incompetence of parents. The caring professions claim to uphold the interests of children and of families, and this may well be their intention. The individuals involved are often motivated by a genuine desire to help. However, they are also members of a distinct profession with its own ideology, values and agenda. No matter how well-meaning, most professional groups promote their own interests, and the parenting and child protection industry is no exception. They have a vested interest in discovering new crises to solve and in inflating problems associated with parenting. Professional intervention often involves putting parents in their place as inept amateurs, which encourages the de-skilling of mothers and fathers. Occasionally it also involves blaming parents for the problems they face. At the very least, professionals demand a privileged status for themselves as experts and make parents dependent upon them.

Creating demand for 'support'

The past decade has seen a concerted campaign to convince the British public that mothers and fathers desperately need the support of parenting professionals. Parents reading shocking surveys of family life are often unaware that what they take to be disinterested studies are actually public relations campaigns designed to raise their awareness about the need for professional advice. It is important to underline the fact that some of the most widely publicized surveys on parenting are explicitly designed to create a demand for the parenting professional. Take the case of a report published by Barnardo's in May 1999. *Attitudes to Parenting* placed great stress on the difficulties faced by British parents and reported widespread demand for parenting education. It is not surprising that this report came to such conclusions, given the way that the survey was framed. Respondents were asked to agree or disagree with such uncontroversial statements as 'Parent support services may help support you in parenting' and 'I know a number of children whose parents would benefit from parent support services.' It is very difficult to imagine how anybody could disagree with that. Who does not know some parent who could use some 'support'? So the report's claim that 68 per cent of its respondents knew of some children whose parents could benefit from support is not exactly a revelation. The report makes clear that it is pleased by the positive demand for parenting support that it has discovered. It notes that 'encouragingly nearly three quarters of parents disagreed that parenting services are only for parents who don't know how to control their children'. It adds that 'even more encouragingly, the overwhelming majority (94 per cent) felt that sometimes it is helpful to talk to another person about problems and issues in parenting'.[1] Given the positive value which this survey attaches to the demand for such support it is surprising that the rate of support was not even higher – say around 99.9 per cent.

The approach reflected in *Attitudes to Parenting* is adopted by other campaigns. In 1997, a survey by the Family Forum concluded that more than two-thirds of children believed that young people should be taught how to parent. A survey carried out to promote the launching of the National Family and Parenting Institute in October 1999 found that half of those questioned wanted to see more teaching about parenting in school, and that 7 out of 10 agreed that support can make a difference if families have a problem. Again, the respondents were implicitly being invited to endorse the need for this new Government-sponsored institute.

It comes as little surprise that so many resources are devoted to creating a demand for the services of parenting professionals. Professionals frequently complain about the relatively small number of busy parents who are interested in their services. A survey of parenting programmes by Celia Smith found a mismatch between what professionals and parents think about the need for support services. Although some of the professionals she interviewed believed that there was the potential for expansion, this was 'not always demonstrated by parents queuing up to attend', and some advertised courses had to be cancelled.[2] Parenting education and associated projects are evidently not demand-led. That is why so much time and energy is devoted to the public promotion of the idea that parents need these services. If mothers and fathers had indeed been queuing up to join parenting classes there would be little need for these public relations campaigns.

Promoting the case for the parenting professional is not confined to Government and specialist agencies. One of the defining features of contemporary child-rearing literature is *the advice to seek more advice*. Parenting manuals no longer merely give advice – they often direct the reader to other sources of support. In effect, instead of offering a practical solution, manuals direct the reader to seek help and support from another professional. Readers who are looking for solutions are offered long lists of helplines and support networks. So if you need advice on what to do about your crying baby, the Health Education Authority manual tells you to 'ask your health visitor'. 'Some areas run a telephone help-line', it advises the anxious parent. Parenting literature always reassures us that 'there is help available' and that 'asking for help and support is a positive step'. Sometimes it seems that providers of child-rearing advice are more interested in convincing parents to seek professional support than in offering practical solutions.

In the past, child-rearing manuals sought to provide advice that could help parents cope with everyday challenges. Although the authors believed that there were limits to what parents could do, they assumed that with sound advice most problems could be solved. Advice providers today take a radically different approach. They not only assume that parents lack common sense and basic knowledge, but that they are unlikely to cope on their own. Informing parents that they cannot cope alone and that therefore they should seek support is a central theme of contemporary child-rearing literature.

One of the arguments used by professionals to create a demand for their services is that parents lack the skills and knowledge necessary for raising children. A major survey carried out by the Canadian Invest in Kids Foundation in April 1999 claimed that parents were woefully ignorant about the 'basic facts necessary for fostering healthy development'. According to Carol Crill-Russell, the vice-president of this organization, parental knowledge is 'a mile wide and an inch deep'.[3] British child professionals take strong exception to the idea that 'parenting is only caught but never taught'. Ed Straw, a trustee of the National Family and Parenting Institute, has published a pamphlet arguing the case for a national programme designed to improve parenting skills in Britain. Straw takes the view that 'our collective knowledge of relationships and parenting is as rudimentary as our medical knowledge was in the nineteenth century'. The main objective of his programme is to create a climate in which more people will want to learn about 'better parenting'.[4] The National Family and Parenting Institute has taken on board Straw's concern and accepts that one of its main tasks is to change public opinion and create a demand for professional services. Its first major publication, The Millennial Family, indicates that there is a 'marketing task' to be done 'to make advice and information on relationships and parenting as routine as antenatal preparation'. It also wants to persuade the media that people could be as interested in programmes about parenting as they are in gardening.[5]

The campaign to expand the demand for parenting services is driven by the conviction that the enlightened professional knows what's best for an ignorant public. Professionals often compare their crusade to previous campaigns against drink-driving or smoking. Tackling public ignorance is undertaken with a zeal that gives this crusade a dogmatic character. The fervour with which they pursue their objective might suggest that there is overwhelming evidence that parenting programmes make a positive difference. Pronouncements about the merits of such programmes are regularly made with a tone of authority that implies that they are of real benefit to mothers and fathers. What parents are never told is that there is no evidence that these programmes actually work.

Extravagant claims about the effectiveness of parent education programmes are not supported by robust evidence. These programmes are rarely evaluated and, when they are, there is little indication that they are effective. American studies indicate that parenting programmes have no significant developmental impact on children. A study in Texas found such programmes made little impact on the children of middle-class parents.[6] Celia Smith's review of British programmes also failed to find evidence that they are effective. Nevertheless, instead of conceding this point, she minimized the absence of evidence-based evaluation by blaming the difficulty of mounting research. So while Smith acknowledged that 'we still do not know enough about the effectiveness of parenting programmes', she felt that this ignorance need not be an obstacle to promoting such initiatives. Smith is too concerned with making a case for parenting projects to pause and reflect on her inability to prove that they work. Instead she insists that the absence of evidence does not mean that parenting programmes are ineffective, but 'rather that their effectiveness has been exceedingly difficult to demonstrate'. In other words she assumes that such programmes are effective – and that it is only a matter of time before the evidence will be found. In the meantime she draws attention to the 'wealth of anecdotal evidence and the practically universal praise from the parents who participate in this project'.[7]

The failure to demonstrate the efficacy of parenting programmes is a source of worry to some child professionals. Roger Smith, Social Policy Manager of the Children's Society, warns that 'parent education and support will only become a major and widely accepted plank of public policy when it has demonstrated much more explicitly its potential benefits'.[8] Maureen Freely has reported that, at a consultation exercise organized by the Family Policy Research Centre in February 1999, many professionals were themselves uncertain about which types of projects worked and which ones did not.[9] Yet, despite such misgivings, more and more energy is devoted towards the promotion of parenting projects. It is a matter of regret that the parenting industry is so zealous in its promotion of initiatives whose value remains unproven.

Given the inconclusive state of research about the impact of parenting on children, and the absence of evidence that parenting programmes work, it is worth asking from where the people involved in these projects derive their expertise. It is certainly not an expertise based on science and research, nor can it be rooted in practical experience. Most professional childcare experts do not advertise themselves as model parents who know every trick in the book. Parenting expertise is one of those mysterious arts that are seldom asked to account for themselves. Sadly, many mothers and fathers who lack confidence in their own resources are prepared to defer to those claiming expert authority. They don't ask the obvious question: 'Why should this person presume to know more than me about the needs of my child?' How long before someone cries out that the Emperor has no clothes?

Disempowering parents

Professionals insist that they are not in the business of judging parents and prescribing formulae. Their advice is often conveyed in non-directive and non-prescriptive language. 'There is no right way to bring up a child', parents are told before being reminded that unless they act according to the guidelines outlined, their child will suffer long-term consequences. Ever since Spock, parents have been told that it is OK to trust yourself. However, it is very difficult to trust your instincts when you are also reminded of the grave consequences that your mistakes can have for the development of your child. The ideas associated with infant determinism have a particularly detrimental effect on the confidence of mothers and fathers. Since so much of a child's future is supposed to be determined in the early years, parents cannot afford to make mistakes. Parents have no second chance to repair the damage, when mistakes made during the first three years of a child's life are said to have incalculable consequences for her long-term development.

The proliferation of advice on every detail of a child's life has the double effect of undermining the confidence of parents and of promoting the authority of the professional. It is hard to trust yourself if you have been advised that a decision you make may have profound consequences for your child. It is difficult to feel empowered when you are given contradictory advice. The main effect of the expansion of this advice culture is to reinforce the dependence of parents on sources of authority outside the family.

Parenting programmes are deliberately packaged to come across as non-authoritarian and sensitive to our needs. The buzzword is partnership – professionals and parents working together. Programme designers contend that they are in the business of involving parents and insist that their role is to facilitate rather than instruct. These claims overlook the fact that parenting programmes assume a relation of inequality, and are based on an agenda formulated in advance by professionals and professionals alone. Parent input is perfunctory and entirely decorative. The parenting profession also appears insensitive to its potential for undermining the confidence of parents, and this is particularly disturbing.

Back in the 1950s, the renowned British child psychiatrist Donald W. Winnicott warned about the danger of allowing professionals to come between a mother and her child. Winnicott feared that professional intrusion into parenting would make matters worse. In 1976, the Committee on Child Health Services reported that the 'growth in the number and variety of professions connected with child rearing, however necessary in our kind of society, has in some measure undermined the self-confidence of parents'. Even two committed advocates of parenting education, writing in 1984, could acknowledge that: 'A recurring theme in talking to groups of parents and reading research reports and accounts of group discussions is that the attitudes of many professionals are tending to undermine parents' self-confidence and their belief in their own parenting abilities.'[10]

In recent years, however, professionals have become far less concerned with the negative impact they may have on parental confidence. One reason is that the parenting industry has become less tolerant of the needs and sensibilities of its clients. Parenting professionals believe that their crusade is far too important for them to worry about the upset they might cause to the life of the odd mother or father. Having vastly inflated the complexity of the task of child-rearing, they also view their own role as indispensable and decisive. In the past professional intervention was focused on problem families where the parents were deemed to be unfit. This relatively modest role has given way to a far more ambitious project designed to 'support' all parents. Time and again, those in authority remind us that every mother and father needs the services of a parenting professional. At meetings and conferences, professionals state the case for universal parent education. From this perspective there are no normal, average parents capable of responsible child-rearing. A responsible parent today is someone who is prepared to solicit the indispensable advice and support offered by the professional.

The very concept of parent education is founded on the premise that mothers and fathers are unlikely to understand their own needs and those of their children, and therefore need to learn these skills from specialists. This teacher–pupil relationship can never be an equal partnership. The National Children's Bureau defines parent education and support as a 'range of educational and supportive measures which help parents and prospective parents to understand their own social, emotional, psychological and physical needs and those of their children and enhance the relationship between them'.[11] It is evidence that parenting education is not a scheme that is designed to provide useful tips and sound practical advice. It assumes a far more ambitious remit of changing the way that mothers and fathers think about themselves and their children. In no other area of life would adults be routinely told that they are not in the best position to decide what are their real needs. And in no other area of life would adults be prepared to put up with lectures from strangers who assume that they have the authority to instruct them about their intimate affairs.

What professionals really think of parents

It is important for mothers and fathers to realize that the parenting industry tends to regard us as either inept amateurs or a potential source of risk to our children. Sometimes they see parents as the problem, and assume that they themselves are the solution. Back in 1930, such professionals expressed these views openly. One British authority, Jean Ayling, was convinced that parents did not have a clue about bringing up children. 'Most of the children of my acquaintance are already badly damaged at an early age', she wrote. Her solution was to limit the role of parents since they have a 'strictly bounded domain of usefulness' and to assign the wider task of child socialization to the helping professions.[12] Ayling's patronizing assumptions about parental incompetence dominated professional thinking in the post-Second World War period. Winnicott alluded to this trend when he warned that 'normal parents' faced 'petty regulations, legal restrictions, and all manner of stupidities' from intrusive professionals. He believed that many professionals were 'by no means uniformly confident in the mother's ability to understand her child better than anyone else can'. And he cautioned that unfortunately 'doctors and nurses are often so impressed with the ignorance and stupidity of some of the parents that they fail to allow for the wisdom of others'.[13]

Today, the caring professions are even more suspicious of parental authority than in the days when Winnicott wrote about their patronizing attitudes. Professionals are so obsessed with exceptional cases of parental neglect and abuse, that they frequently behave as if these were the norm. They act on the premise that a parent is guilty unless he or she can prove that they are a fit and responsible carer. Professionals no longer accept the age-old belief that most adults will become caring and responsible parents. A parenting education manual published by the NSPCC explicitly states that child abuse is not a problem confined to the 'other' parent. It claims that 'almost any parent can get into difficulties if things go wrong'. The aim of the NSPCC-sponsored parenting education programme is to pre-empt abuse.[14] Such mistrust of people's capacity to rear children encourages the NSPCC to dream up schemes for vetting future parents. So the charity has suggested that prospective parents should consider taking an emotional 'health check'. Why? Because a young baby can drive any parent to distraction and they may snap and injure their infant.[15]

Childcare advisers believe that if you do not practise the parenting skills they prescribe, you may not be a fit parent. An emotional health check is one way of imposing quality control over future parents. Another, far more insidious proposal is to weed out the unfit by licensing parents – an idea put forward in Britain by Mukti Jain Campion in her book *Who's Fit to be a Parent?* Campion recommends that parenting should be analysed as if it was a job like being a teacher or social worker. She believes that this parenting-as-a-job framework would make it possible to control prospective parents and refuse mothers and fathers the option of, or continued involvement in, the parenting role. She argues that licensing parents would help protect children against incompetent or abusive parenting.[16]

In Britain, the idea of licensing parents may seem far-fetched. But in the United States, this idea has been taken more seriously. Jack Westman, a professor of psychiatry at the University of Wisconsin, is a vociferous advocate of licensing parents. His proposals have been widely debated by academics, parenting professionals and politicians.[17] Westman, like many professionals in his field, supports the regulation of parenting because he takes the view that children are often damaged by their mothers and fathers. Clearly, if problems were restricted to a small number of deviant adults, the proposal to vet or license all parents would make little sense. However, from the perspective of the caring professional, there is no such thing as a normal parent. This inability to distinguish between the vast majority of responsible and intelligent adults and a tiny minority of out-of-control abusive parents can benefit no one. The very idea that parents need to be vetted sends the message that mothers and fathers cannot be trusted. Such a message inevitably undermines their authority. There is considerable anecdotal evidence that many mothers and fathers have internalized the dim view of contemporary parenthood. This makes it difficult for them to trust other parents. Such parenting pathology sows mistrust and plays a critical role in the making of parental paranoia.

Cannot be taught

The professionalization of parenting has gained strong momentum. The groaning shelves of books and journals about the problems of child-rearing, and the explosion of initiatives designed to support mothers and fathers, suggest that parenting has become a growth industry. Lamentably, we rarely pause and ask the question 'Is this doing any good?' The reluctance to reflect on and to evaluate the role of this industry is all the more surprising since there is little evidence that all this effort has helped people to become better fathers or mothers. On the contrary, it is possible to conclude that the growth of this enterprise has coincided with the intensification of paranoid parenting. Although the professionalization of parenting is not the root cause of this phenomenon, there can be little doubt that it continually exacerbates problems and undermines the confidence of mothers and fathers.

There are several ways in which professional intervention makes parental paranoia worse. Professionals have helped to construct the idea that parents are likely to be incompetent. This belief in parental incompetence is regularly communicated to the public through sensational accounts about the failures of fathers and mothers. The very idea that parenting is a complicated skill has weakened child-carers' confidence and sense of self-sufficiency.

The majority of caring professionals genuinely do their best to support parents. They would claim that they are not in the business of blaming parents, but of reassuring us that we all need help and support. What they fail to realize is that this reassurance is anything but reassuring. Just because all parents are deemed potentially incompetent does not make any individual carer's job easier. On the contrary, the message that you cannot cope on your own makes it clear that society does not trust you to raise your children. Extremist proposals, such as the call to license parents, vividly confirm the lack of confidence that some professionals have in the childcaring potential of grown-up people. But even more moderate proposals that draw attention to a deficit in parenting skills transmit the same message.

Even with the best will in the world, professionals cannot help but undermine the status, confidence and authority of parents. Professional authority competes with the authority of the parent. No parent can be an equal partner with the childcare expert. The terms of any such unequal 'partnership' will be set by the party that possesses the professional expertise. Of course we often have to deal with experts, such as teachers, doctors and car mechanics, who know more than we do. Indeed that is why we go to these specialists, to solve a problem that is beyond us. A parent taking a child to the doctor to treat an allergy has no effect on the parent's self-confidence. He expects the doctor to know more about allergic reactions. Matters are different when it comes to the relationship between a mother and a parenting professional. This involves a direct conflict of authority, about who knows what's in the best interest of her child. Let's look at this relationship more closely.

Effective child-rearing depends on authoritative parenting. The relationship between the child and the parent evolves from a physical one to an emotional and social one. A child's sense of existential security depends on the unconditional trust she develops in her parent. In her early years, the omniscient parent becomes the point of reference through which she makes sense of a bewildering world. What a parent says and does really matters to the infant. In turn, parents rely on their unquestioned authority to nurture and then to encourage independence in a child. That is why the prerequisite of effective parenting is confidence and self-belief in our role as child-rearers. Without this confidence, the exercise of parental authority is fraught with problems.

The role of the parent changes once authority shifts from the child-carer to the professional. The parent now has to listen and defer to outside opinion. The parent is implicitly asked to share authority with people who claim to possess more child-rearing skills. To ignore such expertise is to court public mistrust and the accusation of irresponsibility. However, once authority for parenting is accorded to a group of professionals who exist independently of the family, the status of mothers and fathers is likely to diminish. Parents who are expected to defer to the professional are likely to have a weaker sense of authority than those who are not. It is not possible to share out some of the authority hitherto accorded to the parent without weakening this authority overall.

The pressure to share authority with the child-rearing professional has profound implications for modern parenting. The very existence of an outside source of authority puts parents on permanent trial. Parents are unlikely to have a strong sense of control if they constantly feel the need to prove themselves. Those who are uncertain about their authority are likely to find child-rearing an intensely unsettling and trying task. Even the most confident mother or father is influenced by this trend, since the weakening of the status which society accords to parental authority impacts on the way that all child-carers approach their everyday tasks.

The caring professionals advocate the virtues of responsible parenting. Yet their encroachment on parental authority is likely to have the opposite effect. Why? Because it is not possible to share out such authority without also handing over a measure of responsibility for child-rearing. Take the troublesome problem of discipline. Although they don't say it in so many words, many mothers and fathers sense that they lack the authority effectively to discipline their children, and often feel defeated even before they try. The cry of 'What can I do?' reflects their consciousness of uncertain authority. Unfortunately, too often this expectation of defeat leads parents to look for other sources of authority – teachers and schools – to take responsibility for disciplining the young. The way that parental failure is presented as a normal state of affairs can only lower the expectations that parents have of themselves. The sharing of authority acts as a disincentive to responsible parenting.

The professionalization of parenting impairs the confidence of mothers and fathers. It also promotes an expertise that is of dubious value to our community. We have already noted that much of what constitutes this expertise is prejudice masquerading as science. The lack of substance of this research is not surprising, since the very project of the science of parenting is flawed.

The core assumption of the parenting profession is that child-rearing consists of a set of practices that need to be learnt by mothers and fathers. These practices are represented as skills that can be taught by those who possess the necessary professional qualification. No one could dispute the assertion that child-rearing needs to be learned by mothers and fathers. The forging of every human relationship involves a continual process of learning and gaining an understanding of the other person. A parent needs to learn how to engage the imagination of a child, how to stimulate him and when and how to restrain him from doing something harmful. Effective parents are always learning on the job. However, the most crucial lessons that we are learning are not to do with abstract skills, but about the relationship we have with our children. Learning how to manage this relationship in order to guide a child's development is the crux of effective parenting.

The issue is not whether parenting needs to be learned, but whether it can be taught. Everyday experience suggests that not everything that has to be learned can be taught. Parenting cannot be taught because it is about the forging and managing of an intimate relationship. And when it comes to a relationship, people tend to learn from their own experience. Children and grown-ups are often subjected to very good advice about who they should mix with, and who or how they should love. However, in the end people learn through their interaction with the other party. One reason why well-meaning advice is less than effective is because each relationship contains something unique that is only grasped by those involved. People learn through experiencing the joy and the pain, the exhilaration and the disappointments of their interaction with someone who is significant to their lives.

When it comes to a relationship, learning what is right is an act of individual discovery. Parents learn what is right for their children through interacting with them. Men and women are not born with an innate understanding of parenting. We certainly don't gain such an understanding through books and parenting classes. Until one has a child, even the basic questions to do with parenting remain unfocused and unspecific. As many parents confirm, what they learned from advice books and from professionals actually bears little relationship to their subsequent experience. The birth of their baby throws up the first real problems that they will have to solve. It is at that point that learning begins, and it is the experience of the parent–child relationship that teaches men and women how to go about fulfilling their responsibilities.

When it comes to science, it is possible to teach knowledge without the student having personally to experience and discover the answer for themselves. It is possible to teach skills which can be applied in all scientific experiments. This is not the case with parenting. The very instability of parenting advice and the regularity with which yesterday's authoritative guide is unequivocally dismissed as hopelessly inaccurate indicate that what is going to be taught today will be rejected as irrelevant tomorrow.

People are systematically bombarded with advice about how they should conduct their relationships. The popularity of self-help schemes and advice literature indicates that there is a genuine demand for learning about relationships. Just how much these books and schemes teach us is a matter of debate. There have never been so many publications devoted to instructing people how to have a more fulfilling sex life. There have also never been so many people eagerly seeking to learn from these publications. Have the books helped people to acquire a great sex life? Has all the sex advice taught people to enjoy unprecedented physical and emotional joy? Just posing these questions shows up the ludicrous claim that fulfilment in a sexual relationship can be taught. People can no more be taught to have good loving relationships than how to be good parents.

The very concept of a parenting 'skill' obscures the essence of a child–parent relationship. This technical approach to parenting has little to do with the needs of children. Children do not benefit from the erosion of their parents' authority. The confusion of the conduct of a relationship with skills represents a cultural statement about how adults are viewed. People are less and less trusted to conduct their personal affairs. It is almost as if we expect people to be too immature to handle their relations with one another. Caring professionals and educators now advocate 'relationship education'. There are special schemes afoot to promote relationship skills for married or soon-to-be-married adults. Apprehensions about our ability to manage our private affairs have also led to calls to teach parenting skills to schoolchildren.

Trying to teach schoolchildren about how to become good parents indicates that the caring professions have lost the plot. Schools have an important role in providing children with the education they need to become successful adults. Educated adults with good jobs stand a good chance of learning to become effective parents. Instead of providing lessons about parenting, schools could achieve a lot more by concentrating on the task of making sure that their students become educated adults.

It is very difficult to conduct close and intimate relationships under public scrutiny. A relationship between a parent and child is not only made more complicated by professional intervention, it also changes when it is conducted under scrutiny. A mother or father who is forced to keep one eye on outside authority and the other on their child is forced to play to two different scripts. This distraction can create an unnecessary barrier between parent and child, and weaken the ability of the carer to learn from their special experience. The inexorable consequence is to undermine the confidence of the parent.

There is a case for professional support for families. But that support should be unobtrusive and targeted towards the small minority of parents who have genuinely failed to establish their authority over their children. The failure to distinguish between the problems faced by this small minority and those confronted by most mothers and fathers results from the assumption that all normal parents need support. This approach fails both groups of parents. When all parents are treated as potential failures, it is the children who pay the price.

There is a lot that parents can learn from individuals who possess specialist knowledge. They can learn about practical skills to do with health and nutrition. If they choose, they can learn important insights about child development. But the one thing they cannot learn from anyone else is how to conduct their relationship with their children. Anyone who claims to possess a scientific knowledge of relationships suffers from self-delusion. Mothers and fathers are likely to learn far more from other parents and family members who have shared their experience and whom they trust. But in the end, parents also need to know that most of the time they and they alone possess the knowledge of what is in the best interests of their children.

Eleven

The Politicization of Parenting

The parenting professional has found an eager ally in the politician. During the past decade, parents have found themselves to be the object of increasing public and political interest and discussion. All the main political parties regard the so-called problem of parenting as their issue. The political class has absorbed the ideology of parent determinism. The idea that parenting determines the behaviour of children has become truly politicized. It is frequently proposed that all forms of anti-social behaviour can be linked to poor parenting practices. At one time or another virtually every social problem – crime, drugs, teenage pregnancy, illiteracy and poverty – has been linked to incompetent parenting.

The first major figure to place parent determinism on the political agenda was Sir Keith Joseph. In a 1972 speech, this former Conservative Secretary of State for Social Services argued that poverty and disadvantage was transmitted through the family, and advanced the thesis that more preparation for parenthood could help break this 'cycle of deprivation'. At the time, critics of this approach argued that it was far from clear how deprivation was transmitted through poor parenting. It was also pointed out that it was far from evident how parenting could be modified through policy intervention so as to break this cycle of poverty.

Back in the 1970s and early 1980s the thesis of the cycle of deprivation was generally associated with the politics of the right wing of the Conservative Party. However, in the intervening period, especially since the 1990s, other political interests have jumped on this bandwagon. New Labour, in particular, has thoroughly assimilated the thesis of parent determinism and is now the most robust advocate of bringing child-rearing into the domain of public policy. In October 1996, the Labour Party published its discussion paper *Tackling the Causes of Crime*, which alleged that there were direct links between poor parenting and anti-social behaviour by children. The New Labour Government's 1998 consultation document *Supporting Families* represents, so far, the most ambitious project designed to politicize parenting.

The politicization of parenting is driven by a profound sense of moral malaise. British society is deeply concerned by the prevalence of crime, anti-social behaviour, breakdown of trust and the apparent decline of the family. Many long-established institutions – from the family to the Church – appear exhausted and disoriented. Bewilderment about moral values is widespread and many people feel that British society is losing its way. Such concerns are often generated when life seems unpredictable and out of control. The absence of a sense of community is a constant source of insecurity. We all have a feeling of estrangement at least some of the time and often ask ourselves where we belong.

Moral confusion also unfortunately creates a demand for quick-fix solutions. Parents provide an ideal target for those seeking a ready-made one. It is much easier to personalize a moral problem than to understand it as the erosion of an abstract system of values. Immoral people are simpler to recognize than the failure of institutions to transmit meaningful values about the difference between right and wrong. So we pounce on immoral people. And since most immoral people have been brought up by their parents it is tempting to blame their behaviour on their mothers or fathers. After all, if people's behaviour is determined by the actions of their parents, whom else should we blame?

In the past, politicians were only interested in indicting the so-called problem parent. Sir Keith Joseph's main concern was with the problem posed by a small group of marginalized poor families when he proposed that Government take an interest in parenting. Later, the weakening of the institution of marriage and the apparent decline of the family led some politicians to represent single mothers as the symbol of moral decay. During the 1990s, the deadbeat dad became the subject of moral concern. Gradually, with the intensification of moral uncertainties, other parents were brought into the frame. The yuppie parent who was more concerned about career than family life soon joined the working mother. Today, the scrutiny of the politician is no longer directed at a specific group of mothers and fathers. All potential parents face the attention of policy makers.

Of course, British society does face important moral issues. But to blame parents for the present state of moral malaise is to confuse the symptom with the cause. How parents behave is informed by the cultural, moral and social influences that bear down upon them. The values they transmit to their children are not their personal property, but are ideas that they appropriate from everyday life in their community. Parents can do a lot to prepare their children to become good citizens. But adopting a different child-raising strategy will do little to put right a world uncertain about its moral universe. It is a testimony to the moral illiteracy of the political class that instead of confronting the big questions facing society they prefer to give lectures on parenting skills.

There is also a strong streak of opportunism behind the politicization of parenting. Britain faces a variety of social problems. It is far more expensive to improve the quality of education, health and social services than to exhort parents to spend more time reading to their children, cuddling them or breast-feeding them. No doubt sound parenting practices can have positive effects on children's lives. But these effects pale into insignificance when compared to what can be achieved through an excellent system of childcare and education. Parenting as a tool of social policy is likely to be ineffective but it has the merit of being very cheap.

Politicians have been quick to embrace new ideas about early child development. Childcare experts are now regularly consulted and infant determinism informs the new policy initiatives surrounding intervention in the early years. The parent figures prominently in contemporary social policy making. The professionalization of parenting has become institutionalized through the establishment of the National Family and Parenting Institute.

The politicization of parenting is also influenced by a genuine concern with the many problems associated with family life. Unfortunately, well-meaning and even constructive proposals can do very little to solve the problems faced by parents. State policy is too crude an instrument to deal with the management of intimate emotional relations between parent and child. Parental anxieties and the complex relation between adults and children are not problems that are susceptible to public policy solutions. Why? Because the problems of human relationships are too specific and too personal to be tackled by policies, which are by definition general in character.

Focusing public attention on private troubles has the potential for making matters worse. Even well-meaning intrusive family members can exacerbate an already unsettled situation. In the past it was recognized that such interference could be harmful and that it was important parents were allowed to bring up children in their own way. Today this insight has been lost. Public policy now assumes that intervention in family life can only improve the situation rather than make it worse. Yet public intervention is likely to go much further than the intrusion of busybody relatives in complicating parenting matters. By legitimizing the professionalization of parenting, public policy can have the unintended consequence of disempowering parents further. It is evident that one of the main causes of parental paranoia is the way in which intimate family relationships have become subject to public intervention and scrutiny. Such pressure, whether in the form of 'helpful advice', periodic health warnings, or the intervention of professionals or of politicians, serves to continually erode parental confidence. Those who are genuinely concerned about parents and their children need to realize that this problem is not susceptible to political solutions. Taking the issue of parenting out of the sphere of political life would make a valuable contribution towards restoring the confidence of many parents.

Not the business of the state

Responsible public figures intuitively recognize that the professionalization of parenting is fraught with danger for the conduct of family life. This problem is acknowledged in the Government's consultation document, *Supporting Families*. 'Governments have to be very careful in devising policies that affect our most intimate relationships', it warns.[1] In another passage it calls on Government to 'approach family policy with a strong dose of humility'. Unfortunately, once set in motion, public policy has a tendency to expand. Officialdom, egged on by campaigning professionals and ambitious politicians, is not noted for its ability to exercise self-restraint. Policy making and public intervention have their own inner dynamic. And once parenting becomes a legitimate arena for public intervention, politicians find it difficult to resist the temptation to expand their brief.

Despite its note of caution about exercising care, *Supporting Families* encroaches into areas that directly affect intimate aspects of family life. It outlines the intention of Government to initiate a programme for helping people to prepare for marriage. It proposes to launch projects oriented towards saving marriages. The document also considers policies directed at helping parents cope with the arrival of a baby. On a more ominous note it suggests imposing parenting orders on mothers and fathers who are deemed to have failed to control their children.

Since the publication of *Supporting Families*, the Government has adopted a highly interventionist stance and has politicized parenting. Jack Straw, the Home Secretary, has stated that the culture of parenting needs to be changed so that 'seeking advice and help' is 'seen not as failure but the action of concerned and responsible parents'. No previous Government has sought to promote such an ambitious programme of social engineering in relation to child-rearing.[2] The Government's £540 million Sure Start programme targets deprived families, but it also proposes to educate better-off parents. The recently established National Family and Parenting Institute goes a step further and aims to establish a nationwide network of parenting classes. Officials associated with this institution hope that soon people will regard parenting classes in the same light as ante-natal classes. The Home Office has supported the publication of a booklet, *The Bounty Guide to Fatherhood*, which patronizingly informs fathers about the valuable role they can play in talking to the baby in the womb.

One of the most intrusive initiatives launched by government has been the campaign to promote breast-feeding in spring 2000, discussed in Chapter 9. In addition to the creation of a financial incentive for mothers who breast-fed, it ran a public poster campaign that suggested that mothers who were not breast-feeding their babies were not providing infants with the best. The use of public resources to finance a campaign designed to intimidate mothers to adopt breast-feeding reveals both a patronizing and an authoritarian orientation towards parenting issues.

At present, the authoritarian impulse in public policy is focused on a small group of 'irresponsible parents'. Between September and December 1999, 122 parenting orders were imposed by officialdom. These orders require the parents of convicted children to discipline them and to attend courses on parenting.[3] However, if one group of parents can be compelled to attend mandatory parenting classes, why not others? Once blaming parents becomes institutionalized through public policy, all mothers and fathers can become the legitimate focus of officialdom. If officials assume responsibility for training one group of adults how to parent, how soon before they expand their targeted group? Criminalizing parental failure is the logic of this inexorable expansion of the professionalizing of parenting. The message it conveys to all parents is 'Beware!'

One of the arguments constantly reiterated by government officials and the caring professions is that parenting is one of the most important jobs in the world, and yet so little is done to support it. Jack Straw has bemoaned the fact that parenting is treated as a private matter in British culture, since it is also a public issue with 'implications for children and society'.[4] Parenting is an important matter. So are love affairs, marriages and intimate relations between people. But just because something is important to people and to society does not mean that it requires the regulation of the state. Whenever public policy encroaches into the domain of personal relations it is likely to undermine them. Human relations thrive on emotion and sentiment. They involve personal attachment, commitment and responsibility. Sentiment plays an important role in binding people together. When it becomes subject to formal procedure, sentiment becomes less effective in binding together relations of trust.

The idea that politicians and their officials know what's in the interest of children better than their parents do is also an affront to the dignity of every mother and father. Parents work very hard to fulfil their responsibilities, and most of the time succeed in making a very good job of it. What they do is not the business of the state. Politicians have no authority to claim that they possess a special insight about the conduct of private affairs. The role of public authorities should be confined to those exceptional circumstances when a child faces real harm. Society has a legitimate interest in the protection and welfare of its children. But it has no interest in encouraging the politicization of parenting.

Whenever politics intrudes into the sphere of parenting, problems are exaggerated and mothers and fathers are put on the defensive. The politicization of parenting is a failure of the political imagination. Unable to work out effective social policies that can tackle the real problems facing British society, some politicians have been persuaded that if they can re-educate parents everything would turn out fine. Politicians, who have failed to provide Britain with a decent system of education, somehow assume that nevertheless they are fit to educate parents. Since most of the time parents are intensely defensive about their role, they have remained silent about this affront to their self-respect.

It is important to take politics out of parenting. State intervention into the sphere of parenting offers no solutions. It only fuels parental paranoia. It distracts people from tackling genuine problems and magnifies the problem of parenting. This danger was clearly antici-pated by Winnicott when he warned that 'whatever does not specifi-cally back up the idea that parents are responsible people will in the long run be harmful to the very core of society'.[5] The politicization of parenting serves as an everyday reminder that parents need officialdom to remind them of their responsibility. It has helped create a climate of suspicion and mistrust. The consequence of this for parents and their children is the subject of the final chapter.

Conclusion

Whoever invented the word *parenting* was not primarily interested in the world of children. Until recently the term 'to parent' was used exclusively to refer to the act of begetting a child. Today, it is deployed to describe the behaviour of mothers and fathers. Parenting pertains to modes of adult behaviour. That is why so many of the issues surrounding paranoid parenting have surprisingly little to do with the lives of children. Fears about adult identity are often transferred to the world of children, who then bear the brunt of our anxieties. Public concerns expressed about parenting are grounded in the confusions that adults have about their lives. These confusions have a disproportionate impact upon the lives of those responsible for child-rearing.

Many of the forces that create the condition for the growth of parental anxieties are unrelated to practical issues of child-rearing. The tendency to increase our emotional investment in our children is in part a reflection of difficulties associated with the relations between mature men and women. The process which was previously described as the emptying out of adult identity and the weakening of authority exists independently of childcare issues and shapes the lives of all grown-ups. Of course, the fact that adults find it difficult to conduct their affairs has a significant impact on the way we bring up our children. The decline of adult collaboration and responsibility for the welfare of youngsters has far-reaching implications for this discussion. Insecurity inevitably permeates a parenting culture which relies so heavily on isolated mothers and fathers.

Deprived of the authority they require to carry out their responsibility effectively, parents possess only a weak sense of control over their children's lives. Unfortunately the caring professions and policy makers have not grasped why parents face such a difficult predicament. Even with the best of intentions, childcare professionals add to parents' woes. Their intervention has the effect of disempowering parents, whose status is now contested by a new source of authority. The objective of 'supporting' parents turns into its opposite. Deep inside, every sensible adult knows that the provision of support carries the implication of failure. We support failed schools, failing doctors and failing marriages. When it comes to child-rearing, outside support risks inflicting an irreparable blow to the authority of the parent.

The politician's failure to identify the right problems is not due to a lack of imagination. Policy makers look for problems that they can solve. However, the principal problems confronting parents are not susceptible to political solutions. Grown-ups' confusions are influenced by social, moral and cultural processes. These problems cannot be tackled with a clever law. What we need is a change in attitude by adults towards the socialization of children. Instead of adding to the problems faced by mothers and fathers through transmitting the message of parental incompetence, politicians should address the big question of how to establish a society in which adults are more able to trust others with the welfare of their children.

What can we do?

Understanding the predicament faced by mothers and fathers helps place the individual difficulties faced by parents in perspective. We all need to know that most of the really big issues that plague parents have little to do with problems intrinsic to child-rearing. Today's heightened sense of anxiety towards children is not based on any practical discoveries about their lives. Almost all the forces that fuel paranoid parenting stem from unresolved tensions rooted in the world of adults. The emptying out of adult identity, the depreciation of adulthood, the loss of parental authority, uncertainties about moral values, the professionalization and politicization of parenting and the weakening of adult solidarity are outcomes thrown up by developments in the wider society. These influences serve to disorient and confuse parents who in turn transmit their insecurities through the way they interact with their children. In that sense the wider cultural influences on adulthood have a direct bearing on child-rearing. But these are problems that adults have to sort out amongst themselves and not with their children. Parents can do little to counteract the effects of these cultural influences. But they can take steps to minimize their impact on their family by doing their best to avoid confusing the problem of adulthood with that of childhood. Just remember that when you are about to say 'I could not live with myself if something happened to my child', you are principally concerned with your own state of mind rather than the welfare of your child.

Paranoid parenting can be seen as a collective displacement activity. The failures of grown-up society are visited on children. Lamentably, it is our children who pay the price for the difficulty that we adults have in sorting out our problems.

It is always important to recall that our obsession with our children's safety is likely to be more damaging to them than any risks that they are likely to meet with in their daily encounter with the world. Children can recover from accidents very quickly. In a loving environment, even a traumatic episode need not prevent a child from bouncing back and developing into a confident adult. However, if parents stifle their children with their obsessions and restrict their scope to explore, then the young generation will become socialized to believe that vulnerability is the natural state of affairs. Letting go is always a difficult exercise for parents. However, freeing children from the obsessions of parental paranoia is essential for their healthy development.

There is simply no sensible alternative to letting go. Paranoid parenting actually accomplishes the very opposite of what it sets out to do. When youngsters are protected from risks they miss out on important opportunities to learn sound judgement and build up their confidence and resilience. Such psychological resources ensure their safety far better than the current regime of constant adult supervision.

Instead of teaching children to distrust strangers and to regard the world outside with suspicion, parents need to nourish their child's confidence and self-belief. Children can learn to look after themselves best if they are instilled with a strong sense of what is right and wrong. Instead of concentrating on negative themes such as stranger-danger, parents need to transmit to their children a positive vision of humanity.

We have a responsibility to raise and not lower their expectations about what they can expect of themselves and other people.

One way that parents can temper their fears is by tackling the consequences of the breakdown of adult collaboration. Parents need to take active steps to overcome their isolation. They need to cultivate friends, colleagues and family members to serve as collaborators in the task of child-rearing. In the present climate of suspicion this requires hard work. We need to contact other parents and make friends with them to try to create our own little community of stakeholders in our children's welfare. Some parents have more opportunity than others to construct a network of adult collaborators. But all of us can establish such links, since in every community parents intuitively grasp that they need the help of one another. Parental co-operation helps to minimize the effects of isolation. But it is also the most effective alternative to the disempowering consequences of the professionalization of parenting.

Parenting is not a complex science. It is not even a science at all. It is actually quite a natural undertaking. Sometimes boring, ordinary and even banal, bringing up children is always demanding. Parents can afford to make mistakes, although they would do well to learn from them. As long as you do your best for your child you will probably not need any professional back-up. No one is likely to understand the situation of your child better than you do – so you might as well do what you think is best.

In any case, most professional advice is at best good common sense or at worst someone's prejudice. Usually it is simply someone's opinion. Such advice is formulaic, very general, and nine times out of ten entirely useless. It is often based on prejudice that masquerades as research. You need to be aware that the two principal ideas that dominate today's parenting culture – infant and parent determinism – are fundamentally flawed. They illuminate the job of child-rearing as much as the idea that the world is flat helped overseas explorers in the past. They are today's prejudice. Experience indicates that today's authoritative advice will probably be dismissed in five years as unenlightened opinion, so don't feel worried about not heeding it. The advice of friends and family members is likely to be far more relevant since they are acquainted with your circumstances and actually know a bit about your child. However, in the end it is your call so you might as well follow your instinct. Be prepared to call the childcare expert's bluff.

The aim of this book is not to offer superior advice to the anxious parent. The book is motivated by the conviction that if we can grasp why parenting has been turned into such a troublesome enterprise then we can do something about regaining our self-confidence. Today's parenting culture systematically de-skills mothers and fathers. It places enormous pressures on parents to turn away from what only they can do. The good news is that if we understand the pressures that bear down upon us we can act to insulate ourselves from them. We may still be anxious about our children's well-being, but at least it will be possible to put those fears into a more balanced perspective.

Notes

Introduction

1 See 'Security Concerns Affect Pre-School Choice' in *Parents News*, August 1997.

2 See *The Mirror*, 10 May 2000.

3 Cited in 'Crimes Against Children Drop' in the *Sunday Times*, 11 June 2000.

4 *Observer*, 17 May 1998.

5 See McCaslin, M. & Infanti, H. (1998), 'The Generativity Crisis and the "Scold War": What About Those Parents', *Teachers College Record*, vol. 100, no. 2, pp. 282–3.

6 See 'The Good Parent Test' in the *Daily Telegraph*, 18 January 1997.

One Making Sense of Parental Paranoia

1 For an illustration of this worrying trend see R. Landau (1995) 'The impact of new medical technologies in human reproduction on children's personal safety and well-being in the family', *Marriage and Family Review*, 21 (1–2).

2 NCH Action For Children (1999) *The Internet: A Parents' Guide*, London, p. 2.

3 See 'Computers rot our children's brains: expert', in the *Observer*, 16 April 2000.

4 Strasburger and Donnerstein (1999), p. 129.

5 System Three (1998) *Poll on the Safety of Children in Society in Scotland*, Edinburgh, Stickler and Simons (1995), p. 47.

6 Survey cited in HMSO (1994) *Social Focus on Children* (Central Statistical Office: London).

7 Orpinas and Murray (1999), pp. 774–7.

8 This view is argued by Jean Richardson, Professor of Preventative Medicine at the University of Southern California. She is cited in 'Figuring out when children are ready to stay home alone', *Christian Science Monitor*, 9 July 1996.

9 Alderson (2000), pp. 100–01.

10 NSPCC Press Release, 'NSPCC warns of risks to children this summer', 2 August 1999.

11 Cited in 'Parents rearing "risk-free" generation', *Daily Telegraph*, 27 November 1997.

12 Lindon (1999), p. 9.

13 Hardyment (1995).

14 See 'Children safer despite the worries of parents', *Sunday Times*, 11 June 2000.

15 *The Times*, 10 February 1994.

16 Cited in Amanda Root (1997), p. 128.

17 See Hillman, Adams and Whiteleg (1990), p. 84.

18 Based on reports of research carried out at the University of Coventry. See 'Children safer despite the worries of parents', *Sunday Times*, 11 June 2000.

19 D. Norris (1999) *Protecting our Children: A Guide for Parents*, London, p. 3.

20 See 'Smoke without fire' in the *Guardian*, 12 January 2000.

21 Cited in *The Times*, 10 August 1999.

22 See 'Yes, it's the paedophiles I blame', *Guardian*, 27 July 1999.

23 See *Daily Telegraph*, 26 September 1997.

24 See Salvation Army (1996) *Safe and Sound*, London, p. 2.

25 Interview: Colonel Joy Paxton, 9 September 1998.

26 *Safe from Harm: A Code of Practice for Safeguarding the Welfare of Children in Voluntary Organisations in England and Wales* (1993) Home Office, London, p. 2.

27 *Child Protection: Awareness and Procedures for All Adults Involved in Cricket for Children and Young People* (1999) England and Wales Cricket Board, London, p. 9.

28 See *Daily Telegraph*, 16 May 1998.

29 Cited in *Daily Telegraph*, 25 July 1999.

30 Cited in *Guardian*, 29 August 1998.

31 See 'Lord Puttnam: the arts chose moral ambiguity', in *The Times*, 1 June 2000.

32 Emily Wilson, 'The touchy-feely kids', *Guardian*, 3 November 1999.

33 See NSPCC media release, 'Cruelty to children must stop', 2 August 1999.

34 My thanks to Dr Vanessa Pupavac of Nottingham University for providing details of this incident.
35 See *Guardian*, 21 April 2000.
36 See interview in Furedi and Brown (1997), p. 22.
37 J. Adams, 'Hypermobility', *Prospect*, March 2000.
38 Royal Mail (1999) *The 21st Century Family: A Royal Mail Study on Communication and the Modern Family*, London.

Two The Myth of the Vulnerable Child

1 Furedi (1997), pp. 19–21.
2 Clinton (1996), p. 11.
3 Elliot (1996), p. 42.
4 'You can't play here', *Daily Mail*, 30 May 2000.
5 Alderson (2000), pp. 100–101.
6 See 'Helping children to play stunts creativity', *Independent*, 13 June 2000.
7 'Dare we let them out of our sight?', *Prima*, August 1999.
8 The Mental Health Foundation (1999) *Bright Futures*, London, p. 6.
9 Interview, 1999.
10 See for example Ann Buchanan's claim that child disorders are caused by poor parenting in 'The background' in Buchanan and Hudson (1998), p. 3.
11 See Kagan (1998).
12 These ideas are explored in Scarr and Dunn (1987).
13 Scarr and Dunn (1987), p. 73.
14 K. C. Parker and D. Forrest (1993) 'Attachment disorder: an emerging concern for school counsellors', *Elementary School Guidance and Counselling*, 27 (3) (February).
15 Tizard (1997).
16 J. Bowlby, M. Ainsworth, M. Boston and D. Rosenbluth (1956) 'The effects of mother–child separation: a follow-up study', *British Journal of Medical Psychology*, 29, p. 233.
17 See A. Clarke and A. Clarke in Bernstein and Brannen (1996).
18 S. Ventegodt (1999) 'A prospective study on quality of life and traumatic events in early life – a 30-year follow up', *Child: Care, Health and Development*, 25 (3), pp. 213, 220.
19 Cited in Schaffer (1998a), p. 366.
20 Werner and Smith (1982), p. 159.
21 Schaffer (1998a), pp. 376–9.
22 Cited in Schaffer (1998a), p. 368.

23 Interview, May 2000.

24 Cited in 'The science of cuddles', *Daily Telegraph*, 15 November 1997.

Three Parents as Gods

1 'Over-protective parents may be causing anorexia', in the *Independent*, 1 February 2000.

2 'Parents get blame for terrible twos', *Daily Telegraph*, 30 July 1996.

3 See *Daily Telegraph*, 17 March 1995.

4 Two *Panorama* documentaries, in 1997 and 1999, were devoted to this subject.

5 'Postnatal blues can lower IQ of baby boys', in the *Guardian*, 22 January 2000.

6 See *Observer*, 21 November 1999.

7 See 'Screaming parents "damage" teenagers', in *Independent on Sunday*, 9 April 2000.

8 See 'Children are damaged by quality time', in *The Times*, 13 April 2000.

9 Kagan (1998), p. 146.

10 For a discussion of this event and its wider impact, see Bruer (1999), pp. 1–27.

11 See special edition of *Newsweek* (Spring/Summer 1997) on this subject.

12 *Time*, 3 February 1997.

13 NSPCC Press Release, 'Help for a New Generation of Children', 27 January 2000.

14 See, for example, J. Briscoe (1997) 'Breaking the cycle of violence: a rational approach to at-risk youth', *Federal Probation*, 61 (3).

15 Cited in 'What should children be eating?' *Co-ordinate*, January 1997, p. 10.

16 'Not in front of the children?' *Mother and Baby*, May 2000.

17 Cited in 'Dummies: the pros and cons', *Parents*, September 1997, p. 33. See also 'The truth about dummies', *Prima Baby*, Summer 1998.

18 See 'Breast way forward', in *Mother and Baby*, January 2000, and 'Music to your ears', *Mother and Baby*, April 2000.

19 'Overture for babies', in the *Guardian*, 23 June 2000.

20 'Mental strength', in *Parents*, August 1999.

21 'When they are old enough to . . .', *Prima Baby*, April/May 2000.

22 'Speak', in *Practical Parenting*, April 2000.

23 'Kill your television', in *Baby Magazine*, March 2000.

24 'Enjoy books', in *Prima Baby*, April/May 2000.

25 Bruer (1999), p. 103.

26 Scarr and Dunn (1987), p. 187.

27 Rauscher's research is discussed in the *Lancet*, 28 August 1999, p. 749.

28 Gopnik, Meltzoff and Kuhl (1999), pp. 201–02.

29 Bruer (1999), p. 185.

30 Cited in Bruer (1999), p. 188.

31 Scarr (1992), p. 16.

32 Harris (1998).

33 Duin and Sutcliffe (1992), pp. 114–15.

34 See HMSO (1991).

35 'How to have a brainy baby', *Prima Baby*, June/July 1999.

36 See 'Guide book will tell men how to be a good father', *Daily Telegraph*, 11 September 1999.

37 Naish and Roberts (2000), pp. 9, 11 and 111.

38 J. V. Priya (1992) *Birth Traditions and Modern Pregnancy Care* (Element Books: Dorset).

39 A. Fleissig (1991) 'Unintended pregnancy and the use of contraception: changes from 1984 to 1989', *British Medical Journal*, 302, p. 147.

Four **Parenting on Demand – the New Concept of Child-rearing**

1 Spock (1961), pp. 333–4.

2 Leach (1997), p. 216.

3 Jackson (1999) *Three in a Bed*, pp. 34–5.

4 See Young (1990).

5 Leach (1997), p. 144.

6 D. Rowe, 'Foreword' to Parker and Stimpson (1999), p. 1; Leach (1997), p. 144; and Jackson (1999), p. 41.

7 See Parker and Stimpson (1999), p. 95; D. Rowe, 'Foreword' to Parker and Stimpson (1999), p. 1; and NSPCC (2000), p. 2.

8 J. Kagan, 'Our babies, our selves', in *New Republic*, 5 September 1994.

9 Goleman (1996), p. 199.

10 See J. Gottman, 'Are you a good parent?' *Daily Telegraph*, 18 January 1997.

11 See NSPCC (1998) *Positive Ways of Managing Children's Behaviour: Notes for Group Leaders*, London, p. 6, and Parker and Stimpson (1999), p. 77.

12 Michael Boulton, 'Her growing confidence', in *Mother and Baby*, April 2000.

13 See 'Listen with your heart', *Practical Parenting*, May 2000 and *Baby-Power*, April 2000.

14 See *Practical Parenting*, May 2000 and Jackson (1999), pp. 77–105.

15 'Touch early and often', *Time*, 27 July 1998.

16 Cited in Cassidy (1998), p. 87.

17 Lasch (1977).

18 S. Orbach, 'Holding on to the vision: emotional literacy', paper given at 'Responsible Parenting Requires a Responsible Society', 13 October 1992, p. 49.

19 See Future Foundation (2000), p. 5.

20 See 'Parents take on 7 hours' homework', *Daily Telegraph*, 27 March 2000.

21 Elizabeth Newson (1972) 'Towards an understanding of the parental role,' in *Papers given at the National Children's Bureau's Annual Conference*, September (NCB: London).

22 See 'Teachers threatened by "parents from hell"', *Daily Telegraph*, 27 April 2000.

Five Parenting Turned into an Ordeal

1 *Sunday Times*, 25 May 1997.

2 Cited in 'The myth of quality time', in *Newsweek*, 12 May 1997.

3 'Pushyparent.co.uk going public', *Guardian*, 19 April 2000.

4 Nestlé Family Monitor no. 3, 'The school summer holiday: at home', 1998, p. 2.

5 J. Gershuny (1997) 'Time for the family', *Prospect*, January, p. 56 and 'Men wear the aprons as wives work more', *Daily Telegraph*, 16 April 1998.

6 S. Hofferth (1999) 'Changes in American children's time, 1981–1997', *The Brown University Child and Adolescent Behavior Letter*, 15 (3), pp. 1 and 5.

7 Hofferth, 'Changes in American children's time', p. 5.

8 See Future Foundation (2000).

9 Future Foundation (2000).

10 A. Hochschild, 'There's no place like work', *New York Times Magazine*, 20 April 1997.

11 Health Education Authority (1992).

12 Maushart (1999), p. 10, and Jeffers (1999).

13 Johnson and Johnson Limited Press Release, 13 December 1999, 'An overview analysis and response by psychologist Dr Maureen Marks'.

14 ICM Research, 'Mothercare 2000', Press Release, 10 November 1999.

15 'No kids please, we're modern', *Independent*, 8 July 1998.

Six Why Parents Confuse Their Problems with Those of Their Children

1 See Galinsky (1999).

2 Chernofsky and Gage (1996).

3 Hardyment (1995), p. 299.

4 Health Education Authority (1992), p. 5.

5 Leach (1997), p. 145.

6 Cassidy (1998).

7 Hamand (1994), p. 18.

8 See F. Pittman (1995) 'How to manage your kids', *Psychology Today*, 28 (3), p. 42.

9 Cassidy (1998), p. 43.

10 Zelizer (1985), p. 3.

11 Cited in Zelizer (1994), p. 9.

12 See Elkind (1988).

13 Sennett (1998), p. 146.

14 For an overview of these trends see Family Policy Studies Centre (2000) *Family Change: Guide to the Issues.*

15 Office for National Statistics (1997) *Social Focus on Families.*

16 See Langford (1999), Straw (1998) and Lewis (1999).

17 Firestone (1999).

18 Jenks (1996), p. 107.

19 Zoë Ball's interview in *Marie Claire* is discussed in 'Doomed from the start', *The Times*, 24 March 2000.

20 Beck and Beck-Gernsheim (1995), p. 37.

21 Kagan (1998), p. 129.

22 Zelizer (1985), p. 265.

23 Future Foundation (2000), p. 6.

Seven Confusions about Facing up to Adulthood

1 Jacobson (1996), pp. 582–8, and M. Wolfenstein, 'Fun morality: an analysis of recent American child-training literature', in Mead and Wolfenstein (1955).

2 Hewlett and West (1998), p. 126.

3 Calcutt (1998), p. 236.

Eight The Problem of Holding the Line

1 Bob Franklin, 'The case for children's rights: a progress report', in Franklin (1995), pp. 14–15; and Alderson (2000), pp. 24–5.

2 See Gordon (1975), p. 123; Leach (1997), p. 528; and Ringen (1998).

3 Franklin (1995), p. 14 and Ringen (1998).

4 See *Times Educational Supplement*, 7 January 2000.

5 See 'Fear rules', *Guardian*, 27 June 2000.

6 Parker and Stimpson (1999), p. 171 and J. McCord (1996), p. 832.

7 Baumrind (1996), p. 828.

8 NSPCC (1998) *Positive Ways of Managing Children's Behaviour: Group Activities*, p. 6, and Health Education Authority (1992), p. 40.

9 Cited in D. Barasch, 'Defiance', in *Family Life*, June/July 1999, p. 45.

10 See 'Giving guidance on child discipline', editorial in *British Medical Journal*, 29 January 2000.

11 F. Hamcock, 'Why smack?' *Nursery World*, 29 July 1993.

12 Leach (1997), pp. 528–34.

13 For a discussion of this controversy, see 'This book says you should beat your children, not cuddle them', *Daily Telegraph*, 22 February 1998.

14 Leach (1999), p. 19 and M. Strauss (1996) 'Spanking and the making of a violent society', *Pediatrics*, 98 (4), p. 842.

15 See Hyman (1996) and Eron (1996), p. 822.

16 See 'When to spank', in *U.S. News and World Report*, 13 April 1998.

17 See R. Larzelere (1996) 'A review of the outcomes of parental use of nonabusive or customary physical punishment', *Pediatrics*, 98 (4) and Baumrind (1996).

Nine Unclear Rules – Prejudice Masquerading as Research

1 Isaacs (1960), p. 2.

2 Mead and Wolfenstein (1955), p. 145.

3 Mead and Wolfenstein (1955), p. 145.

4 J. Davey, 'When you feel like smacking', *Parents*, March 1995.

5 See NSPCC (1999).

6 Parker and Stimpson (1999), p. 81.

7 Cited in 'Advise and consent' in *Newsweek*, Spring/Summer 1997, special edition.

8 See the *Guardian*, 17 June 2000.

9 For these conflicting views see 'Lights on at night may harm children's sight', *Daily Telegraph*, 20 May 1999, and 'Nursery lights do not damage young eyes, say scientists', *Daily Telegraph*, 9 March 2000.

10 See 'Dishing out dirt', *Guardian*, 12 October 1999.

11 See K. Carpenter, 'Childcare selections to grow on', *Library Journal*, 8 January 1992.

12 On Spock's views see Etaugh (1980), p. 314. Changing attitudes towards maternal employment are documented by Young (1990), p. 21.

13 A. Carlson, 'Trojan horse of child care', *Executive Speeches*, June/July 1998.

14 See 'Invisible men', *Guardian*, 17 November 1999.

15 See Young (1990), p. 23.

16 See *Baby Magazine*, March 2000 and *Mother and Baby*, May 2000.

17 See 'What's stopping you breastfeeding?', *Prima Baby*, Summer 1997; *Prima Baby*, Summer 1998; 'How to have a brainy baby', *Prima Baby*, June/July 1999; *Parents*, May 1999; *Practical Parenting*, May 2000; and *Mother and Baby*, May 2000.

18 The editorial is cited in 'Baby-friendly frenzy', *Health Visitor*, September 1996.

19 See 'Breast-feeding mothers may pass toxins to babies', *Sunday Times*, 30 April 2000.

20 Jackson (1999), p. 175.

21 For an outline of McKenna's research see M. Small and M. Hellweg, 'A reasonable sleep', *Health and Hygiene*, April 1992. Newburn is cited in 'Should the baby sleep in your bed?' *Express*, 9 December 1999. The Federal Consumer Product Safety Commission's report is discussed in 'Baby in parents' bed in danger? U.S. says yes, but others demur', *New York Times*, 30 September 1999.

22 See 'Off to a good start', *Newsweek*, Summer 1997, special edition.

23 Stilwell is cited in S. Lang, 'Music – good for not only the soul, but the brain', *Human Ecology Forum*, Spring 1999, p. 24. See 'Music beats computers at enhancing childhood development', *Teaching Music*, June 1997.

24 See Smith, Van Loon, De Frates-Densch and Schrader (1998).

25 Anderson (1973), p. 8.

26 Horwood and Fergusson (1999), p. 1023.

27 These points are developed by Dr Alan Prout (1999) 'Living arrows: children's lives and the limits of parenting', *The Parenting Forum*, no. 15; *Practical Parenting*, May 2000; and *Mother and Baby*, May 2000.

28 See Schaffer (1998a), pp. 4–5.

Ten **Professional Power and the Erosion of Parental Authority**

1 Barnardo's (1999) *Attitudes to Parenting*, London, p. 9.
2 C. Smith (1999) *Developing Parenting Programmes*, London, p. 33.
3 Cited in *Alberta Report*, 19 April 1999.
4 Straw (1998), pp. 8 and 21.
5 See National Family and Parenting Institute (1999) *The Millennial Family*, London, p. 6.
6 See M. T. Owen and B. A. Mulvihill (1994) 'Benefits of a parent education and support program in the first three years', *Family Relations*, 43 (2) (April).
7 Smith (1999), op. cit., pp. 93, 97.
8 R. S. Smith (1997) 'Parent education: empowerment or control?' *Children and Society*, 11, pp. 114–15.
9 Freely (2000), p. 187.
10 Pugh and De'Ath (1984), pp. 13–14.
11 See *The Parenting Forum Newsletter*, no. 2, 1996.
12 Ayling (1930), pp. 204, 213.
13 Winnicott (1991), pp. 173–4.
14 NSPCC (1998) *Parenting: A Rough Guide. Group Activities*, London, p. 5.
15 See *Daily Telegraph*, 28 October 1999.
16 See Campion (1995).
17 For an overview of this debate, see *Society*, November 1996.

Eleven **The Politicization of Parenting**

1 *Supporting Families: A Consultation Document*, 1998, Home Office, London, p. 30.
2 'Draft speech for the Home Secretary – launch of the Lords and Commons Family and Child Protection Group's report "Family Matters" ', 23 July 1998, gives an outline of this ambitious programme.
3 *Guardian*, 4 December 1999.
4 Speech delivered at a ministerial seminar on 'Promoting successful parenting', 10 November 1997 at St Ermin's Hotel, London.
5 Winnicott (1991), p. 175.

Select Bibliography

Articles

Baumrind, D. (1991) 'The influence of parenting style on adolescent competence and substance use', *Journal of Early Adolescence*, 11 (1).

Baumrind, D. (1996) 'A blanket injunction against disciplinary use of spanking is not warranted by the data', *Pediatrics*, 98 (4).

Bigner, J. and Yang, R. (1996) 'Parent education in popular literature: 1970–1990', *Family and Consumer Sciences Research Journal*, 25 (1).

Burgess, E. W. 'The family in a changing society', *The American Journal of Sociology*, 53 (6).

Eron, L. (1996) 'Research and public policy', *Pediatrics*, 98 (4).

Etaugh, C. (1980) 'Effects of nonmaternal care on children: research evidence and popular views', *American Psychologist*, 35 (4).

Gardels, N. (1998) 'The crime of quality time', *New Perspectives Quarterly*, 15 (3).

Holloway, S. and Fuller, B. (1999) 'Families and child care: divergent viewpoints', *Annals of the American Academy of Political Science*, 563 (May).

Horwood, L. and Fergusson, D. (1999) 'A longitudinal study of maternal labour force participation and child academic achievement', *Journal of Child Psychology and Psychiatry*, 40 (7).

Hyman, I. (1996) 'Using research to change public policy: reflections on 20 years of effort to eliminate corporal punishment in schools', *Pediatrics*, 98 (4).

Jacobson, L. (1996) 'Revitalizing the American home: children's leisure and the revaluation of play, 1920–1940', *Journal of Social History* (Winter).

McCaslin, M. and Infanti, H. (1998) 'The generativity crisis and the "Scold War": what about those parents?' *Teachers College Record*, 100 (2).

McCord, J. (1996) 'Unintended consequences of punishment', *Pediatrics*, 98 (4).

Mahoney, G. and Kaiser, A. (1999) 'Parent education in early intervention: a call for a renewed focus', *Topics in Early Childhood Education*, 19 (3).

Ojemann, R. (1948) 'A functional analysis of child development material in current newspapers and magazines', *Child Development*, 19.

Orpinas, P. and Murray, N. (1999) 'Parental influences of students' aggressive behaviors and weapon carrying', *Health Education and Behavior*, 26 (6).

Owen, M. T. and Mulvihill, B. A. (1994) 'Benefits of a parent education and support program in the first three years', *Family Relations*, 43 (2) (April).

Powell, D. R. and Diamond, K. (1995) 'Approaches to parent–teacher relationships in U.S. early childhood programs during the twentieth century', *Journal of Education*, 177 (3).

Root, A. (1997) 'Walk: don't drive: why are children's journeys to school increasingly made by car?', *New Economy*, 4 (2).

Rutter, M. (1999) 'Psychosocial adversity and child psychopathology', *British Journal of Psychiatry*, no. 174.

Scarr, S. (1992) 'Developmental theories for the 1990s: development and individual differences', *Child Development*, 63.

Smith, M., Van Loon, P., DeFrates-Densch, N. and Schrader, T. (1998) 'Content changes in parent education books for parents of adolescents', *Family and Consumer Sciences Research Journal*, 27 (2).

Stickler, G. B. (1996) 'Worries of parents and their children', *Clinical Pediatrics*, 35 (4).

Stickler, G. B. and Simons, P. (1995) 'Pediatricians' preferences for anticipatory guidance topics compared with parental anxieties', *Clinical Pediatrics*, 34 (7) (July).

Strasburger, V. and Donnerstein, E. (1999) 'Children, adolescents, and the media: issues and solutions', *Pediatrics*, 103 (1).

Strauss, M. A. (1999) 'Is it time to ban corporal punishment of children?' *Canadian Medical Association Journal*, 161 (7).

Ventegodt, S. (1999) 'A prospective study on quality of life and traumatic events in early life – a 30-year follow up', *Child: Care, Health and Development*, 25 (3).

Young, K. T. (1990) 'American conceptions of infant development from 1955 to 1984: what the experts are telling parents', *Child Development*, 61.

Books

Alderson, P. (2000) *Young Children's Rights: Exploring Beliefs, Principles and Practice* (Jessica Kingsley Publishers: London).

Anderson, M. (ed.) (1973) *Sociology of the Family* (Penguin: Harmondsworth).

Archard, D. (1993) *Children: Rights and Childhood* (Routledge: London).

Ayling, J. (1930) *The Retreat from Parenthood* (Kegan Paul, Trench, Trubner & Co.: London).

Beck, U. and Beck-Gernsheim, E. (1995) *The Normal Chaos of Love* (Polity Press: Cambridge).

Bernstein, B. and Brannen, J. (eds) (1996) *Children, Research and Policy* (Taylor & Francis: London).

Brazelton, B. T. (1981) *On Becoming a Family: The Growth of Attachment* (Delacorte/Seymour Lawrence: Boston).

Braer, J. T. (1999) *The Myth of the First Three Years: A New Understanding of Early Brain Development and Lifelong Learning* (Free Press: New York).

Buchanan, A. and Hudson, B. (1998) *Parenting, Schooling and Children's Behaviour: Interdisciplinary Approaches* (Ashgate Publishing: Aldershot).

Calcutt, A. (1998) *Arrested Development: Popular Culture and the Erosion of Adulthood* (Cassell: London).

Campion, M. J. (1995) *Who's Fit to be a Parent?* (Routledge: London).

Cassidy, A. (1998) *Parents Who Think too Much* (Dell Publishing: New York).

Chernofsky, B. and Gage, D. (1996) *Change Your Child's Behavior by Changing Yours* (Crown Publications: Chicago).

Clinton, R. H. (1996) *It Takes a Village and Other Lessons Chidren Teach Us* (Simon & Schuster: New York).

Damon, W. (1995) *Greater Expectations: Overcoming the Culture of Indulgence in Our Homes and Schools* (Free Press: New York).

Davis, A. (1997) *Confident Parenting: A Hands-on Approach to Children* (Souvenir: Brighton).

Duin, N. and Sutcliffe, J. (1992) *A History of Medicine* (Simon & Schuster: London).

Elkind, D. (1988) *The Hurried Child: Growing up Too Fast Too Soon* (Addison Wesley: New York).

Elliot, M. (1996) *501 Ways to be a Good Parent* (Hodder & Stoughton: London).

Eyer, D. (1996) *Motherguilt: How Our Culture Blames Mothers for What's Wrong with Society* (Random House: New York).

Families for Freedom (1998) *Stranger Danger* (Families for Freedom: London).

Firestone, R. (1999) *The Fear of Intimacy* (American Psychology Association: Boston).

Franklin, B. (1995) *A Handbook of Children's Rights* (Routledge: London).

Freely, M. (2000) *The Parent Trap: Children, Families and the New Morality* (Little Brown: London).

Fukuyama, F. (1997) *The End of Order* (Social Market Foundation: London).

Furedi, F. (1997) *The Culture of Fear: Risk Taking and the Morality of Low Expectations* (Cassell: London).

Furedi, F. and Brown, T. (1997) *Disconnected: Ageing in an Alien World* (Reconnecting: Canterbury).

Future Foundation (2000) *Complicated Lives: A Report by the Future Foundation for Abbey National* (Future Foundation: London).

Galinsky, E. (1999) *Ask the Children: What American Children Really Think about Working Parents* (William Morrow & Company: New York).

Goleman, D. (1996) *Emotional Intelligence: Why it Can Matter More Than I.Q.* (Bloomsbury: London).

Gopnik, A., Meltzoff, A. and Kuhl, P. (1999) *The Scientist in the Crib: Minds, Brains, and How Children Learn* (William Morrow & Company: New York).

Gordon, T. (1975) *P.E.T.: Parenting Effectiveness Training* (Plume Books: New York).

Gottman, J. (1997) *The Heart of Parenting* (Bloomsbury: London).

Hamand, J. (1994) *Father Over Forty* (Optima: London).

Hardyment, C. (1995) *Perfect Parents: Baby-care Advice Past and Present* (Oxford University Press: Oxford).

Harris, J. C. (1998) *The Nurture Assumption: Why Children Turn out the Way They Do* (Bloomsbury: London).

Health Education Authority (1992) *Birth to Five: A Guide to the First Five Years of Being a Parent* (Health Education Authority: London).

Hewlett, S. A. and West, C. (1998) *The War Against Parents: What we Can Do for America's Beleaguered Moms and Dads* (Houghton Mifflin Co.: Boston).

Hilman, M., Adams, J. and Whiteleg, J. (1990) *One False Move . . . A Study of Children's Independent Mobility* (PSI Publishing: London).

HMSO (1991) *Fourth Report of the Health Committee: Maternity Services: Preconception*, vol. 1 (HMSO: London).

Isaacs, S. (1960) *The Nursery Years: The Mind of the Child from Birth to Six Years* (Methuen: London).

Jackson, D. (1999) *Three in a Bed: The Benefits of Sleeping with Your Baby* (Bloomsbury: London).

Jenks, C. (1996) *Childhood* (Routledge: London).

Jeffers, S. (1999) *I'm Okay, You're a Brat! Freeing Ourselves from the Guilt-making Myths of Parenthood* (Hodder & Stoughton: London).

Kagan, J. (1998) *Three Seductive Ideas* (Harvard University Press: Cambridge, Mass.).

La Fontaine, J. (1990) *Child Sexual Abuse* (Polity Press: Cambridge).

Langford, W. (1999) *Revolution of the Heart* (Routledge: London).

Lasch, C. (1977) *Haven in a Heartless World: The Family Besieged* (Basic Books: New York).

Leach, P. (1997) *Your Baby and Child* (Penguin: Harmondsworth).

Leach, P. (1999) *The Physical Punishment of Children: Some Input from Recent Research* (NSPCC: London).

Lewis, J. (1999) *Individualism and Commitment in Marriage and Cohabitation* (Lord Chancellor's Department: London).

Lewis, J., Clark, D. and Morgan, D. (1992) *Whom God Hath Joined Together: The Work of Marriage Guidance* (Routledge: London).

Lindon, J. (1999) *Too Safe for Their Own Good? Helping Children Learn about Risk and Lifeskills* (National Early Years Network: London).

Maccoby, E. and Martin, J. (1983) 'Socialization in the context of the family: parent–child interaction' in E. Heatherington (ed.), *Handbook of Child Psychology*, 4th edn (New York: John Wiley).

Maushart, S. (1999) *The Mask of Motherhood* (Pandora: London).

Mead, M. and Wolfenstein, M. (eds) (1955) *Childhood in Contemporary Cultures* (University of Chicago Press: Chicago).

Naish, F. and Roberts, J. (2000) *Healthy Parents, Better Babies: A Couple's Guide to Natural Preconception Care* (Newleaf: Dublin).

NSPCC (1999) *Get Ready! Preparing Yourself for Your Baby* (NSPCC: London).

NSPCC (2000) *Baby's First Year* (NSPCC: London).

Parker, J. and Stimpson, J. (1999) *Raising Happy Children: What Every Child Needs Their Parents to Know from 0 to 7 Years* (Hodder & Stoughton: London).

Pittman, F. (1994) *Man Enough: Fathers and Sons and the Search for Masculinity* (Perigreen: Los Angeles).

Pugh, G. and De'Ath, E. (1984) *The Needs of Parents, Practice and Policy in Parent Education* (Macmillan: London).

Ringen, S. (1998) *The Family Question* (Demos: London).

Rodger, J. J. (1996) *Family Life and Social Control: A Sociological Perspective* (Macmillan: Basingstoke).

Scarr, S. and Dunn, J. (1987) *Mothercare/Other Care: The Child-care Dilemma for Women and Children* (Penguin Books: Harmondsworth).

Schaffer, H. R. (1998a) *Making Decisions about Children* (Blackwell: Oxford).

Schaffer, H. R. (1998b) *Social Development* (Blackwell: Oxford).

Sennett, R. (1998) *The Personal Consequences of Work in the New Capitalism* (W. W. Norton and Company: New York).

Spock, B. (1961) *Baby and Child Care* (Pocket Books, Inc.: New York).

Straw, E. (1998) *Relative Values: Support for Relationships and Parenting* (Demos: London).

Tizard, B. (1997) *Adoption: A Second Chance* (Open Books: London).

Werner, E. and Smith, R. (1982) *Vulnerable but Invincible: A Longitudinal Study of Resilient Children and Youth* (McGraw Hill: New York).

Winnicott, D. W. (1991) *The Child, the Family, and the Outside World* (Penguin: Harmondsworth).

Woodhead, M., Faulkner, D. and Littlejohn, K. (eds) (1996) *Cultural World of Early Childhood* (Routledge: London).

Zelizer, V. A. (1985) *Pricing the Priceless Child: The Changing Social Value of Children* (Princeton University Press: Princeton, N.J.).

Index